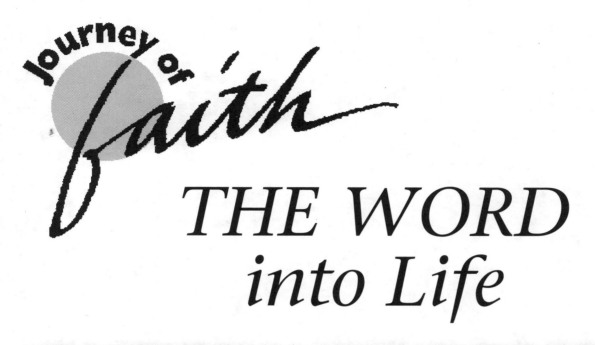

Journey of faith

THE WORD
into Life

A GUIDE FOR GROUP REFLECTION ON SUNDAY SCRIPTURE

CYCLE B

JOHN F. CRAGHAN
ELSIE HAINZ MCGRATH
ANN WOLF

Liguori
ONE LIGUORI DRIVE
LIGUORI MO 63057-9999

Imprimi Potest:
Richard Thibodeau, C.Ss.R.
Provincial, Denver Province
The Redemptorists

ISBN 0-7648-0513-4
Library of Congress Catalog Card Number: 99-71831

Copyright © 1993, 1994, 1999 Liguori Publications
One Liguori Drive
Liguori, Missouri 63057-9999

To order, call 1-800-325-9521
http://www.liguori.org

Scripture quotations are taken from the *New Revised Standard Version Bible,* copyright © 1989, Division of Christian Education of the National Council of Churches of Christ in the United States of America. Reprinted with permission. All rights reserved.

Printed in U.S.A.

Design: Wendy Barnes
Cover photo by Richard Finke

TABLE OF CONTENTS

TABLE OF CONTENTS

THE HISTORICAL DEVELOPMENT

The decision to become a member of the early Christian community was one laden with serious implications. Becoming Christian meant a break with one's background and often required fracturing relationships with the non-Christian members of one's family. In many cases this decision meant a willingness to suffer persecution even unto death. Stories of the early Christians reveal tales of young Christian women, like Perpetua, who was a noblewoman of Carthage and mother of an infant son, and Felicity, who was a pregnant slavewoman. Both refused to denounce Christianity and were subsequently beheaded during the public games in the amphitheater around A.D. 200.

As the decision to be a Christian was not lightly made, neither was the formation process quick and easy. Catechumens were invited into a step-by-step journey of three or more years with the community before full membership was achieved. During this lengthy process they were expected not only to begin to accept Christian beliefs but also to begin to live the Christian faith. The community shared their faith with the catechumens and celebrated each step along the journey with them.

One period of preparation for the catechumens has remained with the Church throughout the centuries, and that is the season of Lent. Originally this time was one of immediate preparation for the catechumens' baptism, which was celebrated at the Easter Vigil on Holy Saturday. During this forty-day retreat, the entire Christian community, most especially the catechumens, devoted themselves to prayer, fasting, and self-scrutiny. For those already Christian, it was a time to remember and renew their original baptismal commitment.

Following the Lenten preparation, the Church celebrated the solemn Easter Vigil, during which the catechumens received the sacraments of initiation and were welcomed into the community. These sacraments were celebrated only once each year, and only at the Easter Vigil. Formation of the new Christians did not end with the rites of Holy Saturday night, however, but continued with further instruction and the daily living out of Christian values.

This ancient process began to change in the year A.D. 313, when the Emperor Constantine mandated religious tolerance throughout the empire. Not only were Christians no longer persecuted but Christianity actually became fashionable, and people entered the catechumenate for political reasons. The standards for formation were relaxed to the point where baptism was received on demand, and by the fifth century the catechumenate had disappeared altogether. Eventually the sacraments of initiation were separated into the rites we know as baptism, confirmation, and Eucharist. Infant baptism became the norm, and the catechumenate vanished.

The Church published the first *Roman Catechism* in 1566, following the Council of Trent. This book of teachings was presented in question-and-answer form and was used for instruction of the faithful. Such *catechisms* later became the foundation for what came to be called *convert classes*. Using a teacher-student model, the priest met with interested parties in order that they might memorize certain prayers and learn the material contained in the catechism. At the end of a four- to six-month period of time, the priest usually determined that the students had mastered enough doctrinal formulations, and baptism was conferred according to parish custom. The duration of the process, the material to be covered, and the format were left to the priest or parish custom, with few outside directives given.

Successful completion of these convert classes meant either baptism or formal reception into the Catholic Church. This event was usually celebrated in a private ceremony, with only close family in attendance. Those newly received into the Church could be confirmed by the bishop at the cathedral; or they could receive the sacrament in their local parish when the bishop came to confirm the school children. Follow-up for the new Catholics, if there was any, might consist of being sent to a formal course in liturgy, Scripture, dogma, or morality.

The first in modern times to call for a change in the formation of new Catholics was the African Church. Following World War II, the African Church began to apply the ancient form of the catechumenate to modern situations, in order to provide stability in formation and a period of time for faith to mature. Then, between 1962 and 1972, a committee that was formed consequential to Vatican Council II engaged in a formal study and revision of the methods leading to baptism or reception into the Catholic Church. This study resulted in promulgation of the *Latin Rite* in 1972, followed by the provisional English text in 1974.

The catechumenate was reborn: a process of formation, sanctified by liturgical rites that mark progress in the journey of faith and culminate in full membership in the Catholic Christian community. An integral part of the revision is the celebration of the liturgical rites in which the catechumens and the parish community participate. These rites mark *closure* of each stage along the faith journey and *transition* into the next.

THE PROCESS

The catechumenate is rightly called a *process*, rather than a *program*, because catechists and sponsors act as guides in the spiritual journey of adults; also because this journey varies according to time, place, and needs of the catechumens. Rather than centering on a mastery of Church doctrine, the process is one of faith development. Catechumens come to a fuller maturity in their relationship with God, a relationship that now begins to express itself in the form of Roman Catholic beliefs. In addition, the process nourishes the building of relationships, not only among the catechumens and catechists but also among the catechumens and the larger Christian community of the parish.

Inquiry

The first stage in the faith journey is called the *inquiry*. During this period inquirers have the opportunity to form relationships with one another and with their catechists. The sessions are informal and often center upon the life stories of God-with-us that have brought each member to this time and place. Questions such as "What is faith?" "Who is God?" "Why does God care about me?" are considered. There is also the opportunity to ask questions related to *things Catholic*: Why are there statues in many churches? What is the role of Mary in the Catholic Church? How much power does the pope have in the Church?

The set of twelve **JOURNEY OF FAITH** *Inquiry Handouts* assist the questioners through this period. They broadly cover basic questions in such specific areas as: what Catholics believe, the meaning of the Mass, the Bible, the saints, prayer, and practices.

This is a time in which each inquirer can take a long and hard look at the Catholic Church—at the ways in which members worship together, at the ways in which they *live* their Catholic Christian faith. First impressions of the parish community, and of all involved with the catechumenate process, are very important in this stage. Its culmination is the inquirer's commitment to *enter* the catechumenate, the period of formal preparation for entrance into full membership in the Catholic Church.

Catechumenate

Marking the end of the inquiry and the beginning of the catechumenate is the *Rite of Becoming a Catechumen*. At this point the inquirers become *catechumens* (those preparing for baptism) or *candidates* (those already baptized but preparing for full membership in the Catholic Church). They publicly state their wish to continue the process of formation, and the community commits their prayerful support to this second step in the faith journey. Selected members of the parish community join the process to serve as sponsors, who act as companions and models of faith and lend personal support to the catechumens and candidates.

During the catechumenate phase of the process, catechesis usually takes place during the Sunday liturgy. The catechumens and candidates may be prayerfully dismissed after the *Prayers of the Faithful*; the catechists, and sometimes the sponsors, join them in reflecting upon the readings for the day and in connecting the Scripture to the faith life of the Church. A set of sixteen *Catechumenate Handouts* aid the learning process during this period. They address catechetical specifics of our faith: the Church, the sacraments, the moral life, and so forth.

The length of this part of formation is determined by the needs of the catechumen/candidate and of the community; it can last anywhere from several months to three years. During this time the catechumens and candidates not only learn Catholic beliefs, but they are exposed to various forms of prayer; they join the community in worship; they participate in the apostolic life of the Church; and they join in community actions.

When the catechumens and candidates are ready to make a formal request for the sacraments of initiation, and when the catechists and sponsors are ready to recommend them to the bishop and to the parish community for full membership, the *Rite of Election* is celebrated. This celebration is held at the cathedral on the first Sunday of Lent. The *Rite of Election* marks the closure of the catechumenate and the beginning of the *Period of Enlightenment*, the time of immediate preparation for reception of the sacraments of initiation at the Easter Vigil on Holy Saturday.

Lent

The beginning of Lent signals a forty-day retreat in which the parish community joins the *elect* (those whom the Church *elected* for full membership during the *Rite of Election*) in preparation for the Easter Vigil. On the third, fourth, and fifth Sundays the *Rites of the Scrutinies* are celebrated during the liturgy. These rites are prayers of healing in which the elect, as well as the faithful, are reminded that all are in need of continued healing, conversion, and reconciliation. The sessions are marked by increased emphasis on prayer rather than on accumulation of knowledge. Aiding both the catechized and the catechists in this process is a series of eight *Lent Handouts*. Vision is focused upon the events of the Easter Vigil and immediate preparation for reception of the sacraments of initiation. Many parishes allow time during Lent for a day of prayer especially designed for the elect and their sponsors.

Mystagogy

The Easter Vigil does not mark the end of the formation process but the beginning of a commitment to a lifelong discovery and living out of the Christian message. The fifty days from Easter to Pentecost are called the period of *mystagogy*, a Greek word meaning *mystery*. In the early Church, the community used this time to explain the mystery of the sacraments the catechumens had experienced. This post-Easter period serves as a time for today's *neophytes* (newly converted) to form a closer relationship with one another and to come to a deeper experiential understanding of God's Word and the sacraments. The neophytes continue to gather to pray, and the sessions may center more on the apostolic or social justice aspects of Catholic Christianity. Eight *Mystagogy Handouts* assist in redirecting the focus of new Catholics—from learning to living. This might be a time to more fully introduce various service organizations of the parish, the parish council, the school board, the education commissions, and so forth. The newly received Catholics are invited to wholly participate in the life of the parish so that their faith may continue to be nourished by the modeling of other parishioners.

The Catechumenate and the Community

The catechumenate process can provide a means of renewal for the entire parish community. It is a constant reminder of our roots, our heritage, and our traditions. Each beginning offers an opportunity for all to re-journey their own path of faith, an opportunity to share the life story of God-with-us, an opportunity to grow into a more mature relationship with God and with one another as community. The catechumenate can facilitate a continuing conversion process in the life of the parish, so that together the members may reflect more clearly the image of the reign of God in our midst.

THE METHODS

Suggestions for Developing a Catechumenate Process

Flexibility is one of the greatest assets of the new *Order of Christian Initiation of Adults*. The presider is given the freedom to accommodate the rites according to his pastoral judgment in order to fit the needs of the parish community, the catechumens, and the candidates. Catechists are encouraged to use their judgment in developing a process of faith formation suited to the needs of both catechumens and candidates. These materials, presented by *Liguori Publications*, are to act as a guide and an aid to that end.

Though one does not have to be a professor of theology or an experienced teacher to be a successful catechist, there are certain techniques and practical suggestions that can make the experience easier and more enjoyable. While a faith-filled experience is the work of God, it takes planning on the part of the catechumenate team to ensure that the process goes smoothly. It is helpful for the team to meet several weeks prior to the beginning of the process. Create a time line and review the materials. Be open to adapting both in order to meet the needs of those who present themselves as catechumens and candidates.

The team should continue to meet monthly throughout the process. It is helpful if each catechist is aware of the topics discussed, materials covered, and questions raised in each session so that there will be continuity between sessions and among presenters. It is also advisable that catechists contact the following week's presenters in order to brief them on any issues that have surfaced and may need to be addressed the following week.

No one can predict the makeup of any particular group. It is possible to have those who have never had any contact with institutionalized religion, those who have been baptized and active in another Christian denomination, and those who were baptized Catholic but not raised in the Church. Persons never baptized are referred to as *catechumens*, while *candidates* describes previously-baptized people. Generally, both can participate together in the same sessions; the major difference between the two comes in the celebration of the *Rites*, where care is taken to separate the two in prayer and sometimes in physical arrangement of the celebration. Refer to the *Rites* for specific instructions in this regard.

In working with adults it is vital that what is presented and discussed be linked with their life experience, especially in the process of faith formation. Catechists are co-learners, catalysts, and partners rather than directors. When catechists openly share the stories of their own faith journey, the catechumens and candidates experience a sense of trust that makes them comfortable in accepting and sharing who they are and where they are in their own journeys.

Again, flexibility is key to working with the catechumenate. Each session should begin with the opportunity for unfinished business to be addressed from the previous week. Often questions come up between sessions that were not obvious to the participants at the moment the topic was presented.

Communication is vital in establishing a sense of trust among participants, and active listening is one of the catechist's greatest tools in establishing this trust. Catechumens and candidates need to be accepted and affirmed for who they are, and this requires a nonjudgmental attitude on the part of all, especially the catechists. It is important to be aware of one's inner reactions to the speaker and to listen with the eyes and the heart.

Active listening requires **empathy**—an acceptance of the uniqueness of each individual, and a willingness to feel *with* them. It requires **sensitivity**—the ability to pick up the feeling level behind the spoken word. This is a feeling *for* the other in which personal prejudices and emotions are controlled.

It requires **attentiveness**—the ability to look at the person and give undivided attention; and **receptiveness**—the desire to genuinely want to hear and the ability to be open to what is said.

Lectionary-Based

The Sunday Lectionary forms the basis for the journey of faith. This is most appropriate since the Word of God tells the story of the faith experienced by the people of God: the relationship between the chosen people and Yahweh, and the relationship between the early Christian community and Jesus of Nazareth. In the process of reflecting upon these faith stories, our own stories of God-with-us become more clearly perceived and articulated. Because Scripture conveys the stories of a community, it is meant to be encountered in the community as we gather to worship and celebrate together. It is also fitting that the catechumens and candidates gather in community to break open the Word of God and to apply it to their own lives in the here and now.

In their reflection and linking of the Scriptures to their own lives, the early Christians began to develop official summaries and teachings regarding the meaning of their communal religious experiences. Since these doctrines and dogmas were born of theological reflection grounded in Scripture, the Church now links these teachings to Scripture in the catechumenate process. Therefore, the sessions begin with Scripture reflection and move toward an encounter with Catholic belief. Since it is primarily through the Sunday liturgy that the community hands on its traditions and beliefs, this becomes the most opportune time for the catechumens and candidates to be formed by the community. Beginning with the period of the catechumenate, it is strongly suggested that they be dismissed from the liturgy following the *Prayers of the Faithful* in order that they may go apart to reflect together upon the Word of God and the teachings of the Church. Several dismissal prayers can be found in the *Rite of Christian Initiation of Adults* book (see No. 67).

A SUGGESTED GUIDELINE FOR A SUNDAY SESSION FOLLOWS:	
30 minutes	Liturgy—all gather in Church. Dismissal after *Prayers of the Faithful*.
10 minutes	Refreshments and settling in.
15 minutes	Prayer and reflection— where are we at this moment?
45 minutes	Reread, reflect upon, and share the Scriptures—either all or the one chosen for this session. Spouses and sponsors can join this session as Eucharist ends.
10 minutes	Evaluation and prayer—how are we going to live the Scripture this week?

Note: During inquiry *or* mystagogy *this format may be adapted for a Sunday morning after Mass or for a weekday evening session.*

Catechist Preparation

In order to prepare for each session, the catechist should make use of both the Scripture commentaries and the handouts covering Catholic beliefs and traditions. For each Sunday a commentary and reflection on the readings is provided. They provide background reading for the catechist in preparing for the session. Throughout the week the catechist should reflect upon the Sunday readings. What are the connections, if any, between the readings? Paying special attention to the gospel reading, who are the characters? What are the sights, sounds, smells, feelings that emerge? Attempt to become a part of the text. What stories of your own faith journey come to the forefront? What is the connection between the readings and the faith-life of today's Church? Are there any questions that are raised in your mind? In between prayer and reflection, the commentary can be consulted. How does the author's reflection resonate with your own prayer and reflection upon the texts? Reread the texts and adapt the discussion questions for your catechumens and candidates.

After you have prayerfully prepared for the session, **relax** and **enjoy** the opportunity to share your faith with those who are eager to be touched by God's Spirit.

THE RITES

Rite of Acceptance Into the Order of Catechumens

This rite marks the first important transition in one's journey of faith—the move from being an interested *inquirer* to becoming a *catechumen*. The importance of this step in one's life is rightly recognized by the Church.

Sponsors have been chosen for all catechumens prior to this initial rite. If the catechumen does not have a particular person in mind to be sponsor, an appropriate person should be selected from among a parish pool of volunteers.

Symbolizing movement into the community, those asking to be received as catechumens, along with their sponsors, usually begin the journey at the doors of the church (see *Rite* 48). The celebrant introduces them to the worshiping community, who asks, "What do you ask of the Church?" They state their desire for initiation, implying their intent to live, learn, and love with the community. The sign of the cross is then marked on each forehead, symbolizing the love and strength of Christ that accompanies each person (see *Rite* 54-55).

This sign of faith may also be marked on their ears, that they may hear the voice of the Lord; on their eyes, that they may see God's glory; on their lips, that they may respond to God's Word; on their heart, that Christ may dwell there by faith; on their shoulders, that they may bear the gentle yoke of Christ; on their hands, that their work may witness Christ; and on their feet, that they may walk in Christ's way (see *Rite* 56).

At the conclusion of the signing, catechumens and sponsors are formally invited to enter the Church and to join in the celebration of the Liturgy of the Word (see *Rite* 60).

Following the readings and homily, it is recommended that the catechumens be called forward and presented with either a book of the gospels or a cross (see *Rite* 64). They then are specially included in the community's intercessory prayers before being formally dismissed from the assembly in order to pray and reflect upon the Scriptures (see *Rite* 65-67).

If some of those seeking full communion in the Church are already baptized, they are to be called *candidates* and the *Rite of Welcoming Baptized but Previously Uncatechized Adults Who are Preparing for Confirmation and/or Eucharist or Reception into the Full Communion of the Catholic Church* is to be used. (See *Rite* 507 and following, Appendix I, for integrating both *candidates* and *catechumens* into the introductory celebration rite.)

Rites of the Catechumenate

Other liturgical rites should take place during the period of the catechumenate: celebrations of the Word of God (see *Rite* 81-89); minor exorcisms (see *Rite* 90-93); blessings (see *Rite* 95-96); anointing (see *Rite* 98-101); sending (see *Rite* 106-117). These rites, although optional, are very important for the continuing faith development of both the catechumens/candidates and the parish community.

Rite of Election

The importance of this rite is accented by the fact that it is celebrated by the bishop (or bishop's representative), generally on the first Sunday of Lent. The rite marks another transition—one duly noted by a change of "title"—from *catechumen* to *elect*. The transition is also noted insofar as godparents have been chosen and approved beforehand.

After all those requesting election have been presented to the bishop (see *Rite* 130) and approved by the entire people of God there present (see *Rite* 131), their names are inscribed in the *Book of Enrollment* (see *Rite* 132). Intercessory prayers and a special blessing for all the *elect* follow this sacred moment.

Rites of the Scrutinies

The *First Scrutiny* takes place on the third Sunday of Lent. Its focus is the gospel of the Samaritan woman at the well. After special intercessory prayers, the celebrant prays that the elect may be exorcised from the powers of sin (see *Rite* 150-156).

During the week that follows, the *Presentation of the Creed* should be formally made to the elect, preferably after the homily within Mass (see *Rite* 157-163).

The *Second Scrutiny* takes place on the fourth Sunday of Lent. Its focus is the gospel of the man born blind. Again, after special intercessory prayers, the celebrant prays that the elect may be exorcised from the powers of sin (see *Rite* 164-170).

The fifth Sunday of Lent brings the *Third Scrutiny*. This Sunday focuses on the raising of Lazarus. Intercessory prayers from all the community and prayers of exorcism from the celebrant again follow (see *Rite* 171-177). During the week after this rite, the *Presentation of the Lord's Prayer* should be formally made to the elect, preferably after the reading of the gospel of the *Lord's Prayer* according to Matthew. Following the homily, which centers on the meaning and importance of the *Lord's Prayer*, the celebrant calls on the worshiping community to silently pray for all the elect. Before their dismissal, the celebrant bestows a special blessing upon the elect (see *Rite* 178-184).

Rites of Preparation

When it is possible to bring the *elect* together on Holy Saturday for reflection and prayer, these are rites that may be considered for use in immediate preparation for the reception of the sacraments (see *Rite* 185 and following). If either the *Presentation of the Creed* or the *Presentation of the Lord's Prayer* has not been celebrated already, they could be celebrated now. An *Ephphetha Rite* (a rite of opening the ears and mouth, symbolizing the hearing and proclaiming of the Word) is a very fitting preparation rite, as is the rite of *Choosing a Baptismal Name*. Any or all of these preparatory rites serve to set the stage for the highlight of the catechumenate experience—the reception of the sacraments of initiation.

Rites of Initiation

Months of sharing the journeys of faith of the elect, their sponsors, and their catechists culminate in this very special parish celebration. Holy Saturday is the night to celebrate, and the Church celebrates in style. In the early Church the Easter Vigil lasted until dawn; today's vigil lasts but a few hours (depending on the parish, generally between two and four). It is the most glorious celebration of the entire liturgical year.

This night begins in total darkness. The parish community may assemble outside for the blessing of the fire. Then, as the celebrant processes into the church, proclaiming the *Light of Christ*, each person lights a taper from the new Easter candle that has been ignited with the new fire. Soon the Church is aglow with tongues of new fire. The Liturgy of the Word begins with only the light of the candles. There are seven readings from the Hebrew Scriptures provided for the occasion, although it is not necessary to proclaim all seven. Psalms are interspersed between each reading.

With the singing of the *Gloria*, the altar candles and electric lights are lit and the Church bells are joyously rung. Then comes the New Testament epistle, the glorious *Alleluia*, the gospel, and the homily. The stage is set for the rites of initiation!

The liturgy of baptism begins with the calling forth of those to be baptized. A litany of the saints follows, and then the celebrant blesses the baptismal water by plunging the Easter candle into the pool. Baptism follows, and each of the newly baptized is clothed with a white garment. Then the whole assembly renews their baptismal vows, and the celebrant ritually sprinkles all with the newly blessed waters of baptism.

Once the baptismal rite is concluded, the candidates for

reception are called forward to profess their belief in the holy Catholic Church. They are joined by the newly baptized, and the rite of confirmation is celebrated with laying on of hands and anointing with chrism.

As the initiation rites conclude and the eucharistic prayer for Holy Saturday begins, new Catholics *(neophytes)* take the place of the *catechumens* and *candidates* who worked and prayed so hard in preparation for this night. They, along with their sponsors and godparents and family members, lead their Church, the people of God, to the festive eucharistic banquet. The goal of initiation is this Eucharist—sharing at the table and being sent forth!

Alleluia! Amen!

HOW TO USE *JOURNEY OF FAITH*

The **JOURNEY OF FAITH** process includes catechetical handouts which are separated into the four phases of Christian initiation:

- The *Inquiry* phase, consisting of twelve 4-page handouts
- The *Catechumenate* phase, consisting of sixteen 4-page handouts
- The *Lent* phase, consisting of eight 4-page handouts
- The *Mystagogy* phase, consisting of eight 4-page handouts

Handouts are available for **adult** initiation in both **English** and **Spanish**.

Handouts in English are also available for the Christian initiation of **children**.

Soon to come, handouts will be available for the Christian initiation of **adolescents** in **English**.

There should be a complete set of handouts for every **leader**, for every **sponsor**, and for every **participant**.

In addition to the handouts, there are **Leaders Guides** available for both the **JOURNEY OF FAITH FOR CHILDREN** and the **JOURNEY OF FAITH FOR ADOLESCENTS**. These books will assist all initiation leaders, whether experienced or novices, through the process of guiding catechumens and candidates into the Church.

This book, **THE WORD into Life**, is available for **each liturgical cycle**. It is intended for use by **all leaders** of Christian initiation groups, whether the participants are adults, adolescents, or children. It is also an excellent resource for the **participants** in *adult* initiation classes. Included in each book are:

- The *readings* for all Sundays of the *liturgical year A, B, or C*, Advent through Christ the King
- The *readings* for the *Easter Triduum*
- The *cycle A readings* for the *third, fourth, and fifth Sundays of Lent*
- The *readings* for those occasional *Sundays that supersede ordinary time* readings
- *Scripture commentary* for every set of readings
- *Discussion and/or reflection questions* for every set of readings
- Every set of readings is *cross-referenced to the catechetical handouts*
- An *overview* of Christian initiation that includes a brief *history* of the process, a depiction of the four *phases* of the process, a *methodology*, a description of the *rites*, and the *how-to's* of this program
- A *thematic index*
- A brief collection of short *gathering prayers* and *dismissal prayers* for each phase of the initiation process

THE WORD into Life is a valuable resource unto itself, of course. Whether you are planning homilies, engaged in biblical academics, involved in small group faith-sharing, or simply searching for further enrichment and knowledge through Scripture, **THE WORD into Life** will make it easier.

The readings are taken from the *New Revised Standard Version Bible* (NRSV), approved for lectionary use by the bishops of both the United States and Canada. We have chosen this translation because of its overwhelming worldwide approval. The most universally familiar and accepted translation available today, it is also used in the *Catechism of the Catholic Church.* Because the readings are taken from the NRSV, there are sometimes discrepancies in numbering. For example, the first reading for the first Sunday of Advent, cycle B, is taken from Is 63:16-17;64:1,3-8 in the NRSV; the numbering system in your Bible or in your missalette may read Is 63:16-17,19;64:2-7. You are alerted to such discrepancies by the (NRSV) reminder at the end of all citations where different numbering occurs.

This book contains readings for all the Sundays of the year. They are arranged so that there are twenty-eight weeks between the first Sunday of Advent and Pentecost; and there are twenty-eight weeks between Trinity Sunday and Christ the King. Themes that emerge from the readings and the commentaries are listed at the end of each commentary with references back to specific **JOURNEY OF FAITH** handouts. Sundays between the first Sunday of Advent and the eighth Sunday in Ordinary Time refer you to handouts from the *Catechumenate* packet; Sundays between the first Sunday of Lent and Easter refer you to handouts from the *Lent* packet; Sundays between the second Sunday of Easter and Pentecost refer you to handouts from the *Mystagogy* packet. Because the twenty-eight weeks between Trinity and Christ the King may be used either for continuing mystagogy or for beginning a new group of inquirers (or both), all the Sundays between Trinity and Christ the King refer you to both the *Mystagogy* and the *Inquiry* packets.

The commentaries, themes, and prayers contained in this book are helps for preparing you to lead inquirers, catechumens and candidates, and neophytes. You are invited and encouraged to familiarize yourself with these resources, in order to both better anticipate and better stimulate questions and discussion. Leading others to Christ is the most important work you will do in your life; your personal preparation for such significant and rewarding work can never be adequately emphasized.

How the handouts are used is up to you and the format your parish wishes to use for initiation. They could be distributed and discussed at the same session; they could be distributed at the end of the session and discussed at the next session; they could be distributed for home study and only discussed to the extent that they may raise questions. Because the themes listed under your weekly commentary refer you back to specific handouts, the handouts are ongoing tools throughout the process.

---

*We give thanks to our God... praying always with joy...
because of your partnership for the gospel....
And this is our prayer: that your love
may increase ever more and more in knowledge
and every kind of perception...
for the glory and praise of God.*
Phil 1:3,4,5,9,11

Enjoy!

Reading 1, Isaiah 63:16-17;64:1,3-8 (NRSV)

You, O Lord, are our father; our Redeemer from of old is your name. Why, O Lord, do you make us stray from your ways and harden our heart, so that we do not fear you? Turn back for the sake of your servants, for the sake of the tribes that are your heritage. O that you would tear open the heavens and come down, so that the mountains would quake at your presence. When you did awesome deeds that we did not expect, you came down, the mountains quaked at your presence. From ages past no one has heard, no ear has perceived, no eye has seen any God besides you, who works for those who wait for him. You meet those who gladly do right, those who remember you in your ways. But you were angry, and we sinned; because you hid yourself we transgressed. We have all become like one who is unclean, and all our righteous deeds are like a filthy cloth. We all fade like a leaf, and our iniquities, like the wind, take us away. There is no one who calls on your name, or attempts to take hold of you; for you have hidden your face from us, and have delivered us into the hand of our iniquity. Yet, O Lord, you are our Father; we are the clay, and you are the potter; we are all the work of your hand.

Psalm 80:1-2,14-15,17-18 (NRSV)

Reading 2, 1 Corinthians 1:3-9

Grace to you and peace from God our Father and the Lord Jesus Christ.

I give thanks to my God always for you because of the grace of God that has been given you in Christ Jesus, for in every way you have been enriched in him, in speech and knowledge of every kind—just as the testimony of Christ has been strengthened among you—so that you are not lacking in any spiritual gift as you wait for the revealing of our Lord Jesus Christ. He will also strengthen you to the end, so that you may be blameless on the day of our Lord Jesus Christ. God is faithful; by him you were called into the fellowship of his Son, Jesus Christ our Lord.

Gospel, Mark 13:33-37

Jesus said to his disciples:

"Beware, keep alert; for you do not know when the time will come. It is like a man going on a journey, when he leaves home and puts his slaves in charge, each with his work, and commands the doorkeeper to be on the watch. Therefore, keep awake—for you do not know when the master of the house will come, in the evening, or at midnight, or at cockcrow, or at dawn, or else he may find you asleep when he comes suddenly. And what I say to you I say to all: Keep awake."

God's Faithfulness

ANN WOLF

God established a covenant with Israel, the people specially chosen to be God's own. Covenant, loosely translated, means treaty, but the treaty (from God's end) is an irrevocable one. The people promise fidelity to Yahweh; Yahweh promises special protection in return for their fidelity. In today's readings we are reminded of God's faithfulness to the covenant—the faithfulness of Yahweh in the Hebrew Scriptures and the renewal of that faithfulness through Jesus of Nazareth in the Christian Scriptures.

In reflecting upon God's faithfulness, we cannot help but reflect upon our own unfaithfulness. Just as the story of the Jewish people is one of the covenant broken and renewed, so we must come to terms with the same process of fidelity and infidelity to God's commandments in our lives today.

In our first reading, the prophet Isaiah speaks to the Jewish people who have recently returned to Jerusalem from their exile in Babylon. When the southern kingdom fell in 587-86 B.C., the Babylonians deported the people. Families were separated from one another, land was seized, the Temple was destroyed. The people were resettled in Babylon, where they were allowed to live in safety but without rights to property, and without the opportunity to worship. For a people whose identity was bound up in land and Temple, to be without these was to exist in living death before God and before one another.

Covenant

Their thoughts turned to remembrance of the salvation Yahweh had gifted them with when they had been delivered from the hands of the Egyptians. The lament called for a renewal of the "awesome deeds" of the past, when the heavens were rent and the mountains quaked. But could the people expect Yahweh to honor the covenant when their hearts had become unclean— when their guilt surrounded them and none remembered to call upon Yahweh's name? How could Yahweh be faithful when the people had turned away?

You are our God, they prayed. "We are the clay and you the potter: we are all the work of your hands" (Is 64:8). The people knew, in the deepest recesses of their hearts, that Yahweh would never abandon them. They were the "chosen ones," the people who were peculiarly Yahweh's own.

In Mark's Gospel, Jesus calls the people to faithfulness. "Beware, keep alert," he warns them (13:33). One never knows when the master will return and call for an accounting. Just as the Jewish people feared that they had wrought Yahweh's anger by their faithlessness, Jesus warns of the master's anger if the servants are caught sleeping. The master has chosen the servants and placed trust in them. A response of faithfulness to the master is demanded.

Saint Paul, in writing to the Corinthians, seems to turn the tables from faithlessness to faithfulness. Corinth was a seaport well known for the loose lifestyle of its inhabitants. In other letters to the Corinthians, Paul warned against visiting prostitutes, engaging in the activities of transvestites, drinking and eating to excess, and other behaviors unbecoming to Christians; but in today's reading he seems to be complimenting his followers and supporting their efforts to engage in clean living in the midst of the squalor of immoral lifestyles: "Just as the testimony of Christ has been strengthened among you" (1:6). Rather than the image of the withered leaves in Isaiah's community, Paul sees a vibrant, faith-filled, and lifegiving community that, because of God's strength, will endure until the Second Coming of Christ upon the earth. In faithfulness to the New Covenant, Christ "will also strengthen you to the end, so that you may be blameless on the day of our Lord Jesus Christ" (1:8).

Our Fickle Fidelity

Often the image we have of God in the Hebrew Scriptures is of the God of *wrath* who is much to be feared, and this picture is contrasted with John's God of *love* in the Christian Scriptures. But far more prominent in the Hebrew Scriptures is the God of *hesed* (steadfast love or loving-kindness) and *rahamim* (tender mercy or compassion). The Hebrew Scriptures are the story of the relationship between God and the "chosen people"; the story of troubled, broken hearts; the story of falling away and returning. This is a relationship that is one day intimate and the next estranged by the faithlessness of the people. So too our story in the Christian Scriptures, and the story of our very lives, is of estrangement and reconciliation. It is a story of dying and rising again. And always it is a story of a God who is faithful to us, even in the midst of our unfaithfulness.

Today's Good News

Advent is a time of *becoming*. It is the season in which we are reminded that we are continually on the journey to wholeness with God. With each life cycle our troubled, broken hearts are healed; we are brought low, and we are raised up. Our many deaths are celebrated in the glory of Resurrection. And always it is the strength of Christ, the *hesed* and *rahamim* of God, that sustains us in the journey.

As we begin a new liturgical year, it is a good time to examine our relationships with God and with one another, to determine those that need to be healed, those that need to be reconciled. We are invited to return from our exile to the material world that bombards us during the pre-Christmas season. We are called to a peace-filled preparation for the advent of new life—the life that will be ours as God renews the covenant with us, the "chosen people" made new in the birth of Jesus of Nazareth, God-with-us.

Points for Reflection and Discussion

1. What are some activities that interfere with the building of relationships in your family during the pre-Christmas season? How can those be turned into peace-filled rather than tension-filled situations?

_____

_____

_____

_____

_____

2. Both Paul and Mark tell us that the end is surely coming. If you knew that this would be your last Advent on earth, what would you do to prepare for Christmas?

_____

_____

_____

_____

_____

Themes

Conversion
  C2, The Sacrament of Baptism
  C3, The Sacrament of Confirmation
Covenant
  C9, The People of God
  C12, History of the Church
Remembrance
  C1, The Sacraments
  C11, The Early Church

Reading 1, Isaiah 40:1-5,9-11

Comfort, O comfort my people, says your God. Speak tenderly to Jerusalem, and cry to her that she has served her term, that her penalty is paid, that she has received from the Lord's hand double for all her sins.

A voice cries out:

"In the wilderness prepare the way of the Lord, make straight in the desert a highway for our God. Every valley shall be lifted up, and every mountain and hill be made low; the uneven ground shall become level, and the rough places a plain. Then the glory of the Lord shall be revealed, and all people shall see it together, for the mouth of the Lord has spoken."

Get you up to a high mountain, O Zion, herald of good tidings; lift up your voice with strength, O Jerusalem, herald of good tidings, lift it up, do not fear; say to the cities of Judah, "Here is your God!" See, the Lord God comes with might, and his arm rules for him; his reward is with him, and his recompense before him. He will feed his flock like a shepherd; he will gather the lambs in his arms, and carry them in his bosom, and gently lead the mother sheep.

Psalm 85:8-9,10-11,12-13 (NRSV)

Reading 2, 2 Peter 3:8-15 (NRSV)

Do not ignore this one fact, beloved, that with the Lord one day is like a thousand years, and a thousand years are like one day. The Lord is not slow about his promise, as some think of slowness, but is patient with you, not wanting any to perish, but all to come to repentance. But the day of the Lord will come like a thief, and then the heavens will pass away with a loud noise, and the elements will be dissolved with fire, and the earth and everything that is done on it will be disclosed.

Since all these things are to be dissolved in this way, what sort of persons ought you to be in leading lives of holiness and godliness, waiting for and hastening the coming of the day of God, because of which the heavens will be set ablaze and dissolved, and the elements will melt with fire? But, in accordance with his promise, we wait for new heavens and a new earth, where righteousness is at home. Therefore, beloved, while you are waiting for these things, strive to be found by him at peace, without spot or blemish; and regard the patience of our Lord.

Gospel, Mark 1:1-8

The beginning of the good news of Jesus Christ, the Son of God. As it is written in the prophet Isaiah,

"See, I am sending my messenger ahead of you, who will prepare your way; the voice of one crying out in the wilderness: 'Prepare the way of the Lord, make his paths straight,' "

John the baptizer appeared in the wilderness, proclaiming a baptism of repentance for the forgiveness of sins. And people from the whole Judean countryside and all the people of Jerusalem were going out to him, and were baptized by him in the river Jordan, confessing their sins. Now John was clothed with camel's hair, with a leather belt around his waist, and he ate locusts and wild honey. He proclaimed, "The one who is more powerful than I is coming after me; I am not worthy to stoop down and untie the thong of his sandals. I have baptized you with water; but he will baptize you with the Holy Spirit."

Prepare The Way Of The Lord

ANN WOLF

This day's readings give us visions of what the "promised land" may be. For Isaiah it was a land in which nature was perfect; for Peter it was a land of cosmological perfection; for Mark it was a land attained through repentance and forgiveness.

Isaiah's message is familiar to those of us who have been surrounded by the beauty of Handel's *Messiah*. The valleys are exalted, the mountains are made low; the highways are made straight, the rough places a plain. All these are events that seem to be far beyond our abilities to accomplish. And so it is that this perfection is achieved through the "mouth of the Lord" (40:5). As all creation came into being through the Word of God, so the perfection of the end of time will come also through the Word.

The message of Isaiah was a beacon of hope for a people brought to despair by the Babylonian exile. Isaiah spoke in the midst of desolation; the "chosen people" were without land and Temple and felt that they were therefore without God. Isaiah's words promised that this situation would not endure: Yahweh's steadfast love would rescue the people from the wasteland, and wholeness would be revealed in the perfect ordering of nature. The desert would yield a highway for God. Zion would herald the glad tidings, and Jerusalem would be the center of good news. Yahweh would come with power to bring vindication to the cities of Judah that had been desecrated by the enemy.

Yahweh is likened to the shepherd who gently caresses his ewes, who protects them from all danger, that they may give birth to future generations and bring forth new life to the flocks. Through the power of Yahweh's Word the glory of the Lord, the reign of God will be revealed—and nature will proclaim its coming.

A New Creation

Rather than a creative perfecting of nature, the Letter of Peter speaks of a new heaven and a new earth coming on the heels of destruction. "The heavens will pass away with a loud noise, and the elements will be dissolved with fire" (3:10). Out of the desolation will emerge a new creation wherein the justice of God will reside. Again, God's power achieves the coming of the reign of God and cosmological events proclaim its imminence.

Those who received this letter from Peter thought that they were already living in the end times. They were sure that the Second Coming would become real during their lifetime. Many thought that God was "delaying" in keeping the promise of the return of Christ. The writer of Peter justified that delay in order for all to repent and come into the fullness of the reign of God. Such repentance was to manifest itself in acts of human justice that would reflect God's justice in the Promised Land.

Repent and Be Saved

The gospel reading focuses not on natural and cosmological signs of the coming of the reign of God, but upon the messenger, the proclaimer of end times. Whereas the mountains, the valleys, the heavens, and the earth proclaimed the coming of the reign of God in the first two readings, a human person proclaims God's coming in the gospel. Whereas God's Word and power brought forth the reign of God in the first two readings, it is the *Word made flesh* and the repentance of the human family that bring forth God's reign in the gospel.

In Isaiah's reading, the "promised land" was one in which chaos was absent in nature. Everything was perfectly ordered. This idea was in concert with the early Hebrew mindset in which God was present in order but absent in chaos. By the time of the prophets, right ordering was achieved through acts of justice. That thought carried through to the Christian Scriptures, especially in the preaching of Jesus of Nazareth. Today John the Baptist gives us a prelude to Jesus' message; he calls for repentance that leads to forgiveness of sins, and in turn leads to the coming of the reign of God. Not only will Jesus' action with and through the Holy Spirit bring the *new* "promised land" this day into reality, but the human family is co-creator by virtue of its acts of repentance.

Today's Good News

Today's proclaimers of the reign of God also call for repentance that leads to a right ordering of society. Peoples of color call for a guarantee of basic human rights that will uphold the dignity of the human person. Any discrimination brought against a human being is an indignity to the image of God. The poor cry out for access to health care, for jobs that provide a just wage, for homes that provide adequate shelter. The children of our world call for stewardship of our resources, which will guarantee that they and their children may simply live. Only human justice can bring about such a society. God can speak to us through the gospels, but God's Word must be proclaimed in action by God's people or the reign of God cannot become a reality in our midst.

Points for Reflection and Discussion

1. What does it mean in your life to be a co-creator with God?

_____

_____

_____

_____

2. Have you ever been treated unjustly by a person, an institution, or a system? Tell about how you felt.

_____

_____

_____

_____

Themes

Justice
   C13, Christian Moral Living
   C14, Social Justice
New Creation
   C10, Who is Jesus Christ?
Reconciliation
   C5, The Sacrament of Penance
   C6, The Sacrament of the Anointing of the Sick

Reading 1, Isaiah 61:1-2,10-11

The spirit of the Lord God is upon me, because the Lord has anointed me; he has sent me to bring good news to the oppressed, to bind up the brokenhearted, to proclaim liberty to the captives, and release to the prisoners; to proclaim the year of the Lord's favor, and the day of vengeance of our God; to comfort all who mourn. I will greatly rejoice in the Lord, my whole being shall exult in my God; for he has clothed me with the garments of salvation, he has covered me with the robe of righteousness, as a bridegroom decks himself with a garland, and as a bride adorns herself with her jewels. For as the earth brings forth its shoots, and as a garden causes what is sown in it to spring up, so the Lord God will cause righteousness and praise to spring up before all the nations.

Luke 1:46-48,49-50,53-54

Reading 2, 1 Thessalonians 5:16-24

Rejoice always, pray without ceasing, give thanks in all circumstances; for this is the will of God in Christ Jesus for you. Do not quench the Spirit. Do not despise the words of prophets, but test everything; hold fast to what is good; abstain from every form of evil. May the God of peace himself sanctify you entirely; and may your spirit and soul and body be kept sound and blameless at the coming of our Lord Jesus Christ. The one who calls you is faithful, and he will do this.

Gospel, John 1:6-8,19-28

There was a man sent from God, whose name was John. He came as a witness to testify to the light, so that all might believe through him. He himself was not the light, but he came to testify to the light.

This is the testimony given by John when the Jews sent priests and Levites from Jerusalem to ask him, "Who are you?" He confessed and did not deny it, but confessed, "I am not the Messiah." And they asked him, "What then? Are you Elijah?" He said, "I am not." "Are you the prophet?" He answered, "No."

Then they said to him, "Who are you? Let us have an answer for those who sent us. What do you say about yourself?" He said, "I am the voice of one crying out in the wilderness, 'Make straight the way of the Lord,' " as the prophet Isaiah said.

Now they had been sent from the Pharisees. They asked him, "Why then are you baptizing if you are neither the Messiah, nor Elijah, nor the prophet?" John answered them, "I baptize with water. Among you stands one whom

you do not know, the one who is coming after me; I am not worthy to untie the thong of his sandal." This took place in Bethany across the Jordan where John was baptizing.

My Soul Rejoices In My God

ANN WOLF

Jesus of Nazareth chose this reading from the prophet Isaiah to begin his public ministry in the synagogue in his hometown. In this way, Jesus linked not only his ministry but his whole person with the downtrodden, the oppressed, the marginalized of society. John the Baptist preached conversion of self, but Jesus went further. Jesus called for a wholly integrated conversion, one that sought reform of societal injustices as well as individual change.

This section of the Book of Isaiah is thought to have been proclaimed by Third Isaiah during the time when the Jewish people were recovering from the Babylonian oppression. In 587-86 B.C. the southern kingdom had fallen to the Babylonians. In keeping with their custom, the Babylonians had deported all leaders and resettled the land with their own people. The Temple had been destroyed. When the Babylonians were defeated by Cyrus the Great of Persia the people were allowed to return to Jerusalem. They believed Yahweh had sent Cyrus to free them from bondage and they rejoiced in their Lord. Salvation meant release of both spirit and body, and Yahweh's saving power surrounded the entire community.

Free at Last

The people found their return to Jerusalem was a time of re-creation. Cyrus had given them both the permission and the financial assistance needed to rebuild the Temple. Sacrifice could once again be offered to Yahweh. But the covenant demanded more than praise and sacrifice because worship without action was unacceptable to Yahweh. The people were once again reminded that they were responsible for joining with Yahweh in the co-creation of a land in which justice and righteousness were to be realized—a land in which captives were liberated and prisoners released.

Life in the Spirit

John the Baptist continued the prophetic tradition in calling his followers to repentance and baptism, but his message pointed to one whose baptism would demand a more radical observance of Mosaic Law, a return to Yahweh's call to justice and righteousness. The baptism of water that John practiced was common among some Jewish sects, especially among the Essenes, a group with which scholars believe John may have been associated. This baptism was practiced often, sometimes several times a day, in order to wash away imperfection. The new baptism, which Jesus would herald, would be more than a cleansing for past misdeeds: In addition to self-conversion, baptism in the Spirit would demand solidarity with the marginalized, and it would require action on their behalf.

Paul echoed Isaiah's theme of praise and thanksgiving before God and through Christ Jesus, and he reminded the early Christians of their prophetic heritage. Do not despise the prophecies, said Paul, even though the prophets may challenge you to difficult tasks. The prophets were not known for giving people a "pat on the back." Rather, their message often was one that "comforted the afflicted and afflicted the comfortable." Perhaps the Thessalonians were among the comfortable. Paul challenged them to be on guard to recognize evil in their midst, and to respond to the Spirit in order that they might "be kept... blameless at the coming of our Lord Jesus Christ" (5:23). Perfection was linked to a preservation of the whole person, "spirit and soul and body" (5:23), and such perfection could not be achieved outside community. Only in community could persons become truly free and reach the perfection to which they were called.

Today's Good News

This day glad tidings are preached to the lowly and brokenhearted; salvation is proclaimed to the captives. But it is not enough to preach and to proclaim such; action must be taken to achieve liberty from all forms of oppression—in society, in church structures, in family. It is easy for North Americans to identify unjust structures in other lands. We can point to governments in South Africa, in Northern Ireland, in Central America that violate human rights through unjust imprisonment or seizure of property. But it is a far more difficult task to identify similar injustices in our own country, in our own cities and towns.

Those who visit the imprisoned are quick to tell us that it is the "lowly" in our midst who are incarcerated. Does that mean that only the poor are judged guilty of crimes? Does it mean that only the poor lack the finances to post bail? What of the forcible relocation of Native Americans for the sake of corporate profits? Are they not imprisoned on land where they cannot herd their sheep, driven into impoverishment? How many elderly are barely surviving, being forced to choose between food and gas or electric? How many Americans crouch behind "security" bars, prisoners in their own homes? How many have no homes?

Points for Reflection and Discussion

1. Who among your parish community would you describe as marginalized? Why would you describe them as such? What does it mean to be in solidarity with them?

_____

_____

_____

_____

_____

2. Can those who are wealthy be marginalized? Why or why not?

_____

_____

_____

_____

_____

Themes

Change of Heart
    C2, The Sacrament of Baptism
Holiness
    C13, Christian Moral Living
    C15, The Consistent Life Ethic
Ministry
    C8, The Sacrament of Holy Orders
    C9, The People of God

Reading 1, 2 Samuel 7:1-5,8-11,16

When King David was settled in his house, and the Lord had given him rest from all his enemies around him, the king said to the prophet Nathan, "See now, I am living in a house of cedar, but the ark of God stays in a tent." Nathan said to the king, "Go, do all that you have in mind; for the Lord is with you." But that same night the word of the Lord came to Nathan:

"Go and tell my servant David: 'Thus says the Lord: I took you from the pasture, from following the sheep to be prince over my people Israel; and I have been with you wherever you went, and have cut off all your enemies from before you; and I will make for you a great name, like the name of the great ones of the earth. And I will appoint a place for my people Israel and will plant them, so that they may live in their own place, and be disturbed no more; and evildoers shall afflict them no more, as formerly, from the time that I appointed judges over my people Israel; and I will give you rest from all your enemies. Moreover the Lord declares to you that the Lord will make you a house. Your house and your kingdom shall be made sure forever before me; your throne shall be established forever.' "

Psalm 89:2-3,4-5,27,29

Reading 2, Romans 16:25-27

To God who is able to strengthen you according to my gospel and the proclamation of Jesus Christ, according to the revelation of the mystery that was kept secret for long ages but is now disclosed, and through the prophetic writings is made known to all the Gentiles, according to the command of the eternal God, to bring about the obedience of faith—to the only wise God, through Jesus Christ, to whom be the glory forever! Amen.

Gospel, Luke 1:26-38

In the sixth month the angel Gabriel was sent by God to a town in Galilee called Nazareth, to a virgin engaged to a man whose name was Joseph, of the house of David. The virgin's name was Mary. And he came to her and said, "Greetings, favored one! The Lord is with you." But she was much perplexed by his words and pondered what sort of greeting this might be. The angel said to her, "Do not be afraid, Mary, for you have found favor with God. And now, you will conceive in your womb and bear a son, and you will name him Jesus. He will be great, and will be called the Son of the Most High, and the Lord God will give to him the throne of his ancestor David. He will reign over the house of Jacob forever, and of his kingdom there will be no end."

Mary said to the angel, "How can this be, since I am a virgin?" The angel said to her, "The Holy Spirit will come upon you, and the power of the Most High will overshadow you; therefore the child to be born will be holy; he will be called Son of God. And now, your relative Elizabeth in her old age has also conceived a son; and this is the sixth month for her who was said to be barren. For nothing will be impossible with God."

Then Mary said, "Here am I, the servant of the Lord; let it be with me according to your word." Then the angel departed from her.

God-With-Us

ANN WOLF

On this last Sunday before Christmas the readings reveal the first proclamation of the Davidic covenant and the promise fulfilled for Christians in the person of Jesus of Nazareth. Paul tells us that the mystery woven through the prophetic writings has become realized in the gospel proclamation. God's Word spoken through Nathan the prophet has been uttered once again, through the appearance of the angel Gabriel to Mary, and the *Word became flesh.*

The first reading from the Book of Samuel tells of David's settlement in the city of Jerusalem after the governments of both the northern and southern kingdoms had pledged allegiance to his rule. David chose Jerusalem as his political capital for two reasons: first because it was located on the border between Israel and Judah, and second because the city was not under the influence of any one tribe. By bringing the Ark of the Covenant to Jerusalem, David also established the city as the religious center of the dynasty. A palace had been built for David, but the Ark remained housed in a tent as had been the custom since the giving of the Mosaic covenant. Thus David began the conversation with his prophet Nathan, stating that surely a fitting "house" (temple) should be erected for the Lord. The oracle of Nathan that follows formed the basis of royal messianism in the Jewish Scriptures: It would not be David who built the "house," but Yahweh.

The House of David

Yahweh had established covenants with Abraham and Sarah, and with Moses. Now a covenant was established with David. In the Davidic covenant, Yahweh promised that the kingdom and the house of David would endure forever. That promise became the basis for the belief that a messiah would one day be born of the house of David, and through his efforts the kingdom of Israel would be reestablished. The early Christians, therefore, took great care in identifying Jesus of Nazareth with the house of David in order to legitimatize their claims that he was the Messiah.

The writer of Luke's Gospel began the story of the Annunciation by telling us that Mary of Nazareth was betrothed to Joseph of the house of David. The child she would conceive would be heir to "the throne of…David" (1:32); he would "reign over the house of Jacob forever," and his kingdom would never end (1:33). The Davidic line was thus established.

Throughout the Hebrew Scriptures, Yahweh was a warrior God, a God who saved the people time and again from suffering and oppression. Yahweh had destroyed all of Israel's enemies and now promised a place of safety for the Israelites. Yahweh was a God of strength and power. When David suggested building a house for Yahweh, it was almost as if God scoffed at him: "I took you from the pasture, from following the sheep to be prince over my people Israel" (2 Sm 7:8). It seemed a bit ridiculous that David would presume to provide the safety and security of housing for Yahweh.

The Ark of the Covenant

When we come to the gospel reading, the tables seem turned. God sends an angel to ask that a young virgin become the mother of God. The Word, by whose power the universe was created, becomes a human being. The Word of Yahweh, "Let my people go!" (Ex 5:1) spoken to the Pharaoh of Egypt, becomes the child of a young girl. The Word, spoken to David, becomes vulnerable to human beings through the Incarnation. "Nothing will be impossible with God" (Lk 1:37), says Gabriel. And so it seems. The God of power and might is born of a woman, to become God-with-us in the most intimate manner imaginable.

Today's Good News

In Mary's time it was not unusual to become a mother at such a young age (Mary was perhaps twelve or fourteen years old). Today, in families of the poorest of the poor, it is still not unusual to have a child at such a young age. What if God were to become so vulnerable to us today? Perhaps it is exactly the poorest of today's poor with whom God would choose to become human. God would become human in the midst of those whom many consider to be subhuman: those who live in streets and ghettos; those who have no health care; those whose children are born with below-normal birthweights; those who go to bed hungry night after night.

Through the Incarnation, God became human, and through our baptism, we say *Yes* to the Incarnation. But this cannot be a once in a lifetime yes—it must be a continual yes: a *Yes* to join ourselves in solidarity with the poor and with Jesus of Nazareth.

Points for Reflection and Discussion

1. Christians are sometimes referred to as the new chosen people. Do you consider yourself to be chosen, and if so, what does it mean for you?

_____

_____

_____

_____

2. Have you ever known a teenaged mother? What are some of the obstacles you suspect she faces in raising children in today's world?

_____

_____

_____

_____

Themes

Ark of the Covenant
    C12, History of the Church
Mother of God
    10, Who is Jesus Christ?
Temple
    C9, The People of God

Reading 1, Sirach 3:2-6,12-14

The Lord honors a father above his children, and he confirms a mother's right over her children. Those who honor their father atone for sins, and those who respect their mother are like those who lay up treasure. Those who honor their father will have joy in their own children, and when they pray they will be heard. Those who respect their father will have long life, and those who honor their mother obey the Lord.

My child, help your father in his old age, and do not grieve him as long as he lives; even if his mind fails, be patient with him; because you have all your faculties do not despise him. For kindness to a father is never forgotten, and will be credited to you against your sins.

Psalm 128:1-2,3,4-5

Reading 2, Colossians 3:12-21

As God's chosen ones, holy and beloved, clothe yourselves with compassion, kindness, humility, meekness, and patience. Bear with one another and, if anyone has a complaint against another, forgive each other; just as the Lord has forgiven you, so you also must forgive. Above all, clothe yourselves with love, which binds everything together in perfect harmony. And let the peace of Christ rule in your hearts, to which indeed you were called in the one body. And be thankful. Let the word of Christ dwell in you richly; teach and admonish one another in all wisdom; and with gratitude in your hearts sing psalms, hymns, and spiritual songs to God. And whatever you do, in word or deed, do everything in the name of the Lord Jesus, giving thanks to God the Father through him.

Wives, be subject to your husbands, as is fitting in the Lord. Husbands, love your wives and never treat them harshly. Children, obey your parents in everything, for this is your acceptable duty in the Lord. Fathers, do not provoke your children, or they may lose heart.

Gospel, Luke 2:22-40

When the time came for their purification according to the law of Moses, Mary and Joseph brought Jesus up to Jerusalem to present him to the Lord (as it is written in the law of the Lord, "Every firstborn male shall be designated as holy to the Lord"), and they offered a sacrifice according to what is stated in the law of the Lord, "a pair of turtledoves or two young pigeons."

Now there was a man in Jerusalem whose name was Simeon; this man was righteous and devout, looking forward to the consolation of Israel, and the Holy Spirit rested on him. It had been revealed to him by the Holy Spirit that he would not see death before he had seen the Lord's Messiah. Guided by the Spirit, Simeon came into the temple; and when the parents brought in the child Jesus, to do for him what was customary under the law, Simeon took him in his arms and praised God, saying, "Master, now you are dismissing your servant in peace, according to your word; for my eyes have seen your salvation, which you have prepared in the presence of all peoples, a light for revelation to the Gentiles and for glory to your people Israel."

And the child's father and mother were amazed at what was being said about him. Then Simeon blessed them and said to his mother Mary, "This child is destined for the falling and the rising of many in Israel, and to be a sign that will be opposed so that the inner thoughts of many will be revealed—and a sword will pierce your own soul too."

There was also a prophet, Anna the daughter of Phanuel, of the tribe of Asher. She was of a great age, having lived with her husband seven years after her marriage, then as a widow to the age of eighty-four. She never left the temple but worshiped there with fasting and prayer night and day. At that moment she came, and began to praise God and to speak about the child to all who were looking for the redemption of Jerusalem.

When they had finished everything required by the law of the Lord, they returned to Galilee, to their own town of Nazareth. The child grew and became strong, filled with wisdom; and the favor of God was upon him.

God Incarnate

ANN WOLF

Today's reading from Luke's Gospel tells us the story of the purification of Mary and the consecration of Jesus to God. It was the Mosaic tradition for Jewish families to appear in the Temple and partake in purification rituals following the birth of a child. It was believed that childbirth rendered a woman unclean, and she was not allowed to participate in community worship until she had been purified. Also, "as is written in the law of the Lord, 'Every firstborn male shall be designated as holy to the Lord'" (2:23). Mary and Joseph brought Jesus to the Temple to seek God's blessings and to offer sacrifice. The wealthy traditionally offered an unblemished lamb. Mary and Joseph offered the sacrifice of the poor: a pair of turtle doves or two young pigeons. The first bird represented a sacrifice of adoration and the second a sin offering.

The Universal Church

Simeon, who was probably a Sadducee, received the baby in his arms. Invoking God's blessing upon the child, he was the first to announce universal salvation through Jesus, "a light for revelation to the Gentiles, and for glory to your people Israel" (2:32). Also praying in the Temple that day was Anna, a highly esteemed widow and prophet. One of only seven women in Rabbinic literature who was linked with prophecy, she "began to praise God and to speak about the child to all who were looking for the redemption of Jerusalem" (2:38).

So the early pages of Luke's Gospel place Jesus of Nazareth within the realm of both the human and the divine. Jesus is linked with all firstborn sons in an external and formal act, signifying possession by the Creator. Mary his mother is one with all womankind in asking God's blessing upon herself and her child. Simeon and Anna set Jesus within the messianic expectation, and Simeon graphically connects Mary with Jesus' redemptive suffering when he describes the sword that will pierce her being.

By the time Luke's Gospel was written, the story of this day had been preserved for many years within the hearts of those who had loved Jesus. It had been repeated in the sorrow of his death and in the glory of his Resurrection. It is the glory of his Resurrection that most colors the remembrance with messianic overtones.

The Model Family

The reading from the Book of Sirach describes the mutuality of parenting as well as the interdependence among family members. "For the Lord honors a father above his children, and he confirms a mother's right over her children" (3:2). The father is gladdened by his children who give reverence and comfort to their mother. Children who care for their parents with kindness and consideration are abundantly blessed by God.

Paul's Letter to the Colossians echoes the call to generosity in family life and adds gifts that are bestowed upon us by the Spirit: "...clothe yourselves with compassion, kindness, humility, meekness, and patience. Bear with one another and...forgive each other; just as the Lord has forgiven you" (3:12,13). These are not merely pious exhortations but basic expectations of those who are "God's chosen ones, holy and beloved" (3:12).

Today's Good News

While it is basic to our Christian faith to believe that Jesus was and remains truly God, we believe also that he took upon himself our humanity in its fullness. And because he was one among us and with us, he experienced every emotion and every physical characteristic that is common to all human beings. He felt the pangs of an empty stomach; he felt the tingle of the cold on his arms; he felt the sweat dripping from his beard. He also felt the joy of loving and being loved, and he felt the pain of being rejected during his greatest hour of need.

We are called to exhibit kindness, compassion, and patience in our world. We are, after all, among those whom Paul counts as "God's chosen ones, holy and beloved." And there is perhaps no other place our power to forgive is tested more than among our families. It is with them that we are most vulnerable. It is with them that we love most surely, and it is also with them that we are most deeply hurt. Kindness, compassion, and patience are virtues that should be honed within our most intimate world of family.

Points for Reflection and Discussion

1. Why is it often easier to forgive our friends than it is to forgive family members?

_____

_____

_____

_____

2. Parents of today's teens grew up with a Leave It to Beaver *image of the family. Today's children grow up with a* Married With Children *family image. What do you think will be the media image of the family for the next generation?*

_____

_____

_____

_____

Themes
Catholic
    C1, The Sacraments
    C12, History of the Church
Family Life
    C7, The Sacrament of Marriage
Messiah
    C10, Who is Jesus Christ?

Reading 1, Isaiah 60:1-6

Arise, shine; for your light has come, and the glory of the Lord has risen upon you. For darkness shall cover the earth, and thick darkness the peoples; but the Lord will arise upon you, and his glory will appear over you. Nations shall come to your light, and kings to the brightness of your dawn. Lift up your eyes and look around; they all gather together, they come to you; your sons shall come from far away, and your daughters shall be carried on their nurses' arms. Then you shall see and be radiant; your heart shall thrill and rejoice, because the abundance of the sea shall be brought to you, the wealth of the nations shall come to you. A multitude of camels shall cover you, the young camels of Midian and Ephah; all those from Sheba shall come. They shall bring gold and frankincense, and shall proclaim the praise of the Lord.

Psalm 72:1-2,7-8,10-11,12-13

Reading 2, Ephesians 3:2-3,5-6

Surely you have already heard of the commission of God's grace that was given me for you, and how the mystery was made known to me by revelation, as I wrote above in a few words. In former generations this mystery was not made known to humankind, as it has now been revealed to his holy apostles and prophets by the Spirit: that is, the Gentiles have become fellow heirs, members of the same body, and sharers in the promise in Christ Jesus through the gospel.

Gospel, Matthew 2:1-12

In the time of King Herod, after Jesus was born in Bethlehem of Judea, wise men from the East came to Jerusalem, asking, "Where is the child who has been born king of the Jews? For we observed his star at its rising, and have come to pay him homage." When King Herod heard this, he was frightened, and all Jerusalem with him; and calling together all the chief priests and scribes of the people, he inquired of them where the Messiah was to be born. They told him, "In Bethlehem of Judea; for so it has been written by the prophet: 'And you, Bethlehem, in the land of Judah, are by no means least among the rulers of Judah; for from you shall come a ruler who is to shepherd my people Israel.' "

Then Herod secretly called for the wise men and learned from them the exact time when the star had appeared. Then he sent them to Bethlehem, saying, "Go and search diligently for the child; and when you have found him, bring me word so that I may also go and pay him homage."

When they had heard the king, they set out; and there, ahead of them, went the star that they had seen at its rising, until it stopped over the place where the child was. When they saw that the star had stopped, they were overwhelmed with joy. On entering the house, they saw the child with Mary his mother; and they knelt down and paid him homage. Then, opening their treasure chests, they offered him gifts of gold, frankincense, and myrrh.

And having been warned in a dream not to return to Herod, they left for their own country by another road.

Already... But Not Yet...

ANN WOLF

One definition of *epiphany* is "a grasp of reality." In a sense, *reality* seems to suggest that which is present, that which is accomplished; but we often deal with a reality that is less than accomplished, that seems to be unfinished. There is this essence of an "already, but not yet" that we find in Paul's theology. It is a feeling of moving toward, an aura of *becoming.* Such movement is always accompanied by change.

Today's reading from the prophet Isaiah is filled with a sense of movement and hope. These words were meant to give inspiration to a people devastated by loss of life, loss of land, and loss of the freedom to worship Yahweh. In 587-86 B.C., the southern kingdom had been overrun by the Babylonians. As was the custom for an invading army, leaders of the captive nation were exiled and the land was resettled by members of the conquering nation. Because families were separated and leadership destroyed, there was no threat of an uprising among those left in Judah. The Temple was devastated, the city was destroyed, and all property and land was confiscated. The Jewish nation was broken. This period in Jewish history is known as the Babylonian captivity, or exile.

In 540 B.C., Babylon surrendered to Cyrus of Persia, and Cyrus was seen by some as the long-awaited messiah. The people were free to return to Jerusalem, and Cyrus even helped to finance the rebuilding of the Temple. The glory of the Lord once again shown upon Jerusalem. The sons and daughters of Abraham and Sarah, who had been exiled to the farthest corners of the earth, came streaming home in jubilation.

A Journey to the Center of the Universe

The writer of Isaiah made Jerusalem a focal point for the world, but this focal point came neither from economic power nor strength in armies. Jerusalem at that point in history was at its weakest. It was in weakness that the city was recognized for being in right relationship with Yahweh.

The reading from the Letter to the Ephesians and the gospel reading from Matthew carry this gathering of the nations one step farther. Not only were the tribes of the Jewish people reunited but the Gentiles were added to their numbers. The image of the three kings that is found in this gospel is often referred to as a symbol of universal salvation. In Christianity there is no separation between Jews or Gentiles or Africans or Arabs: all are reunited into one human family, a new "chosen people" (see Rm 10:12-13; 1 Cor 12:12-13; Gal 3:28-29; Col 3:11).

Today's Good News

Perhaps no other nation in the world better symbolizes a gathering of peoples than does the United States. It was to this land that many came in search of freedom and a better life. Some fled oppressive governments, where worship condemned one to imprisonment and sometimes even death. Some fled countries where starvation ravaged cities and villages alike. Some came for the promise of owning land, the promise of being in control of one's own destiny, the promise of raising children in a place filled with hope. The United States became a *new Jerusalem*, the light shining in the darkness, the beacon of hope in the midst of despair.

It is not uncommon for U.S. citizens to consider themselves the "chosen people," the favored ones of God. They have been richly blessed with natural resources, with freedom to worship, with the opportunity for basic education. They live in a land that has a "work ethic" that tells them that even the most marginalized child can grow up to become president. There is a sense of comfort and safety in knowing that one is a citizen of such a country; but this feeling of being "chosen" can bring a false sense of security.

It may be easy for the U.S. to think that it has all the right answers: that its form of government is the best, its economic structure will meet any needs—that it is, in some sense, the center of the universe. There is, in fact, a danger in any nation believing that *its* will is *God's* will; a danger that it will become an oppressor of others in an attempt to "save them from themselves," to fashion them in its own image. It is difficult for a powerful nation not to impose structures that it considers just, in efforts to remedy injustices it sees in other places. Injustice is not caused by structure, however, but by those who control structure. Universal salvation, which is proclaimed by our readings this day, cannot be dictated by law; it must spring from relationships with one another that are grounded in human dignity.

If any citizens wish to hold their country up as a beacon of hope in a world that has the capacity for self-annihilation, they must ask where their strength lies. Do they measure their power in terms of military and economic superiority, or can they claim a power that springs from being in right relationship with God and with God's people?

Points for Reflection and Discussion

1. At what point do military and economic aid cease to be helpful to another nation and become instead another form of oppression?

_____

_____

_____

_____

2. What things within our society must change before we can consider ourselves as beacons of moral hope?

_____

_____

_____

_____

Themes

Ecumenism
    C13, Christian Moral Living
Epiphany
    C1, The Sacraments
Oppression
    C14, Social Justice
    C16, The Dignity of Life

Reading 1, Isaiah 42:1-4,6-7

Here is my servant, whom I uphold, my chosen, in whom my soul delights; I have put my spirit upon him; he will bring forth justice to the nations. He will not cry or lift up his voice, or make it heard in the street; a bruised reed he will not break, and a dimly burning wick he will not quench; he will faithfully bring forth justice. He will not grow faint or be crushed until he has established justice in the earth; and the coastlands wait for his teaching.

I am the Lord, I have called you in righteousness, I have taken you by the hand and kept you; I have given you as a covenant to the people, a light to the nations, to open the eyes that are blind, to bring out the prisoners from the dungeon, from the prison those who sit in darkness.

Psalm 29:1-2,3-4,3,9-10

Reading 2, Acts 10:34-38

Peter began to speak to them: "I truly understand that God shows no partiality, but in every nation anyone who fears him and does what is right is acceptable to him. You know the message he sent to the people of Israel, preaching peace by Jesus Christ—he is Lord of all. That message spread throughout Judea, beginning in Galilee after the baptism that John announced: how God anointed Jesus of Nazareth with the Holy Spirit and with power; how he went about doing good and healing all who were oppressed by the devil, for God was with him."

Gospel, Mark 1:7-11

John proclaimed, "The one who is more powerful than I is coming after me; I am not worthy to stoop down and untie the thong of his sandals. I have baptized you with water; but he will baptize you with the Holy Spirit."

In those days Jesus came from Nazareth of Galilee and was baptized by John in the Jordan. And just as he was coming up out of the water, he saw the heavens torn apart and the Spirit descending like a dove on him. And a voice came from heaven, "You are my Son, the Beloved; with you I am well pleased."

Power To The People

ANN WOLF

On this feast of the baptism of the Lord, God's Word proclaims power. Isaiah describes the Servant of God who will "bring forth justice to the nations" (Is 42:1); Peter speaks of Jesus being anointed "with the Holy Spirit and with power" (Acts 10:38); and John the Baptist announces Jesus as "the one who is more powerful than I" (Mk 1:7).

The baptism of Jesus immerses him into a public life. The theological significance of this act is so great that it is recorded by all four gospel writers. Today's account comes to us from Mark's Gospel, the first written and a model from which Matthew's and Luke's versions were formed.

Power and the Spirit

Preaching on the bank of the Jordan River, John called for repentance as he cleansed the soul with water. But this would not be enough for true salvation, said John, for someone was to follow him, and that one would baptize in the Holy Spirit; his would be a baptism not only of cleansing, but of empowerment. Such power is clearly embodied in the person of Jesus of Nazareth. "You are my Son, the Beloved; with you I am well pleased" (Mk 1:11).

The Acts of the Apostles preserves the story that Peter told of Jesus' baptism and the beginning of his ministry in Galilee. "God anointed [him] with the Holy Spirit and with power;...he went about doing good and healing all who were oppressed by the devil, for God was with him" (10:38). And the powerful message that Jesus proclaimed was the *Good News* of peace.

The first reading from the Book of Isaiah also describes a person empowered: "I am the Lord, I have called you in righteousness,...as a covenant to the people, a light to the nations" (42:6). This servant of the Lord would not cry out in the streets, nor quench the smoldering wick of fallen armies, but the coastlands would wait for his teaching. The power of the Spirit would enable this person to open the eyes of the blind, to release prisoners, to free those bound in darkness.

Today's Good News

When we think of a powerful person, do we think of one like Jesus of Nazareth? Or is our image more likely to be that of the CEO of a large corporation? Such persons exude an aura of power in their very appearance: three-piece suits or designer dresses are the attire we expect; cars with leather seats and luxury features to carry them to the office. We picture their homes at the end of long driveways, secluded from traffic and noises that surround most city neighborhoods. We imagine them vacationing in mountain retreats or on European beaches. These are the rewards that power bestows.

Perhaps our image of power would include military leaders, people who literally hold the lives of millions within their hands. Battalions stand ready to fulfill their commands. They may even hold it within their power to begin the annihilation of the world with the "touch of a button." Is this what it means to be blessed with the power of the Spirit about which our readings speak?

Can we consider Mother Teresa of Calcutta a powerful person? Those who knew her say her strength came from her unity with the Eucharist; they say she held the heads of the dying in her hands with the same dignity and awe with which she received the Body of Christ in her palm.

What of Archbishop Oscar Romero? Becoming archbishop of El Salvador in a time of great political unrest, he was chosen because he was perceived as "safe"—not likely to call the government and the military to accountability for human rights violations. But as he saw his priests assassinated, his parishioners raped and tortured, his friends disappear, Romero began to claim the power bestowed upon him by baptism: He began to call for an end to the killing and the oppression. Romero paid a price for the power he held among his people. He paid with his life.

Many call Dr. Martin Luther King a person of power. In a time of great racial division in the U.S., a time in which many were calling for justice through violence, Martin Luther King proclaimed the *Good News* of peace. Demanding that all persons be allowed to use restroom facilities, that all persons be allowed safe transportation, that all persons be allowed to buy food, he appealed to a sense of justice wrought by peace-filled witness. King paid a price for the power he held among his people. He paid with his life.

We are all empowered to a sense of justice by our baptism. Most of us will not be called to pay the price with our very lives but the price of witnessing for justice and the dignity of the human person will still seem too great for some. We are all called to die to some form of sin within ourselves, so that we may rise in a new spirit of conversion.

Points for Reflection and Discussion

1. Why do you think the word power *often carries with it a negative connotation?*

_____

_____

_____

_____

2. What abilities must a person have to become powerful in our society?

_____

_____

_____

_____

Themes

Baptism
   C2, The Sacrament of Baptism
Holy Spirit
   C3, The Sacrament of Confirmation
Power
   C14, Social Justice
   C15, The Consistent Life Ethic

Reading 1, 1 Samuel 3:3-10,19

Samuel was lying down in the temple of the Lord, where the ark of God was. Then the Lord called, "Samuel! Samuel!" and he said, "Here I am!" and ran to Eli, and said, "Here I am, for you called me." But he said, "I did not call; lie down again." So he went and lay down. The Lord called again, "Samuel!" Samuel got up and went to Eli, and said, "Here I am, for you called me." But he said, "I did not call, my son; lie down again." Now Samuel did not yet know the Lord, and the word of the Lord had not yet been revealed to him. The Lord called Samuel again, a third time. And he got up and went to Eli, and said, "Here I am, for you called me." Then Eli perceived that the Lord was calling the boy. Therefore Eli said to Samuel, "Go, lie down; and if he calls you, you shall say, 'Speak, Lord, for your servant is listening.' " So Samuel went and lay down in his place. Now the Lord came and stood there, calling as before, "Samuel! Samuel!" And Samuel said, "Speak, for your servant is listening."

As Samuel grew up, the Lord was with him and let none of his words fall to the ground.

Psalm 40:2,4,7-8,8-9,10

Reading 2, 1 Corinthians 6:13-15,17-20

The body is meant not for fornication but for the Lord, and the Lord for the body. And God raised the Lord and will also raise us by his power.

Do you not know that your bodies are members of Christ? Anyone united to the Lord becomes one spirit with him. Shun fornication! Every sin that a person commits is outside the body; but the fornicator sins against the body itself. Or do you not know that your body is a temple of the Holy Spirit within you, which you have from God, and that you are not your own? For you were bought with a price; therefore glorify God in your body.

Gospel, John 1:35-42

John was standing with two of his disciples, and as he watched Jesus walk by, he exclaimed, "Look, here is the Lamb of God!" The two disciples heard him say this, and they followed Jesus. When Jesus turned and saw them following, he said to them, "What are you looking for?" They said to him, "Rabbi" (which translated means Teacher), "where are you staying?" He said to them, "Come and see." They came and saw where he was staying, and they remained with him that day. It was about four o'clock in the afternoon.

One of the two who heard John speak and followed him was Andrew, Simon Peter's brother. He first found his brother Simon and said to him, "We have found the Messiah" (which is translated Anointed). He brought Simon to Jesus, who looked at him and said, "You are Simon son of John. You are to be called Cephas" (which is translated Peter).

Here I Am, Lord

ANN WOLF

We have all heard the phrase: "Many are called, but few are chosen." Would it not be more apt to say: "Many are called, but few choose to respond"? Responding to a call has grave implications, for it involves a sense of vulnerability. It can mean a letting go of plans, of hopes, of dreams. It can mean allowing oneself to be reshaped and molded according to the desires of the one to whom we respond. It necessarily means we are open to being changed, and few of us like the uncertainty of change.

The Call

Our first reading this day tells the story of the call of Samuel. Because Samuel's mother, Hannah, had suffered infertility, he had been consecrated to Yahweh's service in thanksgiving for the gift of his birth. Accordingly, he was raised in the Temple by the priest Eli. Samuel was a child when, in the midst of sleep, he heard someone call his name. Responding with confusion and disorientation, he stumbled into Eli's room, ready to be of service to him. Eli alerted Samuel to the voice of Yahweh, and Samuel responded: "Here I am, Lord." This response changed Samuel's life forever. Our reading ends with the words that "As Samuel grew up, the Lord was with him and let none of his words fall to the ground" (3:19). What kind of effect did Samuel's words have for himself and for his people?

Years later it was Samuel who visited the family of Jesse and chose another young man, David, who became the "anointed one" of God (1 Sm 16:11-13). It was David who successfully united all the tribes of Israel under one government. Yahweh promised that David's reign would be firmly established, and it was from the root of his family tree that the Messiah would spring forth (see Is 11:1-10; also 2 Sm 7:16). Samuel's response to Yahweh's call thus changed the course of Israel's history and laid the foundation for the coming of Jesus the Christ.

Our gospel tells the story of another call to discipleship, that of Simon and his brother Andrew. Both were followers of John the Baptist, and this day they were with him in Bethany when they caught sight of Jesus. "Look, here is the Lamb of God," shouted John (1:36). Simon and Andrew immediately began to follow after Jesus. They had been seeking the Messiah; perhaps this was he whom they sought. "Rabbi, where are you staying?" they asked of Jesus. "Come and see," said he (38,39). And the lives of Jesus, Simon, and Andrew were forever changed with that encounter.

The Name Game

Changing the name was significant in the Hebrew tradition, for when a king was anointed his name was changed to signify the beginning of a new relationship with Yahweh and among the people. Our story tells us that Simon's name was changed to Peter, or *Kephas* (an Aramaic word meaning *the Rock*). At that moment, Peter's life changed from that of a "fisherman" to a "fisher of men." Had Peter known what was in store for him, perhaps he would have chosen to remain with John the Baptist.

To be a disciple (a follower) of a teacher (rabbi) meant to share in the very life of the teacher. Thus responding to Jesus meant leaving behind a settled life with family and friends in order to become a member of a band of followers of an itinerant preacher. It meant becoming marginalized from the Jewish community. It meant accepting the awesome responsibility of leading the first Christian community. Ultimately, it meant Peter's loyalty unto martyrdom for Jesus the Christ.

Paul reminds us in his Letter to the Corinthians that response to the call of Christ cannot be seen as an individual response. Just as Samuel, David, and Peter were all intimately connected to community, the early Christians were called to live out their faith in the midst of community. When we hear the word community today we think of a group of people who hold something in common. For early Christians, community had a far greater significance, for they held everything in common. They were each responsible for one another's very lives. They supported one another financially, nurtured one another's children, cared for one another in sickness, and mourned the loss of one another in death. When Paul spoke of members of a body, the image was indeed descriptive of the first Christian communities; they were that intimately connected.

Today's Good News

Though call and response can cause a certain uneasiness, it can also awaken a sense of excitement within our being. Through baptism, we are empowered by the Holy Spirit with many gifts that enable us to be of service to one another. Often we are unaware of our many talents; it takes the call of another to cause us to more fully develop the gift that we are. It takes the call of another to give us the self-confidence to come forward and accept the challenge.

Points for Reflection and Discussion

1. What is the greatest gift you see within yourself?

_____

_____

_____

_____

_____

2. Have you ever been asked to do something that you thought you were incapable of doing, but you rose to the occasion and accomplished the task? How did you feel? Tell the story.

_____

_____

_____

_____

_____

Themes

Call
    C1, The Sacraments
Confirmation
    C3, The Sacrament of Confirmation
Discipleship
    C9, The People of God
    C13, Christian Moral Living

Reading 1, Jonah 3:1-5,10

The word of the Lord came to Jonah, saying, "Get up, go to Nineveh, that great city, and proclaim to it the message that I tell you." So Jonah set out and went to Nineveh, according to the word of the Lord. Now Nineveh was an exceedingly large city, a three days' walk across. Jonah began to go into the city, going a day's walk. And he cried out, "Forty days more, and Nineveh shall be overthrown!" And the people of Nineveh believed God; they proclaimed a fast, and everyone, great and small, put on sackcloth.

When God saw what they did, how they turned from their evil ways, God changed his mind about the calamity that he had said he would bring upon them; and he did not do it.

Psalm 25:4-5,6-7,8-9

Reading 2, 1 Corinthians 7:29-31

I mean, brothers and sisters, the appointed time has grown short; from now on, let even those who have wives be as though they had none, and those who mourn as though they were not mourning, and those who rejoice as though they were not rejoicing, and those who buy as though they had no possessions, and those who deal with the world as though they had no dealings with it. For the present form of this world is passing away.

Gospel, Mark 1:14-20

After John was arrested, Jesus came to Galilee, proclaiming the good news of God, and saying, "The time is fulfilled, and the kingdom of God has come near; repent, and believe in the good news."

As Jesus passed along the Sea of Galilee, he saw Simon and his brother Andrew casting a net into the sea—for they were fishermen. And Jesus said to them, "Follow me and I will make you fish for people." And immediately they left their nets and followed him. As he went a little farther, he saw James son of Zebedee and his brother John, who were in their boat mending the nets. Immediately he called them; and they left their father Zebedee in the boat with the hired men, and followed him.

Turning

ANN WOLF

This week's readings again focus upon the theme of call, but there is a greater sense of urgency required in the response. Our first reading briefly recounts the mission of Jonah, the prophet whom God sent to Nineveh. Jonah's missionary efforts were highly successful, and from today's account it would appear that he was a quick and ready respondent. But a closer inspection of the text reveals that not only did Jonah hesitate—he altogether refused to journey to Nineveh. Why? The Ninevites were intense enemies of the Jewish people. Jonah would certainly have lost no sleep over Yahweh's threat to annihilate them; what he feared was that they would heed his warnings and be spared! Jonah didn't want to be the instrument of Nineveh's conversion!

But Yahweh was not so easily ignored. As Jonah sought to escape by sailing in the opposite direction, the story tells us that Yahweh sent a great storm. In order to save themselves from certain destruction, the sailors threw Jonah overboard. He was swallowed up by a giant fish who eventually spewed him out—back where he had started.

A Change of Heart

Jonah got the message and set about his task of preaching conversion. He had gone but one-third of the way through Nineveh when the people repented. Theirs was a faith response—a total change of heart. Even the animals were repentant. Much to Jonah's chagrin, Yahweh too had a change of heart: The people of Nineveh were spared.

Few of us would be convinced that this story of Jonah is historical fact. Rather, it is an account of conversion, change of heart, *metanoia*. Paul echoes this same message of repentance in his Letter to the Corinthians: "The appointed time has grown short," he cries with urgency (7:29). The early Christians were certain the end time was imminent. When Jesus promised to return, they took him at his word: They expected a quick return. To live in the early Christian community required a radical change of heart, and this *metanoia* was to be reflected in their daily living. Everything of this world was considered temporary, and those things not conducive to salvation were to be cast aside. Salvation demanded that one turn one's eyes completely away from earthly affairs and cast them only upon the resurrection that was promised.

A Change of Life

Our gospel reading also conveys a sense of turning away, though it is not quite as dramatic as Jonah's preaching and Paul's exhortations. Last week the Gospel of John told the story of the call of Peter and Andrew. This week's version, from Mark, varies slightly. In this account Peter and Andrew were not in the company of John the Baptist, for he had already been arrested. It was Jesus who preached in Galilee, taking up John's cry: "...repent, and believe in the good news" (1:15). In this account it was not Peter and Andrew who sought out Jesus, but Jesus who pursued them. "And immediately they left their nets and followed him" (1:18). Jesus then caught sight of James and John. They too were summoned, and abandoned their nets to follow Jesus.

Today's Good News

We are impressed in all three readings with a sense of urgency and with the quick responses of both the Ninevites and the first disciples of Jesus. In each case, their response was not a minor decision. Rather, it was a commitment—requiring a change of heart—followed by a change in lifestyle. It is difficult for us to imagine that such a radical *Yes!* could come so quickly and easily. Most of us would weigh our options. We would think long and hard before abandoning a comfortable, uncomplicated life in order to follow a call that provided no guarantees. But perhaps the stories are less about quick response than they are about total conversion.

Conversion is a lifelong process for most of us. It is an awakening of our deepest desire to be one with God, and it is the story of our struggle to cast aside all distractions so that we may journey toward wholeness with God. Our lives are cluttered with many distractions that cause our eyes to be clouded and our hearts to be shielded from the vision of God. Sometimes we may feel we are making little progress toward unity with God, and sometimes we may even feel that we are journeying far from God. We are so caught up in the daily pursuit of living that there is little time left for God. Sometimes we are so distracted in our efforts to bring about the reign of God on earth— in our efforts to care for the poor, to feed the hungry, to uphold the dignity of each human person—that we lose sight of God and our task becomes the focus.

Conversion may best be seen as a spiral. It is the winding journey toward wholeness that builds upon relationship with God. The nourishing of that relationship requires a constant reevaluation and refocusing of our priorities in order to leave behind that which distracts us and to embrace that which brings us into more intimacy with God. This is not quickly, nor easily, accomplished. But it is a journey that one day ends, placing us firmly in the open arms of the God who calls us.

Points for Reflection and Discussion

1. What is the greatest distraction in your life that interferes with your ability to build and nourish your relationship with God?

_____

_____

_____

_____

2. Can you give an example of a noble cause that might distract us from God rather than bring us closer?

_____

_____

_____

_____

Themes
Prophet
    C9, The People of God
Rebirth
    C3, The Sacrament of Confirmation
Repentance
    C5, The Sacrament of Penance

Reading 1, Deuteronomy 18:15-20

Moses said to the people:

The Lord your God will raise up for you a prophet like me from among your own people; you shall heed such a prophet. This is what you requested of the Lord your God at Horeb on the day of the assembly when you said: "If I hear the voice of the Lord my God any more, or ever again see this great fire, I will die." Then the Lord replied to me: "They are right in what they have said. I will raise up for them a prophet like you from among their own people; I will put my words in the mouth of the prophet, who shall speak to them everything that I command. Anyone who does not heed the words that the prophet shall speak in my name, I myself will hold accountable. But any prophet who speaks in the name of other gods, or who presumes to speak in my name a word that I have not commanded the prophet to speak—that prophet shall die."

Psalm 95:1-2,6-7,7-9

Reading 2, 1 Corinthians 7:32-35

I want you to be free from anxieties. The unmarried man is anxious about the affairs of the Lord, how to please the Lord; but the married man is anxious about the affairs of the world, how to please his wife, and his interests are divided. And the unmarried woman and the virgin are anxious about the affairs of the Lord, so that they may be holy in body and spirit; but the married woman is anxious about the affairs of the world, how to please her husband. I say this for your own benefit, not to put any restraint upon you, but to promote good order and unhindered devotion to the Lord.

Gospel, Mark 1:21-28

They went to Capernaum; and when the sabbath came, Jesus entered the synagogue and taught. They were astounded at his teaching, for he taught them as one having authority, and not as the scribes.

Just then there was in their synagogue a man with an unclean spirit, and he cried out, "What have you to do with us, Jesus of Nazareth? Have you come to destroy us? I know who you are, the Holy One of God." But Jesus rebuked him, saying, "Be silent, and come out of him!" And the unclean spirit, convulsing him and crying with a loud voice, came out of him. They were all amazed, and they kept on asking one another, "What is this? A new teaching—with authority! He commands even the unclean spirits, and they obey him." At once his fame began to spread throughout the surrounding region of Galilee.

Priest, Prophet, King

ANN WOLF

What does it mean to be among God's faithful people? Each of today's readings give us a clue, and when pieced together we have an image that partially reflects what the call to discipleship might include in today's world. The first reading speaks of the role of the prophet; the second reading examines the lifestyle of the married as opposed to the unmarried; and the gospel gives us a glimpse of the person of Jesus as we read the first Markan account of his divine power of healing.

A Priestly People

In the reading from Deuteronomy, Moses speaks to Yahweh's people about prophecy, but in the section immediately prior to this reading there is a description of what it meant to be of the house of Levi, that is the priestly class. For the Israelites, priesthood and covenant were closely linked. Because the Israelite nation was chosen by God, they were a holy nation and a kingdom of priests. Because the covenant was with all, the designation of an official priestly office did not exclude any from a special relationship with God. The priests only represented the whole of the people in public worship; they did not replace the community in offering praise to Yahweh.

Because the people often lacked the holiness to present themselves before Yahweh, eventually the priestly class came to be looked upon as models of sanctity and the ones worthy to represent the nation before Yahweh.

In the later development of Judaism, the priestly class took on a three-tiered hierarchy. The Levites were the lowest in stature, and served in the sanctuary. They became the representatives of the firstborn sons who were to be consecrated to God. Next on the hierarchical ladder were the sons of Aaron, who were specifically consecrated as priests; they represented the nation in sacrificial worship. The high priest bore the names of all twelve tribes of Israel on his breastplate, and he represented the whole of the nation when he entered the sanctuary. Only he could enter the Holy of Holies, and only once a year, to offer atonement for the sins of the nation. Thus the function of the Levitical priesthood was to maintain the holiness of the "chosen people" and to constantly reestablish the covenant relationship with Yahweh. In a sense, they acted as mediators between Yahweh and the people.

A Prophetic People

In the reading for this day, Moses speaks of another mediator: the "prophet." The early prophets were the "cult" prophets, or those attached to the Temple. We saw the prophetic role of Samuel in the anointing of David as king. Nathan, the prophet of David, also was attached to the Temple. Prophets established a link between the king and Yahweh; when the monarch deviated from faithful service to Yahweh, the prophet called him back.

In examining the roles of eighth-century prophets (Amos, Micah, Hosea), we see a shift in the mediation—no longer was the prophet attached to the Temple, and no longer did he speak to the king. These prophets were raised up from among the people, and it was their task to call the people to faithfulness. The prophets were "radical," in that they called for a return to the "spirit" of the law when the people had strayed.

There is little mention of the families of any of the prophets in the Hebrew Scriptures. It seems they followed a lifestyle similar to that of Jesus of Nazareth, that is, they were "itinerant preachers" of a sort—not a style conducive to family life. Paul picks up on the theme of discipleship and family in his second reading. It is difficult, he says, amid the cares of everyday life, to be faithful to God. Loyalties are divided because there is never enough time to meet the needs of family and of God. In the early Church, and even in more recent times, it was common to hold up the unmarried state as the choice of those who were serious about being true followers of Christ. The secular world was seen as a hindrance to spirituality. If one wanted to develop an intimate relationship with God, it required separation from the world.

Today's Good News

Vatican Council II has reemphasized the rightful place of the laity in the Church, calling upon all the baptized to fulfill the function of priest, prophet, and king. We have already seen that the priestly role was one of worship. The prophetic role was one of witness and faithfulness to the spirit of the law. Jesus gives us an example today of one of the roles of kingship: to act with both authority and compassion.

What does it mean today to be priest, prophet, and king? Surely, even for the unmarried, there is a constant struggle to balance the responsibilities of family, work, and relationship with God. Since few persons have a calling to live a monastic lifestyle, most of us find it a constant struggle to integrate spirituality into our lives. And yet, it is here that we can be the most faithful witnesses to gospel values.

Points for Reflection and Discussion

1. Do you think it is easier to maintain a spiritual life as a married or unmarried person in today's society?

_____

_____

_____

_____

2. Most people struggle to find quiet time to "be with" God. What has been successful for you?

_____

_____

_____

_____

Themes
Authority
   C12, History of the Church
Holy Orders
   C8, The Sacrament of Holy Orders
Marriage
   C7, The Sacrament of Marriage

Reading 1, Job 7:1-4,6-7

Job spoke:

Do not human beings have a hard service on earth, and are not their days like the days of a laborer? Like a slave who longs for the shadow, and like laborers who look for their wages, so I am allotted months of emptiness, and nights of misery are apportioned to me. When I lie down I say, "When shall I rise?" But the night is long, and I am full of tossing until dawn. My days are swifter than a weaver's shuttle, and come to their end without hope. Remember that my life is a breath; my eye will never again see good.

Psalm 147:1-2,3-4,5-6

Reading 2, 1 Corinthians 9:16-19,22-23

If I proclaim the gospel, this gives me no ground for boasting, for an obligation is laid on me, and woe to me if I do not proclaim the gospel! For if I do this of my own will, I have a reward; but if not of my own will, I am entrusted with a commission. What then is my reward? Just this: that in my proclamation I may make the gospel free of charge, so as not to make full use of my rights in the gospel.

For though I am free with respect to all, I have made myself a slave to all, so that I might win more of them. To the weak I became weak, so that I might win the weak. I have become all things to all people, that I might by all means save some. I do it all for the sake of the gospel, so that I may share in its blessings.

Gospel, Mark 1:29-39

As soon as they left the synagogue, they entered the house of Simon and Andrew, with James and John. Now Simon's mother-in-law was in bed with a fever, and they told Jesus about her at once. He came and took her by the hand and lifted her up. Then the fever left her, and she began to serve them.

That evening, at sundown, they brought to him all who were sick or possessed with demons. And the whole city was gathered around the door. And he cured many who were sick with various diseases, and cast out many demons; and he would not permit the demons to speak, because they knew him. In the morning, while it was still very dark, he got up and went out to a deserted place, and there he prayed. And Simon and his companions hunted for him. When they found him, they said to him, "Everyone is searching for you." He answered, "Let us go on to the neighboring towns, so that I may proclaim the message there also; for that is what I came out to do." And

he went throughout Galilee, proclaiming the message in their synagogues and casting out demons.

When Bad Things Happen To Good People

ANN WOLF

In the Israelite tradition, Yahweh was a God of justice. Those who were faithful to the covenant could expect blessings and rewards; those who were disloyal experienced the other side of justice—destruction. In early Judaism there was no belief in resurrection or afterlife; rewards and punishments were received in this life. This idea carried over into the New Testament world, and we see an example in the story of the man born blind. Jesus' disciples asked him if the blindness was a result of the man's sin or the sin of his parents. Illness, birth defects, and demonic possession were commonly perceived as punishment for sin.

The Book of Job was a contradiction to the image of Yahweh's justice, for Job appeared to be a holy man. Why would Yahweh allow his destruction? Would not Yahweh bless him for his faithfulness? In today's reading we witness one of Job's laments. He calls his life a drudgery. He is like a slave laboring in the scorching sun, looking for a moment of rest in the shade. Taking to his bed, overcome with bone-wrenching tiredness, Job is unable to rest. He tosses and turns all night, waiting for the dawn. But he knows that the sunrise will not bring him relief from his distress; it will only herald the beginning of another day of suffering. Although there is no relief, at least the days pass swiftly. Their passing reminds Job that his life, too, passes like the wind.

Job has lost his family and his possessions; his body is covered with boils and open wounds. Job laments his predicament; he tries to reason with God; he pleads for mercy. Job searches his life for signs of unfaithfulness, yet he has been an upright man. He has tried to serve Yahweh. Why has he not been blessed? Why has he been cursed? Is this story perhaps not one of blessings and curses, but rather one of faithfulness?

The Jewish people lived among various ancient near-eastern tribes. Within some of those tribes was the belief that human beings had been created as mere playthings of the gods; others believed that human beings were created as servants for the gods. The Jewish belief in free will was unique. Perhaps the story of Job was meant to be a lesson in freedom. What would the covenant mean if humans did not have the freedom to enter into a covenant relationship with Yahweh? Would it be valid if humans were robotic? On the other hand, if humans were free to reject God, would not their faithfulness be a true sign of desire to be in relationship with Yahweh? And what better way to test faithfulness than in time of trial? It is easy to praise God when one is blessed; it is not so easy when one feels abandoned and cursed by God.

While the gospel reading does not imply that Peter's mother-in-law was sinful because she had been overtaken with illness, there is some sense of that in the others who presented themselves for healing. Some were afflicted with bodily ailments, others with demonic possession. They came from everywhere to beg Jesus to surround them with his healing power; they came seeking wholeness, seeking to recover their bodies and their spirits from evil forces that threatened to devour them. Like Job, they suffered. Like Job, their lives were filled with drudgery and a sense of hopelessness. Most importantly, like Job, they were faithful. Ultimately, it was their faithfulness that freed them from the ravage of evil in their lives.

Today's Good News

Why do good people suffer? Why are the poor exploited and people of color discriminated against? Why are babies killed and old folks ignored? Why? Why? Why?

The problem of evil is inherent in our world, and with evil comes suffering. But with suffering can come growth and with growth can come faithfulness and with faithfulness can come faith and with faith can come meaning. Ultimately, as Viktor Frankl said, "suffering ceases to be when one finds a meaning for it."

The healing that Job experienced, and the healing that Jesus effected in people began within the persons themselves. They took a risk, became vulnerable to the people and the circumstances in their lives. The process brought them to faith and healing.

We cannot eliminate suffering because we cannot eliminate evil. We cannot explain suffering because we cannot explain evil. But we can transcend suffering because we can transcend evil. We are called to risk fame and fortune for the sake of the Name, and to encourage others by our witness. We who have faith, who have found meaning in our own suffering, are the healers in our world.

Points for Reflection and Discussion

1. How can one be a model of "Christian service" without feeling abused and "taken advantage of"?

_____

_____

_____

_____

_____

2. Perhaps you have known someone who was "on fire with the Spirit." Were you drawn to them, or were you somewhat alienated from their witness?

_____

_____

_____

_____

_____

Themes

Healing
   C6, The Sacrament of the Anointing of the Sick
Persecution
   C16, The Dignity of Life
Solidarity
   C14, Social Justice

Reading 1, Leviticus 13:1-2,44-46

The Lord spoke to Moses and Aaron, saying: When a person has on the skin of his body a swelling or an eruption or a spot, and it turns into a leprous disease on the skin of his body, he shall be brought to Aaron the priest or to one of his sons the priests. The priest shall pronounce him unclean; the disease is on his head.

The person who has the leprous disease shall wear torn clothes and let the hair of his head be disheveled; and he shall cover his upper lip and cry out, "Unclean, unclean." He shall remain unclean as long as he has the disease; he is unclean. He shall live alone; his dwelling shall be outside the camp.

Psalm 32:1-2,5,11

Reading 2, 1 Corinthians 10:31—11:1

Whether you eat or drink, or whatever you do, do everything for the glory of God. Give no offense to Jews or to Greeks or to the church of God, just as I try to please everyone in everything I do, not seeking my own advantage, but that of many, so that they may be saved. Be imitators of me, as I am of Christ.

Gospel, Mark 1:40-45

A leper came to Jesus begging him, and kneeling he said to him, "If you choose, you can make me clean." Moved with pity, Jesus stretched out his hand and touched him, and said to him, "I do choose. Be made clean!" Immediately the leprosy left him, and he was made clean. After sternly warning him he sent him away at once, saying to him, "See that you say nothing to anyone; but go, show yourself to the priest, and offer for your cleansing what Moses commanded, as a testimony to them." But he went out and began to proclaim it freely, and to spread the word, so that Jesus could no longer go into a town openly, but stayed out in the country; and people came to him from every quarter.

Sin And Suffering

ANN WOLF

A common thread running through the readings for this day is that of ritual purity. The first reading tells us that the priests immediately ostracized the lepers from the community because of ritual impurity. In Paul's letter he speaks of offending the Greeks and Jews who had specific dietary customs. And Jesus again raises the issue of ritual purity in the healing of the leper.

To be afflicted with leprosy was perhaps the worst curse a person could incur during ancient times. The disease was not only debilitating but also extremely disfiguring. Death was the only relief from suffering for a person afflicted with certain kinds of leprosies, like the one we know today as Hanson's disease. When death finally came, one no longer bore any resemblance to one's former self.

Because illness was seen as punishment for sins, any type of illness or physical deformity rendered a person "unclean" and unable to participate in community worship. Those afflicted were to tear their clothing. In addition, those afflicted with bodily deformity were ostracized from the community, for association with an unclean person rendered all parties unclean.

Sin Offerings

Even normal bodily functions were seen as defilements and caused one to be exiled from the worshiping community. (Recall the ritual of purification that Mary of Nazareth performed in the Temple following the birth of Jesus.) Any woman who gave birth to a child was considered unclean until she had been purified by sacrifice and prayers in the Temple.

No matter what the affliction or illness, the priest was the only one who would attest to ritual purity. None who were in need of purification could reenter the worshiping community until the priest had certified them to do so. That is why Jesus told the leper to present himself to the priest and to offer what Moses prescribed in return for the cure. Without confirmation from the priest, the healed leper would have continued to be ostracized from the Temple.

The Divine Physician

New Testament theology presents a complete reversal of the idea of ostracizing the so-called sinner. If bodily affliction were a sign of sin, Jesus appears to have spent most of his time in the company of sinners. Indeed, he says that he has not come to save the "healthy," but to save the sinner. In a time when priests disassociated themselves from the marginalized, Jesus must have seemed a remarkable figure to the downtrodden. They were accustomed to being shunned not only by society but also by religious leaders. Here was a person who welcomed them into his presence.

Today's Good News

This is a question that we still struggle with today. Why are holy people afflicted with debilitating illness? Why are men and women and children afflicted with our modern-day form of leprosy, Acquired Immune Deficiency Syndrome (AIDS)? It doesn't seem fair. People awaiting transplants die before their name hits the top of the list. Children suffer illnesses because their parents are too poor to provide treatment for them.

We find evidences of Jesus healing many people in the gospel stories. But we often overlook the suffering that persisted—even Jesus' own suffering. All signs of evil did not disappear when the Son of God walked this earth. His example of redemptive suffering was a witness for everyone everywhere—because there is suffering in every human life. To suffer for another is to save the other, and to suffer with another is to know the other. We often try to explain away illness and suffering. We blame original sin; we talk about systemic and societal sin. But the causes of suffering cannot be explained away, and responsibility for it cannot be laid at the feet of others. Ultimately, we all have to live with sin and suffering. Can we suffer compassionately and obediently, as Jesus did, and so carry on his redemptive work in the lives of the many and come to know God in our own lives?

Points for Reflection and Discussion

1. Have you ever experienced an illness as a blessing? Tell why you considered it a blessing rather than a curse.

_____

_____

_____

_____

2. Do you know anyone afflicted with AIDS? How can you cause them to feel embraced rather than rejected? What can the Catholic community do to address their feelings of isolation?

_____

_____

_____

_____

_____

Themes
Renewal
   C6, The Sacrament of the Anointing of the Sick
Sin
   C5, The Sacrament of Penance
Suffering
   C16, The Dignity of Life

Reading 1, Isaiah 43:18-19,21-22,24-25

The Lord spoke:

Do not remember the former things, or consider the things of old. I am about to do a new thing; now it springs forth, do you not perceive it? I will make a way in the wilderness and rivers in the desert. The people I formed for myself so that they might declare my praise. Yet you did not call upon me, O Jacob; but you have been weary of me, O Israel! You have not bought me sweet cane with money, or satisfied me with the fat of your sacrifices. But you have burdened me with your sins; you have wearied me with your iniquities. I, I am he who blots out your transgressions for my own sake, and I will not remember your sins.

Psalm 41:2-3,4-5,13-14

Reading 2, 2 Corinthians 1:18-22

As surely as God is faithful, our word to you has not been "Yes and No." For the Son of God, Jesus Christ, whom we proclaimed among you, Silvanus and Timothy and I, was not "Yes and No"; but in him it is always "Yes." For in him every one of God's promises is a "Yes." For this reason it is through him that we say the "Amen," to the glory of God. But it is God who establishes us with you in Christ and has anointed us, by putting his seal on us and giving us his Spirit in our hearts as a first installment.

Gospel, Mark 2:1-12

When Jesus returned to Capernaum after some days, it was reported that he was at home. So many gathered around that there was no longer room for them, not even in front of the door; and he was speaking the word to them. Then some people came, bringing to him a paralyzed man, carried by four of them. And when they could not bring him to Jesus because of the crowd, they removed the roof above him; and after having dug through it, they let down the mat on which the paralytic lay. When Jesus saw their faith, he said to the paralytic, "Son, your sins are forgiven." Now some of the scribes were sitting there, questioning in their hearts, "Why does this fellow speak in this way? It is blasphemy! Who can forgive sins but God alone?" At once Jesus perceived in his spirit that they were discussing these questions among themselves; and he said to them, "Why do you raise such questions in your hearts? Which is easier, to say to the paralytic, 'Your sins are forgiven,' or to say, 'Stand up and take your mat and walk'? But so that you may know that the Son of Man has authority on earth to forgive sins"—he said to the paralytic—"I say to you, stand up, take your mat and go to your home." And he stood up, and immediately took the mat and went out before all of them; so that they were all amazed and glorified God, saying, "We have never seen anything like this!"

A New Thing

ANN WOLF

All three of this day's readings speak of newness, of hopefulness. The Jewish people were on the verge of being liberated for new life in Jerusalem when God spoke to them in the first reading. Paul proclaims a new concept of God in the second reading. And the gospel proclaims wholeness and new life in the forgiveness of sins.

The first reading from the Book of Isaiah announces liberation for the Jewish people held captive in Babylon. Cyrus the Great of Persia was in the process of overtaking the Babylonian forces, and deliverance was at hand. The people could not know what their future held, but they hoped for freedom—freedom to repossess their land, freedom to once again worship Yahweh in the Temple. Some of their dreams were to be realized. Though they would never again claim the power that was theirs under David and Solomon, they would be allowed to return to their holy city and to rebuild a Temple for their God.

I Will Never Forget You, My People

For the Jewish people, life was one of remembrances. In the midst of suffering and slavery their thoughts always turned to the mighty deeds that God had wrought in the past—deliverance from the hands of Pharaoh in Egypt. The Exodus was not just an event of the past; it was relived every year in the Passover feast. Never were those saving events more remembered and hoped for than during times of oppression.

But Yahweh was calling the people to move beyond those remembrances now. Something new was about to happen—something more wonderful than they could imagine. And this wondrous event would be in spite of Israel's faithlessness. Even though they had forgotten Yahweh, Yahweh had not forgotten them. Yahweh would be faithful for all time.

Paul also reminded the Corinthians of Yahweh's faithfulness. God had not been like those saying *yes* one moment and *no* the next. Neither did Paul change his story when he proclaimed that Jesus was the Son of God. Paul's arguments pointed to Jesus as the fulfillment of God's Word. But the early Christian community must have had many questions regarding this person, Jesus of Nazareth. Never before had God become a human person. Never before had God been truly one among them. This was beyond their experience.

Because we believe Jesus to be the fulfillment of God's Word, we affirm our belief in the Creator through our belief in Christ. It is through Christ that we say *Amen* to God. And it was through Christ that God affirmed these people as a new creation, a gathering of Jews and Gentiles into a new people of God. Not only did the Creator join Christ in affirming this new people, but through the gift of the Spirit they were sealed and anointed in faith.

In struggling to define Jesus of Nazareth as the person of God among us, the writers of the gospels sought examples from his earthly life in order to document their claims. Today's gospel reading is an example of such documentation. Because the Jewish people believed that illness was a punishment inflicted by God upon those who had sinned, Jesus' healing miracles were interpreted as not only the healing of bodily ills but also the healing of spiritual illness. Today's story is such an example.

Ask, And It Shall Be Given To You

Jesus was teaching in a home in Capernaum. His followers were so numerous that they filled the tiny house and spilled out into the streets. There was no way to approach Jesus to ask for healing, especially since the paralyzed man was confined to some form of carrier that made movement within the crowd impossible. Not easily discouraged, his friends removed a section of the thatched roof and lowered the man—right under the nose of Jesus. Their faith did not go unrewarded: Not only did Jesus heal the paralytic, but he forgave his sins—an action that was reserved to God alone. Thus the writer of the gospel used this instance to equate Jesus with God, and also to associate forgiveness of sins with faith.

Paul links faith with belief in God's Word, and in Jesus as the fulfillment of that Word. Faith in God means not only anticipation of bodily health, but receptivity to God's healing Word. It is that sense of spiritual healing that comes from the forgiveness of sins.

Today's Good News

While the scribes and Pharisees believed that only God could forgive (Mk 2:7), the New Testament encourages the Christian community to forgive one another (see Mt 6:12; Lk 11:4). While sacramental forgiveness is reserved to the clergy, the power to heal broken relationships is given to all. It is with the same faith of the paralytic who came before Jesus that we share our Lord's Prayer and present ourselves to one another. It is our willingness to make ourselves receptive to the healing Word of God, our willingness to make ourselves vulnerable to the forgiving power of another human person,

that allows God to re-create the *Word* made flesh among us once again.

Points for Reflection and Discussion

1. Recall an experience in which it was difficult for you to ask forgiveness from another person. Why was it so difficult?

_____

_____

_____

_____

2. Do you think that there is more to "going to confession" than just asking God to forgive your sins through the priest?

_____

_____

_____

_____

Themes

Anointing
    C6, The Sacrament of the Anointing of the Sick
Christology
    C10, Who is Jesus Christ?
Forgiveness
    C5, The Sacrament of Penance

Reading 1, Hosea 2:14,15,19-20 (NRSV)

Thus says the Lord:
I will bring her into the wilderness, and speak tenderly to her. There she shall respond as in the days of her youth, as at the time when she came out of the land of Egypt.

And I will take you for my wife forever; I will take you for my wife in righteousness and in justice, in steadfast love, and in mercy. I will take you for my wife in faithfulness; and you shall know the Lord.

Psalm 103:1-2,3-4,8,10,12-13

Reading 2, 2 Corinthians 3:1-6

Surely we do not need, as some do, letters of recommendation to you or from you, do we? You yourselves are our letter, written on our hearts, to be known and read by all; and you show that you are a letter of Christ, prepared by us, written not with ink but with the Spirit of the living God, not on tablets of stone but on tablets of human hearts.

Such is the confidence that we have through Christ toward God. Not that we are competent of ourselves to claim anything as coming from us; our competence is from God, who has made us competent to be ministers of a new covenant, not of letter but of spirit; for the letter kills, but the Spirit gives life.

Gospel, Mark 2:18-22

John's disciples and the Pharisees were fasting; and people came and said to him, "Why do John's disciples and the disciples of the Pharisees fast, but your disciples do not fast?" Jesus said to them, "The wedding guests cannot fast while the bridegroom is with them, can they? As long as they have the bridegroom with them, they cannot fast. The days will come when the bridegroom is taken away from them, and then they will fast on that day.

"No one sews a piece of unshrunk cloth on an old cloak; otherwise, the patch pulls away from it, the new from the old, and a worse tear is made. And no one puts new wine into old wineskins; otherwise, the wine will burst the skins, and the wine is lost, and so are the skins; but one puts new wine into fresh wineskins."

A Covenant Never Revoked

ANN WOLF

There are many metaphors within Scripture that speak of God's covenant with the people. The readings of this day reveal both the images of covenant and the creative tensions that covenants tend to produce.

The Book of Hosea relates the tale of the stormy marriage between the prophet and his wife, Gomer. Filled with symbols of Canaanite religious practices and fertility rites, the book tells the story of Gomer's unfaithfulness and Hosea's neverending love for her. It is no accident that Hosea uses the image of marriage and infidelity to refer to Israel's worship of the Canaanite gods. In actual fact many Israelites were committing adultery by participating in Canaanite fertility rites; but the greater evil was the notion that they could "hedge their bets" by worshiping both Yahweh and Baal at the same time. Hosea is calling Israel to make a decision to come back to Yahweh alone.

The Lord mourned the loss of the people and remembered the wilderness experience that had nourished the relationship between Yahweh and the people. Yahweh dreamed of leading the people into the desert—of speaking to them in their hearts, and of receiving the same loving response from them that they had given in their youth. Yahweh yearned to return to the making of the covenant: "...I will say...'You are my people'; and he shall say, 'You are my God' " (2:23). How quickly they had forgotten!

I Will Espouse You to Me Forever

Paul speaks of the *new* covenant that has been established between God and the people through the person of Jesus of Nazareth. No longer does the covenant rest upon the law, says Paul, but upon the Spirit of the living God. The law is not written upon stone but upon the fleshy tablets of the heart. The people themselves have become signs of the covenant. It is not through any effort of their own that they have been chosen; through God's goodness and mercy they have been made ministers of this new covenant.

While the old covenant bound the people to dietary laws and ritual prescriptions, the new covenant would bind them in spirit. John's disciples were bound to the old law; Jesus' followers were bound to move beyond the letter of the law, to approach the spirit. No longer would they rejoice only in the written law of the Lord; rather, Christians would rejoice in their relationship with Christ. That relationship would call them to lives based on justice, love, and mercy—*hesed* and *rahamim*—those same virtues that had formed the foundation for the old covenant. But to follow Christ would include even more. The day would come when the bridegroom was gone, and fasting would follow. To be consecrated to Jesus would mean to follow in the footsteps of his suffering.

Of Old Things and New

Mark's Gospel reading this day is filled with images of tensions between the old and the new. An old and tattered garment is used as an example. Mark tells us not to look on Jesus as a new patch on our old comfortable behaviors because it won't work. Jesus is a brand new garment that we must put on. Similarly the new wine that heralds a new time of celebration reminds us that Jesus does not simply continue old celebrations of bygone times; he is the host to a new banquet, a messianic celebration.

The marriage feast symbolized Yahweh's faithfulness even though, time and again, the people had strayed; the Passover feast re-created Yahweh's saving power among the people. Jesus chose the celebration of the old covenant meal of Passover to establish the new covenant meal of Eucharist, which is both a sign of faithfulness and of salvation.

Today's Good News

Hosea makes the point that Yahweh does not act as society acts: Yahweh remains faithful, no matter what. Mark makes the point that Jesus does not act as rabbis act: Jesus is new wine, calling us to a whole new way of life. Paul makes the point that Christians do not act as followers of the Law act: A new covenant has been established between God and the people, through the person of Jesus, the Spirit of the living God.

In celebrating the Eucharist, we re-create our liberation and salvation through the death/resurrection event. When Israel *remembered* the Exodus event they made it a *present reality*. In the same way as the Jewish people continue to consider the Passover an event of present time, we celebrate Eucharist as our share in the suffering and rising of Jesus. When we gather to celebrate Eucharist, we not only call to mind the night Jesus celebrated with his disciples, but we *reenact* the consecration of the bread and wine into his Body and Blood. Jesus is *re-membered*: He becomes *truly present* among us.

Eucharist, consequently, is not just a ritual to be celebrated in a church: It is an event that calls us to a daily living out of the covenant it symbolizes. Eucharist is not celebrated in isolation; it is an event of community because the living out of the new covenant cannot be done alone. We are called to bring Eucharist to our homes, to the marketplace, and to the workplace. We are called to be signs of justice, love, and mercy to prisoners, and to the sick, and to the homeless. We are called to be

different and to make a difference—to be faithful to the *new covenant* that is symbolized in the *Real Presence* of the Eucharist.

Points for Reflection and Discussion

1. What is one practical suggestion that you can offer to link Sunday worship with Monday living?

_____

_____

_____

_____

2. How can we revive the image of marriage as covenant in our world?

_____

_____

_____

_____

_____

Themes
Eucharist
    C4, The Eucharist
    C11, The Early Church
Liturgy
    C9, The People of God
    C12, History of the Church
Love
    C7, The Sacrament of Marriage

Reading 1, Genesis 9:8-15

God said to Noah and to his sons with him, "As for me, I am establishing my covenant with you and your descendants after you, and with every living creature that is with you, the birds, the domestic animals, and every animal of the earth with you, as many as came out of the ark. I establish my covenant with you, that never again shall all flesh be cut off by the waters of a flood, and never again shall there be a flood to destroy the earth."

God said, "This is the sign of the covenant that I make between me and you and every living creature that is with you, for all future generations: I have set my bow in the clouds, and it shall be a sign of the covenant between me and the earth. When I bring clouds over the earth and the bow is seen in the clouds, I will remember my covenant that is between me and you and every living creature of all flesh; and the waters shall never again become a flood to destroy all flesh."

Psalm 25:4-5,6-7,8-9

Reading 2, 1 Peter 3:18-22

Christ suffered for sins once for all, the righteous for the unrighteous, in order to bring you to God. He was put to death in the flesh, but made alive in the spirit, in which also he went and made a proclamation to the spirits in prison, who in former times did not obey, when God waited patiently in the days of Noah, during the building of the ark, in which a few, that is, eight persons, were saved through water. And baptism, which this prefigured, now saves you—not as a removal of dirt from the body, but as an appeal to God for a good conscience, through the resurrection of Jesus Christ, who has gone into heaven and is at the right hand of God, with angels, authorities, and powers made subject to him.

Gospel, Mark 1:12-15

The Spirit drove Jesus out into the wilderness. He was in the wilderness forty days, tempted by Satan; and he was with the wild beasts; and the angels waited on him.

Now after John was arrested, Jesus came to Galilee, proclaiming the good news of God, and saying, "The time is fulfilled, and the kingdom of God has come near; repent, and believe in the good news."

A New Age—A New Lifestyle

JOHN F. CRAGHAN

We profess that Jesus introduced a new age with his proclamation of the kingdom about two thousand years ago. But for us the newness seems to have worn off. Thus we do not feel the urgency to live in a way befitting the newness of that message. We conclude that our present lifestyle is adequate.

Today's readings introduce us to the challenge of Lent. They recall sweeping changes, both in the history of Israel and in the history of the Church, which ushered in radical shifts in living. They urge us to reassess our present manner of living. In effect, they support a new age—a new lifestyle.

A Rainbow of Promise

The priestly writer of this section of Genesis offers a message of hope to the despairing exilic community. The flood brought chaos (see Gn 7:11), but God's covenant with Noah effects a new age—ultimately restoration to the land of Israel. Although the rainbow originally symbolized a warrior god to the ancients, it here presented a message of hope to a very fragile world. When the Israelites beheld the rainbow in the sky, they remembered God's promise that the waters of chaos would never return (9:11,15).

With the new age came a new way of life. In the priestly tradition of the Pentateuch, Israel was challenged to renew its sense of values. The priestly creation account accentuated the Sabbath celebration (Gn 2:2-3). The flood account stressed an avoidance of violence and the reckless oppression of humans (Gn 6:11,13; see also Ez 7:23-24). They, and many other priestly writings, insisted: a new age—a new lifestyle.

Writing from Rome some eighty years after Christ's death and Resurrection, the author of First Peter sought to strengthen the faith of believers in the northern part of present-day Turkey. After mentioning the death/Resurrection experience of Jesus, the writer dwelt on the victory over the fallen angels who had so corrupted the earth that God was compelled to send the flood. Although these spirits seduce humanity, Jesus controls their power of evil by means of his passion, death, and Resurrection.

The new age inaugurated by Christ demands a special way of life. Baptism is not a mere "removal of dirt from the body" (3:21); it is initiation into an experience that demands personal transformation. Ultimately it is a way of life in keeping with the new creation brought about by Christ. The author supports the teaching: a new age—a new lifestyle.

The Desert Experience

Mark clearly links the temptations of Jesus with his baptism by John. In baptism, Jesus accepts his messianic mission from the Father. In the temptations, Jesus begins to grapple with the means of achieving that mission. Mark's use of a tradition that spoke of angels and wild beasts suggests that Jesus had to deal with popular messianic expectations, but he goes on to show that only death and resurrection would ultimately accomplish God's mission.

In Jesus, God's definitive intervention in human history is taking place. This is a new age that calls for a new response. Jesus challenges his audience to reshape their lives in a radical fashion ("repent") and to trust in the Good News that is ultimately grounded in the life-and-death style of Jesus. For Mark, the teaching is clear: a new age—a new lifestyle.

Today's Good News

The beginning of Lent is the traditional time for making Lenten resolutions. We recall the penances we performed in past Lents and rack our brain for some new practice, something different. Today's readings may suggest that we look more deeply into our lifestyles and only then determine our Lenten practices.

What is the basic flaw in our lifestyle? What is that radical problem that seems to be at the bottom of other "lesser" problems? What keeps us from being that total person we want to be and indeed should be? Whether it is the inability to love more deeply or to trust more fully, today's readings prompt us to assess that basic fault against the background of God's supreme intervention in human history—the life of Jesus culminating in death and Resurrection.

It must be that overwhelming demonstration of love that must compel us to alter our lives. A new age—a new lifestyle.

Points for Reflection and Discussion

1. Jesus' desert experience was a time of facing temptations head-on. What temptations in your life continue to plague you? Would this Lent be a good time to face them head-on?

_____

_____

_____

_____

2. Today's stories all prepare us for something new by emphasizing change. What do you need to change in your own life in order to prepare for something new?

_____

_____

_____

_____

_____

Themes
Lent
   L1, What is Lent?
Temptation
   L3, Take a Look

Reading 1, Genesis 22:1-2,9,10-13,15-18

God tested Abraham. He said to him, "Abraham!" And he said, "Here I am." He said, "Take your son, your only son Isaac, whom you love, and go to the land of Moriah, and offer him there as a burnt offering on one of the mountains that I shall show you."

When they came to the place that God had shown him, Abraham built an altar there and laid the wood in order. Then Abraham reached out his hand and took the knife to kill his son. But the angel of the Lord called to him from heaven, and said, "Abraham, Abraham!" And he said, "Here I am." He said, "Do not lay your hand on the boy or do anything to him; for now I know that you fear God, since you have not withheld your son, your only son, from me." And Abraham looked up and saw a ram, caught in a thicket by its horns. Abraham went and took the ram and offered it up as a burnt offering instead of his son.

The angel of the Lord called to Abraham a second time from heaven, and said, "By myself I have sworn, says the Lord: Because you have done this, and have not withheld your son, your only son, I will indeed bless you, and I will make your offspring as numerous as the stars of heaven and as the sand that is on the seashore. And your offspring shall possess the gate of their enemies, and by your offspring shall all the nations of the earth gain blessing for themselves, because you have obeyed my voice."

Psalm 116:10,15,16-17,18-19

Reading 2, Romans 8:31-34

If God is for us, who is against us? He who did not withhold his own Son, but gave him up for all of us, will he not with him also give us everything else? Who will bring any charge against God's elect? It is God who justifies. Who is to condemn? It is Christ Jesus, who died, yes, who was raised, who is at the right hand of God, who indeed intercedes for us.

Gospel, Mark 9:2-10

Jesus took with him Peter and James and John, and led them up a high mountain apart, by themselves. And he was transfigured before them, and his clothes became dazzling white, such as no one on earth could bleach them. And there appeared to them Elijah with Moses, who were talking with Jesus. Then Peter said to Jesus, "Rabbi, it is good for us to be here; let us make three dwellings, one for you, one for Moses, and one for Elijah." He did not know what to say, for they were terrified. Then a cloud overshadowed them, and from the cloud there came a voice, "This is my Son, the Beloved; listen to him!" Suddenly when they looked around, they saw no one with them any more, but only Jesus.

As they were coming down the mountain, he ordered them to tell no one about what they had seen, until after the Son of Man had risen from the dead. So they kept the matter to themselves, questioning what this rising from the dead could mean.

Love Means Letting Go

JOHN F. CRAGHAN

Love means letting go. How easily we bandy about the word *love*. We love pizza, we love our city, we love our friends. But to what lengths will we go to demonstrate the depth of our love? Are we willing to place restrictions on ourselves? Do we easily accept the statement that love means letting go?

Today's readings provide classical examples of the capacity to love. They see love not as a momentary emotion but as a lifelong commitment to a person or persons. Indeed they take the object of love so seriously that nothing is too demanding to show one's profound concern and dedication. They maintain that love means letting go.

Do You Love Me?

In the present arrangement of the Book of Genesis, this account of the sacrifice of Isaac intends to edify the reader by stressing the virtues of Abraham. Up to this point, God has been promising Abraham a host of descendants and possession of a great land (see Gn 15:15,18-21). Now the promise seems to be in jeopardy because God asks Abraham to sacrifice Isaac. By his willingness to do even that, Abraham thus appears as the patron saint of utter obedience and trust.

The author captures the depth of Abraham's allegiance in these words: "Now I know that you fear God, since you have not withheld your son" (22:12). When the reader recalls Abraham's desperate desire to have an heir (see Gn 15:3), the scene takes on an added degree of pathos. "Offer him as a burnt offering" is pitted against "your only son, whom you love." In the author's view, Abraham's love of God seemingly takes precedence over his love for his son. Love means letting go.

In the Letter to the Romans, Paul examines the foundation of Christian hope, especially by speaking of the role of the Spirit. At this point he launches into a hymn about God's everlasting love. In response to the question about future opposition, he remarks: "If God is for us, who is against us?" (8:31). To dramatize the extent of

God's willingness to assist the Christian, Paul appeals to a specific kind of love, not simply to a commonplace demonstration of affection. He writes: "He who did not withhold his own Son, but gave him up for all of us, will he not with him also give us everything else?" (8:32).

It is possible that in using the expression "did not withhold his Son," Paul was alluding to Abraham's sacrifice of Isaac. Certainly, today's readings being so arranged recall Abraham's action for us. The Father and Abraham show a common interest in that they refuse to set limits to their capacity to love. Love means letting go.

It Is Good that We Are Here

Mark's account of the transfiguration is part of his disclosure of Jesus' messianic identity. Mark also includes all Christians in this process of identification. Jesus had already informed the apostles that he must suffer, die, and only then rise again (Mk 8:31). To follow Jesus, one must deny one's very self; to find oneself, one must lose oneself (Mk 8:35). In this setting the transfiguration relates to change, to transformation through giving of self—both for Jesus and for all Christians.

Although historically the transfiguration may have been a moment of intense prayer for Jesus, Mark sees it as a divine revelation linked to the baptism (see Mk 1:9-11) and the Gethsemane experience (see Mk 14:32-42). As at the baptism, Jesus is God's beloved Son. As in the Gethsemane experience, Jesus is God's beloved Son who is willing to accept the Father's will, even to the point of death. It is this ultimate self-giving that the disciples find so hard to accept. Their discussion about "rising from the dead" (9:10) is Mark's way of showing that the Lord of Easter Sunday must first be the Servant of Good Friday. For Mark, love means letting go.

Today's Good News

Letting go can cover a variety of situations. It may mean letting go of an unhealthy pursuit of career if spouse and family might suffer. It may mean letting go of alcohol or other addictions if our health and community are jeopardized. It may mean letting go of purely selfish interests if our skills and talents are needed by the community. It may mean letting go of our own convenience if the problems and pains of others demand our attention. These are but a few examples of that central reality in life: love means letting go.

Points for Reflection and Discussion

1. Have you ever experienced an "it is good that we are here!" feeling? Did letting go of it transform you?

_____

_____

_____

_____

_____

2. Is there an obstacle to transformation in your life right now? Are you willing to let go of it?

_____

_____

_____

_____

_____

Themes

Change
    L2, Saying Yes to Jesus
Lifegiving
    L3, Take a Look
Love
    L5, The Way of the Cross

Reading 1, Exodus 20:1-17

God spoke all these words: I am the Lord your God, who brought you out of the land of Egypt, out of the house of slavery; you shall have no other gods before me. You shall not make for yourself an idol, whether in the form of anything that is in heaven above, or that is on the earth beneath, or that is in the water under the earth. You shall not bow down to them or worship them; for I the Lord your God am a jealous God, punishing children for the iniquity of parents, to the third and the fourth generation of those who reject me, but showing steadfast love to the thousandth generation of those who love me and keep my commandments.

You shall not make wrongful use of the name of the Lord your God, for the Lord will not acquit anyone who misuses his name.

Remember the sabbath day, and keep it holy. Six days you shall labor and do all your work. But the seventh day is a sabbath to the Lord your God; you shall not do any work—you, your son or your daughter, your male or female slave, your livestock, or the alien resident in your towns. For in six days the Lord made heaven and earth, the sea, and all that is in them, but rested the seventh day; therefore the Lord blessed the sabbath day and consecrated it.

Honor your father and your mother, so that your days may be long in the land that the Lord your God is giving you.

You shall not murder.

You shall not commit adultery.

You shall not steal.

You shall not bear false witness against your neighbor.

You shall not covet your neighbor's house; you shall not covet your neighbor's wife, or male or female slave, or ox, or donkey, or anything that belongs to your neighbor.

Psalm 19:7,8,9,10 (NRSV)

Reading 2, 1 Corinthians 1:22-25

Jews demand signs and Greeks desire wisdom, but we proclaim Christ crucified, a stumbling block to Jews and foolishness to Gentiles, but to those who are the called, both Jews and Greeks, Christ the power of God and the wisdom of God. For God's foolishness is wiser than human wisdom, and God's weakness is stronger than human strength.

Gospel, John 2:13-25

The Passover of the Jews was near, and Jesus went up to Jerusalem. In the temple he found people selling cattle, sheep, and doves, and the money changers seated at their tables. Making a whip of cords, he drove all of them out of the temple, both the sheep and the cattle. He also poured out the coins of the money changers and overturned their tables. He told those who were selling the doves, "Take these things out of here! Stop making my Father's house a marketplace!" His disciples remembered that it was written, "Zeal for your house will consume me."

The Jews then said to him, "What sign can you show us for doing this?" Jesus answered them, "Destroy this temple, and in three days I will raise it up." The Jews then said, "This temple has been under construction for forty-six years, and will you raise it up in three days?" But he was speaking of the temple of his body. After he was raised from the dead, his disciples remembered that he had said this; and they believed the scripture and the word that Jesus had spoken.

When he was in Jerusalem during the Passover festival, many believed in his name because they saw the signs that he was doing. But Jesus on his part would not entrust himself to them, because he knew all people and needed no one to testify about anyone; for he himself knew what was in everyone.

* Please note that the *Cycle A* readings for the third Sunday of Lent (page 140) may be substituted for these readings.

Trust

JOHN F. CRAGHAN

Before we decide to trust someone, we often look for credentials or tangible proof that will in turn dictate the extent of our confidence in that person. When we have no such credentials or tangible proof, we have no trust. Without realizing it, we are articulating the truth that we want our trust to rest on a foundation of experience.

Today's readings deal with the perennial problem of trust. They address the issue of trust by referring to its foundations. They look to concrete historical events that serve as proof of the reasonableness of trust.

Seven of the ten commandments are a form of tribal wisdom. They are expressions of the practice of the tribal community, sanctioned by tribal authority, and aimed at the good of the community (see Jer 35:6-10). As such, they came before Moses and the Exodus experience. They stemmed from a recognition that some actions promote community while other actions harm community.

Whom Do You Trust?

In the commandments, the older regulations are ratified as accepted legislation. It is no longer a question of obeying the tribal elders, although that is certainly commendable. The stamp of approval by God makes them a matter of loyalty to God. "I am the Lord your God, who brought you out of the land of Egypt, out of the house of slavery" (Ex 20:2) captures God's intervention in history on behalf of Israel. It reminds the people of God's credentials and offers tangible proof. God has the right to impose law, and God's law is worthy of trust.

In dealing with his Corinthian community, Paul has to face the issue of credibility and trust. The Greeks desire some form of revelation that they can debate as worthy of rational acceptance. The Jews seek some sign or miracle that will provide a basis for confidence. Confronted by these requests for credentials, Paul offers only one: "We proclaim Christ crucified, a stumbling block to Jews and foolishness to Gentiles" (1:23).

For Paul, the cross is so central that the gospel message is unintelligible without it. It is that historical event that summarizes the whole plan of salvation. As Paul writes elsewhere, "...the Son of God, who loved me and gave himself for me" (Gal 2:20). Only this divine folly and this divine weakness can account for the loyalty of the Christian. For Paul, the cross is the foundation for trust.

Rebuilding the Temple

In the cleansing of the Temple, Jesus appears as a latter-day Jeremiah who addresses the abuses of God's dwelling place (see Jer 7:1-15;26:1-19). He also seems to appeal to the text from Zechariah concerning the second Temple: "And there shall no longer be traders in the house of the Lord of hosts on that day" (14:21). If those in charge of the Temple continue to destroy it after the manner of their forebears, then Jesus will raise up a new but unspecified Temple in a brief period of time (see Tb 14:5).

The author of the gospel has adapted the original event to speak about the foundation of trust. Jesus' zeal for the Temple is the reason for his death, and his resurrected Body becomes the new Temple. The demand for a sign (and thus for Jesus' credibility) is answered in terms of Jesus' death/Resurrection experience.

Today's Good News

Today's believer can ask timely questions about his or her reason for performing or neglecting duties. Is obedience to civil and Church laws grounded in Jesus who suffered, died, and rose again? Are we really loyal to Jesus because he has demonstrated concern and, therefore, is worthy of our trust? Are we really conscious of this foundation as we interact with the members of our community? Are they deserving of loyalty because Jesus suffered, died, and rose for them?

In the same line of reasoning, do we choose to imitate Jesus' self-giving and thereby offer concrete proof of our trustworthiness? Do we win loyalty by reaching out to others and meeting their needs, or do we simply demand trust and confidence unconditionally? Do we treat our family with a respect that shows itself in action? For the author of the Ten Commandments, for Paul, and for John, trust is a response to an experience of trustworthiness.

Points for Reflection and Discussion

1. Do you know someone who is completely trustworthy? What qualities make them so? Are you completely trustworthy?

_____

_____

_____

_____

_____

2. Do you believe the Ten Commandments are valid laws in today's world? Why or why not?

_____

_____

_____

_____

_____

Themes
Cross
    L5, The Way of the Cross
Law
    L4, The Nicene Creed
Trust
    L2, Saying Yes to Jesus

Reading 1, 2 Chronicles 36:14-17,19-23

All the leading priests and the people also were exceedingly unfaithful, following all the abominations of the nations; and they polluted the house of the Lord that he had consecrated in Jerusalem.

The Lord, the God of their ancestors, sent persistently to them by his messengers, because he had compassion on his people and on his dwelling place; but they kept mocking the messengers of God, despising his words, and scoffing at his prophets, until the wrath of the Lord against his people became so great that there was no remedy. Therefore he brought up against them the king of the Chaldeans, who killed their youths with the sword in the house of their sanctuary, and had no compassion on young man or young woman, the aged or the feeble; he gave them all into his hand. They burned the house of God, broke down the wall of Jerusalem, burned all its palaces with fire, and destroyed all its precious vessels. He took into exile in Babylon those who had escaped from the sword, and they became servants to him and to his sons until the establishment of the kingdom of Persia, to fulfill the word of the Lord by the mouth of Jeremiah, until the land had made up for its sabbaths. All the days that it lay desolate it kept sabbath, to fulfill seventy years.

In the first year of King Cyrus of Persia, in fulfillment of the word of the Lord spoken by Jeremiah, the Lord stirred up the spirit of King Cyrus of Persia so that he sent a herald throughout all his kingdom and also declared in a written edict: "Thus says King Cyrus of Persia: The Lord, the God of heaven, has given me all the kingdoms of the earth, and he has charged me to build him a house at Jerusalem, which is in Judah. Whoever is among you of all his people, may the Lord his God be with him! Let him go up."

Psalm 137:1-2,3,4-5,6

Reading 2, Ephesians 2:4-10

God, who is rich in mercy, out of the great love with which he loved us even when we were dead through our trespasses, made us alive together with Christ—by grace you have been saved—and raised us up with him and seated us with him in the heavenly places in Christ Jesus, so that in the ages to come he might show the immeasurable riches of his grace in kindness toward us in Christ Jesus. For by grace you have been saved through faith, and this is not your own doing; it is the gift of God—not the result of works, so that no one may boast. For we are what he has made us, created in Christ Jesus for good works, which God prepared beforehand to be our way of life.

Gospel, John 3:14-21

Jesus said to Nicodemus:

Just as Moses lifted up the serpent in the wilderness, so must the Son of Man be lifted up, that whoever believes in him may have eternal life. For God so loved the world that he gave his only Son, so that everyone who believes in him may not perish but may have eternal life. Indeed, God did not send the Son into the world to condemn the world, but in order that the world might be saved through him. Those who believe in him are not condemned; but those who do not believe are condemned already, because they have not believed in the name of the only Son of God. And this is the judgment, that the light has come into the world, and people loved darkness rather than light because their deeds were evil. For all who do evil hate the light and do not come to the light, so that their deeds may not be exposed. But those who do what is true come to the light, so that it may be clearly seen that their deeds have been done in God.

* **Please note that** *Cycle A* **readings for the fourth Sunday of Lent (page 142) may be substituted for these readings.**

Family Traits

JOHN F. CRAGHAN

In everyday life we meet the weak and the strong, the unfit and the fit. We applaud the successes of the strong and the accomplishments of the fit. But how do we react to the failures of the weak and the debacles of the unfit? Do we endorse the notion that only the fit survive or is there room for compassion?

Today's readings are a study in compassion. They reveal a God who chooses to identify with the weak and the unfit, a God who refuses to make success and accomplishments the ultimate criterion for God's elect. They are an ever timely appeal to the believing community: Be compassionate—it's a family trait.

The Chronicler (the author of First and Second Chronicles, Ezra, and Nehemiah) paints a dismal picture of the events surrounding the destruction of Jerusalem in 586 B.C. and the subsequent exile. God's people repeatedly rejected the message of the prophets and continued in their sinfulness, although God "had compassion on his people and on his dwelling place" (36:15). As a result, God was forced to use the Chaldeans (the neo-Babylonians) as the agents of God's displeasure with the people. Citing the seventy years mentioned by Jeremiah (25:12), the author sees the exile as the fulfillment of the prophet's message.

A God of Compassion

Destruction, however, is not the final chapter in the story of God's dealings with people. Using the Persian king Cyrus as spokesperson in 538 B.C., Yahweh offers the possibility of renewal and reconciliation. The return to Jerusalem is an example of God's relentless relationship with God's people. Indeed it is only fitting that the last verses form the conclusion of the Hebrew Bible (2 Chr 36:22-23—taken from Ezr 1:1-3). Be compassionate—it's a family trait.

The author of Ephesians begins this chapter by mentioning sinfulness, which is characterized as a form of death. In the face of these obvious weaknesses, the author presses on to note God's compassion: "...God, who is rich in mercy" (2:4). This concept is developed via reference to the community's participation in the mystery of Christ. With Christ they are brought to life together (2:5), raised up together, and enthroned together (2:6). As the author further remarks, such compassion is God's gift (2:8).

The experience of God's compassion is not a past event that one easily forgets. The author reminds the people that they in turn are to show the same concern to others. To receive compassion means to mediate compassion: "...be kind to one another, tenderhearted, forgiving one another, as God in Christ has forgiven you" (Eph 4:32). Be compassionate—it's a family trait.

God So Loved the World

This gospel passage is part of Jesus' conversation with Nicodemus (Jn 3:1-21). John points out that to be begotten of the Spirit (3:8) depends on Jesus' passion/death/Resurrection experience. The comparison with Moses' bronze serpent (see Nm 21:9) indicates that to be "lifted up" (3:14) means nothing less than the crucifixion (see Jn 12:32-33). Ultimately this being "lifted up" brings life to all believers (see Jn 7:37-39).

John also accentuates compassion in this passage. After the manner of Abraham, the Father loves the world to such an extent that he gives his *only* Son (see Gn 22:2,12,18). This giving makes eternal life possible for the believer. Be compassionate—it's a family trait.

Today's Good News

The weak and the unfit come in many shapes and sizes. We know all too well of the alcoholics, the AIDS victims, the homeless, the handicapped, and so forth. Usually our first reaction to their plight is pity. Our reaction to their needs is perhaps referral to some governmental or charitable institution. At this point we may excuse ourselves and think that we have exhausted our capacity for compassion.

Yet the Gospel of John suggests that we be willing to give of ourselves and inject ourselves into their problems. Such giving links us to the Trinity. The world's problems become ours as well. Be compassionate—it's a family trait.

Points for Reflection and Discussion

1. Do you see a difference between "pity" and "compassion"? Is one better than the other? Discuss the two.

_____

_____

_____

_____

_____

2. Is compassion a trait in your family? In your parish family? Discuss the two.

_____

_____

_____

_____

_____

Themes

Compassion
  L5, The Way of the Cross
Family
  L2, Saying Yes to Jesus

Reading 1, Jeremiah 31:31-34

The days are surely coming, says the Lord, when I will make a new covenant with the house of Israel and the house of Judah. It will not be like the covenant that I made with their ancestors when I took them by the hand to bring them out of the land of Egypt—a covenant that they broke, though I was their husband, says the Lord. But this is the covenant that I will make with the house of Israel after those days, says the Lord: I will put my law within them, and I will write it on their hearts; and I will be their God, and they shall be my people. No longer shall they teach one another, or say to each other, "Know the Lord," for they shall all know me, from the least of them to the greatest, says the Lord; for I will forgive their iniquity, and remember their sin no more.

Psalm 51:1-2,10-11,12-13 (NRSV)

Reading 2, Hebrews 5:7-9

In the days of his flesh, Jesus offered up prayers and supplications, with loud cries and tears, to the one who was able to save him from death, and he was heard because of his reverent submission. Although he was a Son, he learned obedience through what he suffered; and having been made perfect, he became the source of eternal salvation for all who obey him.

Gospel, John 12:20-33

Among those who went up to worship at the festival were some Greeks. They came to Philip, who was from Bethsaida in Galilee, and said to him, "Sir, we wish to see Jesus." Philip went and told Andrew; then Andrew and Philip went and told Jesus. Jesus answered them, "The hour has come for the Son of Man to be glorified. Very truly, I tell you, unless a grain of wheat falls into the earth and dies, it remains just a single grain; but if it dies, it bears much fruit. Those who love their life lose it, and those who hate their life in this world will keep it for eternal life. Whoever serves me must follow me, and where I am, there will my servant be also. Whoever serves me, the Father will honor.

"Now my soul is troubled. And what should I say— 'Father, save me from this hour'? No, it is for this reason that I have come to this hour. Father, glorify your name." Then a voice came from heaven, "I have glorified it, and I will glorify it again." The crowd standing there heard it and said that it was thunder. Others said, "An angel has spoken to him."

Jesus answered, "This voice has come for your sake, not for mine. Now is the judgment of this world; now the ruler of this world will be driven out. And I, when I am lifted up from the earth, will draw all people to myself." He said this to indicate the kind of death he was to die.

---

* Please note that *Cycle A* readings for the fifth Sunday of Lent (page 144) may be substituted for these readings.

God's Concern Is Our Concern

JOHN F. CRAGHAN

It is so tempting to remain aloof, unattached, and uninvolved. We see problems and needs on all sides. But all too often we do not see them as *our* problems and *our* needs. We cannot help but notice the hurting and the depressed. But we rationalize they are God's concern, not ours. It seems almost too much to imagine that God's concern is our concern.

Today's readings stress the reality of relationships. They understand people against the background of covenant. People relate to God by relating to one another. These readings imply that to worship God is to meet the needs of God's people. God's concern is our concern.

Written on Their Hearts

It is likely that Jeremiah originally addressed this message of hope to the northern kingdom of Israel during the time of national revival around 624-623 B.C. (Later editors adapted the message to suit the needs of the southern kingdom of Judah.) The prophet believed things had gotten so bad that Yahweh's direct intervention was needed to remedy the situation. In this renewal, Yahweh would effect a profound interior change among the people. The change would be so extensive that the people would not require any instruction. This change was to be ultimately the result of Yahweh's intention to forgive and forget human sinfulness.

As a prophet, Jeremiah made God's problem his problem. This problem, namely, the communication of God's intention to the community, demanded that Jeremiah announce both the sinfulness of his audience and God's willingness to forgive. As other parts of the Book of Jeremiah show, the prophet suffered enormously in the discharge of his office, but Jeremiah understood that if Yahweh was to be the God of this people in a new way (31:33), then Yahweh needed Jeremiah to articulate Yahweh's plan. Here, God's concern is Jeremiah's concern.

The High Priest Glorified

In today's passage from Hebrews, the author discusses the high priesthood of Jesus. This is an office that God as Father bestows on him for the benefit of others. As high priest, Jesus represents people before God. He makes a sin offering for them. He intercedes for them. As the unique high priest, however, he assumes the responsibility of winning salvation for sinful humanity.

By making God's problem (salvation) his problem, Jesus experiences pain and frustration. When confronted with the reality of his own death, he must address his Father with loud cries and tears (5:7). Indeed the pain and frustration teach him obedience so that he can accomplish his Father's will. It is this loving acceptance that will constitute him high priest. Here, God's concern is Jesus' concern.

For John, the word *hour* encapsulates the entire process of crucifixion, resurrection, and ascension. This *hour* also includes the salvation of the Gentiles ("some Greeks" in 12:20). Jesus is willing to lay down his life for all peoples. This moment, however, is also a temptation for Jesus to do his own will, not his Father's.

In chapter twelve of his gospel, John gives his version of Jesus' agony in the garden. There is his poignant expression of pain: "Now my soul is troubled" (12:27; see also Mk 14:34). Yet Jesus prays that his Father's will be done: "Father, glorify your name" (12:28; see also Mk 14:35-36). To this the Father responds that the acceptance of this aspect of the *hour* will result in Jesus' exaltation with him (12:28). In effect, John has Jesus respond to his Father's will: God's concern is Jesus' concern.

Today's Good News

Our response to making God's concern our concern does not entail enormous scrutiny or research. Perhaps we do best to look at the relationships we have with our spouses, our families, our local communities, our parishes, and so forth. If we are on good terms with them we are on good terms with God. If our spouses or families are hurting, God is concerned and so should we be. We cannot remain aloof and unconcerned.

Like Jesus and Jeremiah, we are tempted to flee the scene and abdicate our responsibility. We want the hurting to be helped, but we want our God to do it alone. By accepting the implications of our relationships, we take on the loud cries and tears of Jesus and Jeremiah. But we cannot have it any other way. To accept this God is to accept God's extended family. Hence, God's concern is our concern.

Points for Reflection and Discussion

1. Is there anyone in your immediate family who is hurting? Is there something you can do to alleviate his or her pain? Have you tried?

_____

_____

_____

_____

2. If God's concern is our concern, then God's family is our family. Are there people in God's family whom you find unacceptable? How do you reconcile this?

_____

_____

_____

_____

Themes

Forgiveness
     L3, Take a Look
Suffering
     L5, The Way of the Cross

Procession With Palms, Mark 11:1-10 *

When they were approaching Jerusalem, at Bethphage and Bethany, near the Mount of Olives, Jesus sent two of his disciples and said to them, "Go into the village ahead of you, and immediately as you enter it, you will find tied there a colt that has never been ridden; untie it and bring it. If anyone says to you, 'Why are you doing this?' just say this, 'The Lord needs it and will send it back here immediately.' " They went away and found a colt tied near a door, outside in the street. As they were untying it, some of the bystanders said to them, "What are you doing, untying the colt?" They told them what Jesus had said; and they allowed them to take it. Then they brought the colt to Jesus and threw their cloaks on it; and he sat on it. Many people spread their cloaks on the road, and others spread leafy branches that they had cut in the fields. Then those who went ahead and those who followed were shouting,

>*"Hosanna! Blessed is the one who comes in the name of the Lord! Blessed is the coming kingdom of our ancestor David! Hosanna in the highest heaven!"*

* alternate reading - Procession With Palms, John 12:12-16

Reading 1, Isaiah 50:4-7

The Lord God has given me the tongue of a teacher, that I may know how to sustain the weary with a word. Morning by morning he wakens—wakens my ear to listen as those who are taught. The Lord God has opened my ear, and I was not rebellious, I did not turn backward. I gave my back to those who struck me, and my cheeks to those who pulled out the beard; I did not hide my face from insult and spitting. The Lord God helps me; therefore I have not been disgraced; therefore I have set my face like flint, and I know that I shall not be put to shame.

Psalm 22:7-8,16-17,18-19,22-23 (NRSV)

Reading 2, Philippians 2:5-11 (NRSV)

Let the same mind be in you that was in Christ Jesus, who, though he was in the form of God, did not regard equality with God as something to be exploited, but emptied himself, taking the form of a slave, being born in human likeness. And being found in human form, he humbled himself and became obedient to the point of death—even death on a cross. Therefore God also highly exalted him and gave him the name that is above every name, so that at the name of Jesus every knee should bend, in heaven and on earth and under the earth, and every tongue should confess that Jesus Christ is Lord, to the glory of God the Father.

Gospel, Mark 14:1—15:47

It was two days before the Passover and the festival of Unleavened Bread. The chief priests and the scribes were looking for a way to arrest Jesus by stealth and kill him; for they said, "Not during the festival, or there may be a riot among the people."

While he was at Bethany in the house of Simon the leper, as he sat at the table, a woman came with an alabaster jar of very costly ointment of nard, and she broke open the jar and poured the ointment on his head. But some were there who said to one another in anger, "Why was the ointment wasted in this way? For this ointment could have been sold for more than three hundred denarii, and the money given to the poor." And they scolded her. But Jesus said, "Let her alone; why do you trouble her? She has performed a good service for me. For you always have the poor with you, and you can show kindness to them whenever you wish; but you will not always have me. She has done what she could; she has anointed my body beforehand for its burial. Truly I tell you, wherever the good news is proclaimed in the whole world, what she has done will be told in remembrance of her."

Then Judas Iscariot, who was one of the twelve, went to the chief priests in order to betray him to them. When they heard it, they were greatly pleased, and promised to give him money. So he began to look for an opportunity to betray him.

On the first day of Unleavened Bread, when the Passover lamb is sacrificed, his disciples said to him, "Where do you want us to go and make the preparations for you to eat the Passover?" So he sent two of his disciples, saying to them, "Go into the city, and a man carrying a jar of water will meet you; follow him, and wherever he enters, say to the owner of the house, 'The Teacher asks, Where is my guest room where I may eat the Passover with my disciples?' He will show you a large room upstairs, furnished and ready. Make preparations for us there." So the disciples set out and went to the city, and found everything as he had told them; and they prepared the Passover meal.

When it was evening, he came with the twelve. And when they had taken their places and were eating, Jesus said, "Truly I tell you, one of you will betray me, one who is eating with me." They began to be distressed and to say to him one after another, "Surely, not I?" He said to them, "It is one of the twelve, one who is dipping bread into the bowl with me. For the Son of Man goes as it is written of him, but woe to that one by whom the Son of Man is betrayed! It would have been better for that one not to have been born."

While they were eating, he took a loaf of bread, and after blessing it he broke it, gave it to them, and said,

"Take; this is my body." Then he took a cup, and after giving thanks he gave it to them, and all of them drank from it. He said to them, "This is my blood of the covenant, which is poured out for many. Truly I tell you, I will never again drink of the fruit of the vine until that day when I drink it new in the kingdom of God."

When they had sung the hymn, they went out to the Mount of Olives. And Jesus said to them, "You will all become deserters; for it is written, 'I will strike the shepherd, and the sheep will be scattered.' But after I am raised up, I will go before you to Galilee." Peter said to him, "Even though all become deserters, I will not." Jesus said to him, "Truly I tell you, this day, this very night, before the cock crows twice, you will deny me three times." But he said vehemently, "Even though I must die with you, I will not deny you." And all of them said the same.

They went to a place called Gethsemane; and he said to his disciples, "Sit here while I pray." He took with him Peter and James and John, and began to be distressed and agitated. And said to them, "I am deeply grieved, even to death; remain here, and keep awake." And going a little farther, he threw himself on the ground and prayed that, if it were possible, the hour might pass from him. He said, "Abba, Father, for you all things are possible; remove this cup from me; yet, not what I want, but what you want." He came and found them sleeping; and he said to Peter, "Simon, are you asleep? Could you not keep awake one hour? Keep awake and pray that you may not come into the time of trial; the spirit indeed is willing, but the flesh is weak." And again he went away and prayed, saying the same words. And once more he came and found them sleeping, for their eyes were very heavy; and they did not know what to say to him. He came a third time and said to them, "Are you still sleeping and taking your rest? Enough! The hour has come; the Son of Man is betrayed into the hands of sinners. Get up, let us be going. See, my betrayer is at hand."

Immediately, while he was still speaking, Judas, one of the twelve, arrived; and with him there was a crowd with swords and clubs, from the chief priests, the scribes, and the elders. Now the betrayer had given them a sign, saying, "The one I will kiss is the man; arrest him and lead him away under guard." So when he came, he went up to him at once and said, "Rabbi!" and kissed him. Then they laid hands on him and arrested him. But one of those who stood near drew his sword and struck the slave of the high priest, cutting off his ear. Then Jesus said to them, "Have you come out with swords and clubs to arrest me as though I were a bandit? Day after day I was with you in the temple teaching, and you did not arrest me. But let the scriptures be fulfilled." All of them deserted him and fled.

A certain young man was following him, wearing nothing but a linen cloth. They caught hold of him, but he left the linen cloth and ran off naked.

They took Jesus to the high priest; and all the chief priests, the elders, and the scribes were assembled. Peter had followed him at a distance, right into the courtyard of the high priest; and he was sitting with the guards, warming himself at the fire. Now the chief priests and the whole council were looking for testimony against Jesus to put him to death; but they found none. For many gave false testimony against him, and their testimony did not agree. Some stood up and gave false testimony against him, saying, "We heard him say, 'I will destroy this temple that is made with hands, and in three days I will build another, not made with hands.' " But even on this point their testimony did not agree.

Then the high priest stood up before them and asked Jesus, "Have you no answer? What is it that they testify against you?" But he was silent and did not answer. Again the high priest asked him, "Are you the Messiah, the Son of the Blessed One?" Jesus said, "I am; and 'you will see the Son of Man seated at the right hand of the Power,' and 'coming with the clouds of heaven.' " Then the high priest tore his clothes and said, "Why do we still need witnesses? You have heard his blasphemy! What is your decision?" All of them condemned him as deserving death. Some began to spit on him, to blindfold him, and to strike him, saying to him, "Prophesy!" The guards also took him over and beat him.

While Peter was below in the courtyard, one of the servant-girls of the high priest came by. When she saw Peter warming himself, she stared at him and said, "You also were with Jesus, the man from Nazareth." But he denied it, saying, "I do not know or understand what you are talking about." And he went out into the forecourt. Then the cock crowed. And the servant-girl, on seeing him, began again to say to the bystanders, "This man is one of them." But again he denied it. Then after a little while the bystanders again said to Peter, "Certainly you are one of them; for you are a Galilean." But he began to curse, and he swore an oath, "I do not know this man you are talking about." At that moment the cock crowed for the second time. Then Peter remembered that Jesus had said to him, "Before the cock crows twice, you will deny me three times." And he broke down and wept.

As soon as it was morning, the chief priests held a consultation with the elders and scribes and the whole council. They bound Jesus, led him away, and handed him over to Pilate. Pilate asked him, "Are you the King of the Jews?" He answered him, "You say so." Then the chief priests accused him of many things. Pilate asked him again, "Have you no answer? See how many charges they bring against you." But Jesus made no further reply, so that Pilate was amazed.

Now at the festival he used to release a prisoner for them, anyone for whom they asked. Now a man called Barabbas was in prison with the rebels who had committed murder during the insurrection. So the crowd came and began to ask Pilate to do for them according to his custom. Then he answered them, "Do you want me to release for you the King of the Jews?" For he realized that it was out of jealousy that the chief priests had handed him over. But the chief priests stirred up the crowd to have him release Barabbas for them instead. Pilate spoke to them again, "Then what do you wish me to do with the man you call the King of the Jews?" They shouted back, "Crucify him!" Pilate asked them, "Why, what evil has he done?" But they shouted all the more, "Crucify him!" So Pilate, wishing to satisfy the crowd, released Barabbas for them; and after flogging Jesus, he handed him over to be crucified.

Then the soldiers led him into the courtyard of the palace (that is, the governor's headquarters); and they called together the whole cohort. And they clothed him in a purple cloak; and after twisting some thorns into a crown, they put it on him. And they began saluting him, "Hail, King of the Jews!" They struck his head with a reed, spat upon him, and knelt down in homage to him. After mocking him, they stripped him of the purple cloak and put his own clothes on him. Then they led him out to crucify him. They compelled a passer-by, who was coming in from the country, to carry his cross; it was Simon of Cyrene, the father of Alexander and Rufus. Then they brought Jesus to the place called Golgotha (which means the place of a skull). And they offered him wine mixed with myrrh; but he did not take it. And they crucified him, and divided his clothes among them, casting lots to decide what each should take. It was nine o'clock in the morning when they crucified him. The inscription of the charge against him read, "The King of the Jews."

And with him they crucified two bandits, one on his right and one on his left. Those who passed by derided him, shaking their heads and saying, "Aha! You who would destroy the temple and build it in three days, save yourself, and come down from the cross!" In the same way the chief priests, along with the scribes, were also mocking him among themselves and saying, "He saved others; he cannot save himself. Let the Messiah, the King of Israel, come down from the cross now, so that we may see and believe." Those who were crucified with him also taunted him.

When it was noon, darkness came over the whole land until three in the afternoon. At three o'clock Jesus cried out with a loud voice, "Eloi, Eloi, lema sabachthani?" which means, "My God, my God, why have you forsaken me?" When some of the bystanders heard it, they said, "Listen, he is calling for Elijah." And someone ran, filled a sponge with sour wine, put it on a stick, and gave it to him to drink, saying, "Wait, let us see whether Elijah will come to take him down."

Then Jesus gave a loud cry and breathed his last. And the curtain of the temple was torn in two, from top to bottom. Now when the centurion, who stood facing him, saw that in this way he breathed his last, he said, "Truly this man was God's Son!" There were also women looking on from a distance; among them were Mary Magdalene, and Mary the mother of James the younger and of Joses, and Salome. These used to follow him and provided for him when he was in Galilee; and there were many other women who had come up with him to Jerusalem.

When evening had come, and since it was the day of Preparation, that is, the day before the sabbath, Joseph of Arimathea, a respected member of the council, who was also himself waiting expectantly for the kingdom of God, went boldly to Pilate and asked for the body of Jesus. Then Pilate wondered if he were already dead; and summoning the centurion, he asked him whether he had been dead for some time. When he learned from the centurion that he was dead, he granted the body to Joseph. Then Joseph bought a linen cloth, and taking down the body, wrapped it in the linen cloth, and laid it in a tomb that had been hewn out of the rock. He then rolled a stone against the door of the tomb. Mary Magdalene and Mary the mother of Joses saw where the body was laid.

The Measure Of Success

JOHN F. CRAGHAN

Self-giving is the measure of success. Each day we calculate our achievements. We may look at our bank balance. We may consider the admiration of our public. We may note the flattering use of our name. We may reflect on our power and authority. But how accurate are these criteria?

Today's readings powerfully suggest that we opt for a more objective and realistic norm. They announce that we direct our attention and energies to focus on others. They maintain that the proper gauge of achievement is the service of others. Here, self-giving is the measure of success.

The passage from Isaiah is part of the third Suffering Servant Song (Is 50:4-9). Spoken toward the end of exile in Babylon, this song reveals Israel as a prophetic figure obedient to the Word of God. Unfortunately not all responded to the message of this prophet. Indeed their lack of response expresses itself in reprisals. Beating, plucking of the beard, buffeting, and spitting are some of the ways in which the unwilling audience reacted to the forlorn prophet.

I Am Not Disgraced

This passage contrasts the prophet's seeming failure with his unshakable confidence. He boldly proclaims that God is his support and hence he will not be disgraced. With God on his side who can possibly be against him? Rejecting his apparently dismal performance and seeing his mistreatment as a gauge of his dedication, he solemnly attests that self-giving is the measure of success.

Jesus Christ Is Lord

Borrowing a Jewish-Christian hymn and making some adaptations, Paul sings of humanity as God intended it. Although Jesus should not have been subject to death and corruption (see Wis 2:23), he put aside the privileges of divine honor and embraced a life of pain and frustration ("emptied himself," 2:7). Though he was the same as all other humans in nature ("in human likeness," *ibid*) , he was nonetheless different ("found in human form," *ibid*). The difference was that he did not have to be reconciled to God. Notwithstanding, he experienced death.

Paul quickly notes that death did not have the last word. By emptying himself, Jesus fulfilled himself. God exalted him and conferred on him the title and authority previously reserved to the Father. Consequently everyone must acknowledge that Jesus is Lord (see Is 45:23).

Mark provides a shocking exposé of the events leading to the death of Jesus. At the same time, he sees the passion account as the moment for appreciating the full identity of his hero. This is the Jesus who said earlier: "Whoever wishes to be first among you must be slave of all. For the Son of Man came not to be served but to serve, and to give his life a ransom for many" (Mk 10:44-45). The passion narrative is simply the unfolding of this startling paradox.

The Jewish trial (14:53—15:1) establishes not Jesus' guilt but his unique dignity (Messiah, Son of the Blessed One, and exalted Son of Man). But the revelation results in the cry of blasphemy and abuse. The Roman trial (15:2-20) proclaims Jesus the king of the Jews. But the proclamation provokes only the "homage" of the soldiers. The crucifixion scene elicits the title of "the Messiah, the king of Israel." Flanked by criminals on his right and left, however, Jesus dies abandoned by most of his disciples and seemingly deserted by his Father. Despite it all, the centurion confesses: "Truly this man was God's Son!" (15:39). In the light of Easter morning, that profession states unequivocally that self-giving is the measure of success.

Today's Good News

The cross must be the real test of achievement, not the bank balance, not the admiration, not the power or authority. The lonely figure mounted on the Roman form of capital punishment serves to direct our attention to our hurting world. To be a follower of the Messiah is to show concern for the Messiah's extended family. To be a disciple of the exalted Son of Man is to reveal empathy for the Son of Man's charges. To be a devotee of the king of the Jews is to show devotion to the king's subjects.

Mark shows us that the lofty titles of Jesus are genuine only to the extent that he gives his life as "a ransom for many." The titles we bear and the hats we wear are real only insofar as they provoke us to reach out to others. Self-giving is the measure of success.

Points for Reflection and Discussion

1. Are you a successful person? What is your greatest achievement?

_____

_____

_____

_____

2. How do you respond to ridicule? How does it make you feel (the ridicule and your response)?

_____

_____

_____

_____

Themes
Death
    L1, What is Lent?
Prophecy
    L7, The Meaning of Holy Week

Reading 1, Acts of the Apostles 10:34,37-43

Peter began to speak to them: The message spread throughout Judea, beginning in Galilee after the baptism that John announced: how God anointed Jesus of Nazareth with the Holy Spirit and with power; how he went about doing good and healing all who were oppressed by the devil, for God was with him. We are witnesses to all that he did both in Judea and in Jerusalem. They put him to death by hanging him on a tree; but God raised him on the third day and allowed him to appear, not to all the people but to us who were chosen by God as witnesses, and who ate and drank with him after he rose from the dead. He commanded us to preach to the people and to testify that he is the one ordained by God as judge of the living and the dead. All the prophets testify about him that everyone who believes in him receives forgiveness of sins through his name.

Psalm 118:1-2,16-17,22-23

Reading 2, Colossians 3:1-4 *

If you have been raised with Christ, seek the things that are above, where Christ is, seated at the right hand of God. Set your minds on things that are above, not on things that are on earth, for you have died, and your life is hidden with Christ in God. When Christ who is your life is revealed, then you also will be revealed with him in glory.

*alternate reading - 1 Corinthians 5:6-8

Gospel, John 20:1-9 **

Early on the first day of the week, while it was still dark, Mary Magdalene came to the tomb and saw that the stone had been removed from the tomb. So she ran and went to Simon Peter and the other disciple, the one whom Jesus loved, and said to them, "They have taken the Lord out of the tomb, and we do not know where they have laid him." Then Peter and the other disciple set out and went toward the tomb. The two were running together, but the other disciple outran Peter and reached the tomb first. He bent down to look in and saw the linen wrappings lying there, but he did not go in. Then Simon Peter came, following him, and went into the tomb. He saw the linen wrappings lying there, and the cloth that had been on Jesus' head, not lying with the linen wrappings but rolled up in a place by itself. Then the other disciple, who reached the tomb first, also went in, and he saw and believed; for as yet they did not understand the scripture, that he must rise from the dead.

**alternate reading - Mark 16:1-8

The Paradox Of Easter

JOHN F. CRAGHAN

We become so used to the *alleluias* of Easter Sunday. We hear the Good News that the Father has saved the Son. But does it really strike us as news? We seem resigned to accept the fact that the tomb is actually empty. But what does the empty tomb really mean?

Today's readings are studies in paradox. They focus on statements that seem contradictory or opposed to common sense. They upset us by pointing out that we should reassess those divine ways that don't seem to go together. They boldly proclaim that Easter is a paradox.

Today's passage from the Acts of the Apostles is the beginning of the mission to the Gentiles. Peter explains to the Gentile Cornelius and his household that the Jewish Jesus now reaches out to non-Jews (see Lk 4:16-30). The proclamation of the Good News and Jesus' anointing with the Spirit envision all of humanity. Jesus of Nazareth now impacts the Gentile community.

An Easter People

This speech is also an example of Easter paradox. After a brief summary of Jesus' ministry (10:37-39), there is mention of Good Friday, the killing of Jesus (see also Acts 2:23-24;4:10). God, however, transforms this act of murder into the beautiful reality of new life. By raising up Jesus, the Father makes possible the sharing of that new life with believers. Good Friday is overcome by Easter Sunday. The paradox of Easter.

Paul tells the people of Colossae that baptism into Christ gives us a mystical share in the death and resurrection experience: "...if you have been raised with Christ..." (3:1); "for you have died..." (3:3); "When Christ...is revealed,...you also will be revealed with him in glory" (3:4). This is not a question of *material* versus *spiritual*. We are *both*, in the here-and-now, and our present resurrected state is challenge rather than comfort. We are an Easter people. We are paradox.

Of Stones and Cornerstones

Mary of Magdala is the first witness to the empty tomb, but she thinks Jesus' body has been stolen and she leaves. Peter is the first one to enter the tomb, and he witnesses the burial cloths with the head covering rolled up in a separate place. "Then the other disciple...also went in" (Jn 20:8). This *other disciple* is found only in the Gospel of John, and only in four scenes: at the Last Supper (13:23), beside the cross (19:26), and in a subsequent Resurrection account (21:7). He is identified only as "the disciple whom Jesus loved," perhaps offered as a model for us. The author credits him with being the first to come to faith: "and he saw and believed" (20:8). What did he see that Peter missed? Why didn't Mary see it? The faith of Easter is a paradox.

The Resurrection breaks into everyday human history at specific times and places, confronting and calling each of us. Easter faith is neither wishful thinking nor mass delusion. By telling his story of the first Easter morning, the author of John's Gospel shows that Christianity's central belief is grounded upon three separate kinds of evidence, and each is sufficient unto itself. There is factual testimony (of an empty tomb); there is personal witness (of Peter and the other disciple); and there is biblical prophecy (Jn 20:9; see Lk 24:26; 1 Cor 15:4; also Ps 16:10; Hos 6:2; Jon 2:1,2,11).

Today's Good News

The message of Easter is the challenge to turn our own lives around. As we review our lives, we immediately conjure up the failures, the mistakes, those less-than-glorious moments. To learn of the empty tomb is to begin to fill the void in our lives. The Risen One reminds us that God strengthens the weak and supports the frail. To start to rebuild our lives is to begin the journey that goes from Good Friday to Easter Sunday.

The message of Easter is also the challenge to turn the lives of others around. As we look about, we easily recall the misfits, the despondent, the homeless, the aging, and so forth. Their lives seem to be aimless, fruitless, directionless. On Easter we are compelled to believe in a God who invites us to announce the empty tomb by filling the lives of others with purpose and meaning. Our faith that the Crucified One has been raised is the call that our sisters and brothers must also be raised. Discarded building stones do become cornerstones. If we are an Easter people, the paradox continues.

Points for Reflection and Discussion

1. What do you think of when you hear the words: "We are an Easter people"?

_____

_____

_____

_____

_____

2. Does the joy of Easter ever overshadow or obliterate the challenge of Easter for you? Does the paradox of Easter ever leave you more in doubt than in faith?

_____

_____

_____

_____

_____

Themes
Easter
    L7, The Meaning of Holy Week
Faith
    L4, The Nicene Creed
Resurrection
    L8, Catechumenate Retreat Day

Reading 1, Acts of the Apostles 4:32-35

Now the whole group of those who believed were of one heart and soul, and no one claimed private ownership of any possessions, but everything they owned was held in common. With great power the apostles gave their testimony to the resurrection of the Lord Jesus, and great grace was upon them all. There was not a needy person among them, for as many as owned lands or houses sold them and brought the proceeds of what was sold. They laid it at the apostles' feet, and it was distributed to each as any had need.

Psalm 118:2-4,13-15,22-24

Reading 2, 1 John 5:1-6

Everyone who believes that Jesus is the Christ has been born of God, and everyone who loves the parent loves the child. By this we know that we love the children of God, when we love God and obey his commandments. For the love of God is this, that we obey his commandments. And his commandments are not burdensome, for whatever is born of God conquers the world. And this is the victory that conquers the world, our faith. Who is it that conquers the world but the one who believes that Jesus is the Son of God? This is the one who came by water and blood, Jesus Christ, not with the water only but with the water and the blood. And the Spirit is the one that testifies, for the Spirit is the truth.

Gospel, John 20:19-31

When it was evening on that day, the first day of the week, and the doors of the house where the disciples had met were locked for fear of the Jews, Jesus came and stood among them and said, "Peace be with you." After he said this, he showed them his hands and his side. Then the disciples rejoiced when they saw the Lord.

Jesus said to them again, "Peace be with you. As the Father has sent me, so I send you."

When he had said this, he breathed on them and said to them, "Receive the Holy Spirit. If you forgive the sins of any, they are forgiven them; if you retain the sins of any, they are retained."

But Thomas (who was called the Twin), one of the twelve, was not with them when Jesus came. So the other disciples told him, "We have seen the Lord." But he said to them, "Unless I see the mark of the nails in his hands, and put my finger in the mark of the nails and my hand in his side, I will not believe."

A week later his disciples were again in the house, and Thomas was with them. Although the doors were shut,

Jesus came and stood among them and said, "Peace be with you." Then he said to Thomas, "Put your finger here and see my hands. Reach out your hand and put it in my side. Do not doubt but believe." Thomas answered him, "My Lord and my God!"

Jesus said to him, "Have you believed because you have seen me? Blessed are those who have not seen and yet have come to believe."

Now Jesus did many other signs in the presence of his disciples, which are not written in this book. But these are written so that you may come to believe that Jesus is the Messiah, the Son of God, and that through believing you may have life in his name.

Doing Is Believing

JOHN F. CRAGHAN

We usually put down the doubting Thomas. For him and his followers, seeing is believing. On the contrary, we like to think that we believe without seeing the evidence. But do we perhaps fail in another direction? Is our believing such that it impels us outward to act on behalf of others? Is our believing so dynamic that it necessarily includes others? Do we endorse the notion that *doing* is believing?

Today's readings are a profound study in the joint action of faith and works. They see believing not as an *exclusive* union—with God—but as an *inclusive* one—with God *and* others. They powerfully remind us that faith involves movement from the world of God into the world of God's people. Here, *doing* is believing.

Today's passage from Acts is one of Luke's three major summaries (see also Acts 2:42-47;5:11-16). Here Luke brings together two different but interrelated notions: He states that the earliest Christians owned all things in common (4:32); and he depicts individuals selling their property and making the proceeds available to the needy of the community (4:34-35; see also Acts 4:36-37; 5:1-10). Between the two, he speaks of the apostles' witness and credibility (4:33).

A Community of Believers

What is striking in Luke's account is the motivation he gives for the community's generosity. In the Greco-Roman world in which they lived, people would expect repayment for whatever they gave to others, even if the recipients were good friends. Here the basis for giving is faith ("the whole group of those who believed," 4:32). It is such faith-filled charity that Luke suggests to his audience as the ideal Christian response.

The author of First John, writing circa A.D. 100, addresses the members of his community. There has been serious disagreement within the community, and some have broken away. It is not unlikely that the protestors were wealthy members of the community; hence their departure may have left the community destitute. There is a sharp difference of opinion concerning Christian doctrine. First John appears to be a short treatise on theological ideas.

Go and Do the Same

Today's epistle passage is linked to 1 John 4:20-21. Therein the author stated that to love God *means* to love one's sisters and brothers. (There is really only one commandment; contrast Mk 12:29-31.) Such love is a corollary of faith. In today's reading, verse 1 says, "Everyone who believes that Jesus is the Christ has been born of God, and everyone who loves the parent loves the child."

The gospel passage consists of two episodes plus a conclusion. In the first episode (Jn 20:19-23), Jesus appears to the disciples minus Thomas; in the second episode (20:24-29), Jesus appears to the disciples with Thomas. It is likely that the second episode is an expansion of the first, that is, doubting Thomas is an example who meets the needs of the community. In the conclusion (20:30-31), the author directs his attention to those Christians who had not known, nor would ever know, the historical Jesus.

The first episode is significant for the faith-inspired mission of the disciples. They react to the risen Jesus in faith: "...the disciples rejoiced when they saw the Lord" (20:20). Jesus then makes his relationship with the Father the model for their own mission (20:21). Jesus' lifegiving breath is the gift of the Spirit of Pentecost that jump-starts that mission. They are to continue the mission of Jesus, offering life to all believers. Here, doing is believing.

Today's Good News

As we gather for Eucharist, we profess our faith: "We believe in one God...." We also share a sign of peace. Today's readings remind us that we must carry our professions of faith and signs of peace into settings outside of church. They insist that we see our gift of faith as precisely that—a gift—and thus something to be shared in wider community. They also make clear that sharing our faith (mission) means more than merely religious instruction or a theology lecture. Sharing our faith means seeing the image of God in all those persons who make up the fabric of our lives. Seeing the image of God means reverencing and imitating God in our words and works—whether at work or at play, whether at home or away. Doing is believing.

Points for Reflection and Discussion

1. Do you fully believe that your faith is a gift from God? If so, how do you reconcile your attempts to "instill faith" in others? When you meet those who "believe" differently than you do, are you frustrated at their "ignorance"?

_____

_____

_____

_____

_____

2. Concentrate on the "doing is believing" concept. How do you feel when you think about its implications within your life?

_____

_____

_____

_____

_____

Themes

Charity
   M2, The Laity: Called To Build God's Kingdom
Faith
   M1, Conversion: A Lifelong Process

Reading 1, Acts of the Apostles 3:13-15,17-19

Peter addressed the people:

"The God of Abraham, the God of Isaac, and the God of Jacob, the God of our ancestors has glorified his servant Jesus, whom you handed over and rejected in the presence of Pilate, though he had decided to release him. But you rejected the Holy and Righteous One and asked to have a murderer given to you, and you killed the Author of life, whom God raised from the dead. To this we are witnesses.

"And now, friends, I know that you acted in ignorance, as did also your rulers. In this way God fulfilled what he had foretold through all the prophets, that his Messiah would suffer. Repent therefore, and turn to God so that your sins may be wiped out."

Psalm 4:1,3,6-7,8 (NRSV)

Reading 2, 1 John 2:1-5

My little children, I am writing these things to you so that you may not sin. But if anyone does sin, we have an advocate with the Father, Jesus Christ the righteous; and he is the atoning sacrifice for our sins, and not for ours only but also for the sins of the whole world. Now by this we may be sure that we know him, if we obey his commandments. Whoever says, "I have come to know him," but does not obey his commandments, is a liar, and in such a person the truth does not exist; but whoever obeys his word, truly in this person the love of God has reached perfection.

Gospel, Luke 24:35-48

The disciples told what had happened on the road, and how he had been made known to them in the breaking of the bread.

While they were talking about this, Jesus himself stood among them and said to them, "Peace be with you." They were startled and terrified, and thought that they were seeing a ghost. He said to them, "Why are you frightened, and why do doubts arise in your hearts? Look at my hands and my feet; see that it is I myself. Touch me and see; for a ghost does not have flesh and bones as you see that I have." And when he had said this, he showed them his hands and his feet. While in their joy they were disbelieving and still wondering, he said to them, "Have you anything here to eat?" They gave him a piece of broiled fish, and he took it and ate in their presence. Then he said to them, "These are my words that I spoke to you while I was still with you—that everything written about me in the law of Moses, the prophets, and the psalms must be fulfilled."

Then he opened their minds to understand the scriptures, and he said to them, "Thus it is written, that the Messiah is to suffer and to rise from the dead on the third day, and that repentance and forgiveness of sins is to be proclaimed in his name to all nations, beginning from Jerusalem. You are witnesses of these things."

The Forgiving Community

JOHN F. CRAGHAN

The Christian community is a forgiving community. All too often we fester in our own hurt. Others offend us, perhaps grievously, and if they eventually come to us for forgiveness, we often choose to reject their request. Oddly, we prefer to wallow in our self-pity. We may judge that it is better to preserve our sense of pride than to free a repentant brother or sister from the heavy burden of guilt. In such circumstances it is hard to believe that the Christian community is a forgiving community.

Today's readings deal with the Christian community's innate sense of reaching out in forgiveness. They present scenes in which the graciousness of pardon outweighs the enormity of sin. They challenge the modern believer to focus on the penitents, not on the lingering ache of personal injury. They show that the Christian community is a forgiving community.

Today's passage from the Acts of the Apostles is part of Peter's Temple sermon (Acts 3:12-26). Peter uses a variety of titles to link Israel with the Christian Church. The God of the patriarchs has glorified Jesus the Suffering Servant (3:13; see Is 52:13). This same Jesus is the Holy and Righteous One and the Author of Life (3:14-15). But the people sinned; they chose a murderer over Jesus and were thus responsible for his death (3:14-15). With Jesus' Resurrection, God took charge (3:15).

Repent and Be Saved

In calling for conversion, Peter refers to the ignorance of the audience (3:17). He goes on to mention two closely connected moments in their conversion process. They are to turn *from* their evil way and turn *to* God (3:19). Though the killing of Jesus is a serious sin, it can yet be forgiven.

The first two verses of today's passage from First John are intimately related to the preceeding section (1 Jn 1:6-10). Those who have broken away from the community have falsely claimed that they have communion with God, though they walk in darkness (1:6). They also boast that they are free of the guilt of sin (1:8). Indeed they deny the fact that they have actually sinned (1:10). To these false statements the author replies that his community walks in light (1:7) and publicly confesses the likelihood of sin (2:1).

Only Say the Word...

By having communion with one another, the community is able to experience the cleansing from sin that Jesus has made possible (1:7). Indeed it is the bloody death of Jesus *(ibid)* that makes forgiveness possible. Transcending the victim on the Day of Atonement (see Lv, chapter 16), "...he is the atoning sacrifice for our sins, and not for ours only but also for the sins of the whole world" (2:2).

The gospel passage is part of Luke's account of the revelation of Jesus to the apostolic circle (Lk 24:36-53). It has two components: the appearance (24:36-43) and instruction (24:44-49). While Luke emphasizes the necessity of the revealing Word, he also deals with penance and forgiveness.

In the scene, Jesus appears as a typical Christian missionary, greeting the community and accepting food (see Lk 10:5-7). The household meal is especially significant since it is linked to those meals where Jesus' forgiveness played such a central role (see Lk 5:32;7:39,48;19:10). In the instruction scene, Jesus directs the universal preaching of the community (24:47). For Luke, the Christian community is a forgiving community.

Today's Good News

All too often we hear words such as these: "I will *never* forgive him (or her)!" On occasion, we have probably uttered such words ourselves. They may describe our unwillingness to forgive; they may also describe our difficulty in forgiving. Today we are reminded that we are not isolated individuals. Our Christian calling is to imitate the community to which we belong—the community that experiences the love of Jesus of Nazareth. By belonging to that community, we impose upon ourselves the awesome responsibility of continuing the ways of Jesus. To say "I forgive you" is to say "I love my community and, therefore, I love you." To reconcile an estranged sister or brother is to profess that the Christian community is a forgiving community.

Points for Reflection and Discussion

1. Have you ever been denied forgiveness by a person you've wronged? Have you forgiven all who have wronged you?

_____

_____

_____

_____

2. Do you believe there are any "unforgivable" sins? Why or why not?

_____

_____

_____

_____

_____

Themes

Conversion
    M1, Conversion: A Lifelong Process
Forgiveness
    M2, The Laity: Called To Build God's Kingdom
Sin
    M6, Discernment

Reading 1, Acts of the Apostles 4:8-12

Peter, filled with the Holy Spirit, said to them, "Rulers of the people and elders, if we are questioned today because of a good deed done to someone who was sick and are asked how this man has been healed, let it be known to all of you, and to all the people of Israel, that this man is standing before you in good health by the name of Jesus Christ of Nazareth, whom you crucified, whom God raised from the dead. This Jesus is 'the stone that was rejected by you, the builders; it has become the cornerstone.' There is salvation in no one else, for there is no other name under heaven given among mortals by which we must be saved."

Psalm 118:1,8-9,21-23,26,21,29

Reading 2, 1 John 3:1-2

See what love the Father has given us, that we should be called children of God; and that is what we are. The reason the world does not know us is that it did not know him. Beloved, we are God's children now; what we will be has not yet been revealed. What we do know is this: when he is revealed, we will be like him, for we will see him as he is.

Gospel, John 10:11-18

I am the good shepherd. The good shepherd lays down his life for the sheep. The hired hand, who is not the shepherd and does not own the sheep, sees the wolf coming and leaves the sheep and runs away—and the wolf snatches them and scatters them. The hired hand runs away because a hired hand does not care for the sheep.

I am the good shepherd. I know my own and my own know me, just as the Father knows me and I know the Father. And I lay down my life for the sheep. I have other sheep that do not belong to this fold. I must bring them also, and they will listen to my voice. So there will be one flock, one shepherd. For this reason the Father loves me, because I lay down my life in order to take it up again. No one takes it from me, but I lay it down of my own accord. I have power to lay it down, and I have power to take it up again. I have received this command from my Father.

Just The Facts

JOHN F. CRAGHAN

Everyday events happen all around us. We know of political successes and disasters. We hear of personal happiness and tragedy. We learn of great feats and failures. Our tendency is to accept these without reflecting on their meaning, without interpreting their significance.

Today's readings are a study in interpretation. They challenge us, not only to tabulate the facts but also to uncover the meaning of the facts. They impose upon us the somewhat demanding task of going beyond surface observation to penetrate the deeper dimensions of life. They advocate that believers interpret the facts.

The scene in Acts is of Peter's first speech after the healing of the cripple (Acts 3:1-10). Moved by the Spirit, Peter addresses the highest Jewish authority, the Sanhedrin. Immediately the passage moves to a level of interpretation. The facts are the events surrounding the cure of the cripple, but the key issue is clearly the interpretation of the cure.

In the Name of Jesus

Peter points to a higher level. It is no longer a question of restoration to health (4:9) and physical soundness (4:10) but of salvation (4:12). The Jesus whom the people rejected in the crucifixion has been raised by God (see Ps 118). It is only because of *this* reversal that the cripple now enjoys good health. Implicitly, Peter challenges his audience by interpreting the facts.

Today's well-known responsorial Psalm (118) deals with a king's miraculous escape from powerful enemies. As a whole, the psalm is a liturgical celebration in which the king describes his dreadful ordeal (118:10-13) and then interprets it. The only adequate explanation for this radical turn of events is the intervention of Yahweh, the God of Israel (118:21). The psalmist illustrates this reversal by using the metaphor of the rejected building stone. When the people see the king no longer as discarded stone but as the very cornerstone of the edifice (118:22), they must indeed acknowledge that this is God's doing. The psalmist resolutely interprets the facts.

And Mine Know Me

In an atmosphere charged with conflict, the author of today's gospel reading contrasts Jesus with Israel's leaders (see the rejection of the man born blind in chapter 9 of John). In the first parable (Jn 10:11-13), Jesus the ideal shepherd does not hesitate to lay down his life for the sheep (the Pharisees are probably the hired hands). In the second parable (10:14-16), Jesus has a deep personal relationship with his sheep ("I know my own and my own know me," 10:14). The purpose of this knowing is to effect union among all of Jesus' followers (10:16). Jesus freely lays down his life. It is this self-giving that is at the heart of the Gentile mission. By this connection the author of John interprets the facts.

Today's Good News

The modern believer is called upon to react to the evil in society. Exploitation, oppression, abuse of power, and so forth are not merely the undesirable results of immutable economic laws. The believer is challenged to uncover those responsible for the dehumanizing of persons made in the image of God. This implies a call to action. From a Christian perspective the wretchedness of human existence indicates that the power of Jesus' death and resurrection has not yet penetrated those situations. Believers must interpret the facts.

The modern believer is also called upon to react to the good in society. We need to applaud the unstinting efforts of leaders to improve the quality of human life. We must acknowledge the diverse variety of human gifts and praise all use of those gifts for the benefit of others. We should proclaim the joy of human friendship and the depth of human cooperation. In these and similar situations, the believer becomes ever more aware of a generous God who interacts with generous humans. By finding evidence of the impact of the passion/death/resurrection of Jesus in everyday life, believers interpret facts.

Points for Reflection and Discussion

1. Do you see those who lobby for the disenfranchised as "meddlers"? Could they be "interpreters of facts"?

_____

_____

_____

_____

2. Sheep only respond to one voice—that of their shepherd. How radically would your life change if you responded only to the voice of your Shepherd? Would you become a better "interpreter of facts"?

_____

_____

_____

_____

Themes

Interpretation
    M6, Discernment
Reality
    M3, Your Special Gifts
Relationships
    M4, Family Life

Reading 1, Acts of the Apostles 9:26-31

When Saul had come to Jerusalem, he attempted to join the disciples; and they were all afraid of him, for they did not believe that he was a disciple. But Barnabas took him, brought him to the apostles, and described for them how on the road he had seen the Lord, who had spoken to him, and how in Damascus he had spoken boldly in the name of Jesus. So he went in and out among them in Jerusalem, speaking boldly in the name of the Lord. He spoke and argued with the Hellenists; but they were attempting to kill him. When the believers learned of it, they brought him down to Caesarea and sent him off to Tarsus.

Meanwhile the church throughout Judea, Galilee, and Samaria had peace and was built up. Living in the fear of the Lord and in the comfort of the Holy Spirit, it increased in numbers.

Psalm 22:25-26,27,29,30-31 (NRSV)

Reading 2, 1 John 3:18-24

Little children, let us love, not in word or speech, but in truth and action. And by this we will know that we are from the truth and will reassure our hearts before him whenever our hearts condemn us; for God is greater than our hearts, and he knows everything.

Beloved, if our hearts do not condemn us, we have boldness before God; and we receive from him whatever we ask, because we obey his commandments and do what pleases him. And this is his commandment, that we should believe in the name of his Son Jesus Christ and love one another, just as he has commanded us. All who obey his commandments abide in him, and he abides in them. And by this we know that he abides in us, by the Spirit that he has given us.

Gospel, John 15:1-8

Jesus said to his disciples:

I am the true vine, and my Father is the vinegrower. He removes every branch in me that bears no fruit. Every branch that bears fruit he prunes to make it bear more fruit. You have already been cleansed by the word that I have spoken to you. Abide in me as I abide in you. Just as the branch cannot bear fruit by itself unless it abides in the vine, neither can you unless you abide in me. I am the vine, you are the branches. Those who abide in me and I in them bear much fruit, because apart from me you can do nothing. Whoever does not abide in me is thrown away like a branch and withers; such branches are gathered, thrown into the fire, and burned. If you abide in me, and my words abide in you, ask for whatever you wish, and it will be done for you. My Father is glorified by this, that you bear much fruit and become my disciples.

A Call To Action

JOHN F. CRAGHAN

Today's readings perceive the Christian life as a call to action. They reflect the obligations inherent in the reception of baptism. To belong to Jesus and his community means to live according to the teachings of Jesus in community. The genuine Christian is the active Christian.

From Sinner to Saint

Today's passage from Acts shows how the Jerusalem community found it difficult to imagine that Saul had actually become a Christian. Their unwillingness to accept the new convert prompted Barnabas to introduce him as a fellow believer. He pointed out that Saul's vision of the risen Lord led to his fearless proclamation of the Christian message in Damascus. The former persecutor was now their brother in Christ.

Luke goes on to develop the impact Saul's acceptance of Christianity had on non-Christians. "...he went in and out among them in Jerusalem, speaking boldly in the name of the Lord" (9:28). "He spoke and argued with the Hellenists" (those Jews who spoke only Greek, 9:29). Their response to Saul's overtures was to attempt to kill him—an action that prompted the Christians to send him to his native Tarsus (9:29-30). In this compelling scene, Saul models the fact that genuine Christian conversion leads to action.

Moved to Act

Earlier the author of First John had condemned the actions of those who had broken away from the community. Here he accentuates the positive aspects of Christianity. He points out that love must show itself in action (3:18). After encouraging his audience to have confidence in God (3:19-21), the author says that they will receive from God whatever they ask because they "obey his commandments and do what pleases him" (3:22).

The author indicates that Christians must be motivated by two realities: Jesus' divine sonship and caring love for one another "as he has commanded us" (3:23). Belief in Jesus and mutual love go hand in hand. To love sisters and brothers is to continue the love that God initiated in sending Jesus (see 1 Jn 4:9-10). Here acceptance of a creed is not sufficient unto itself; only an acceptance that incorporates active love of others "abide in him, and he abides in them" (3:24).

Abide in Me...

Today's gospel teaches via a parable that employs the Hebrew image of God's people as a vine (see, for example, Jer 2:21;6:9;8:13;12:10). Here, however, the new Israel is actually part of the vine (the branches). As the real vine, Jesus brings true life from the Father. Failure to bear fruit means our failure to share in that divine life. Sharing in that vine-life means sharing it with others (Jn 15:2). The Christian's response, to "abide in me" (15:4), is essentially a commitment to productivity "because apart from me you can do nothing" (15:5). And "Whoever does not abide in me is thrown away like a branch and withers" (15:6).

Jesus' farewell discourse to his disciples, given at the Last Supper, began in Chapter 14 of John's Gospel. Now that Jesus has basically completed his parable of the vine (himself) and the branches (the disciples), he relates it to the present setting. The disciples will receive whatever they ask so long as they remain wedded to Jesus (15:7). It is by their fruitfulness that they are disciples, and it is in that fruitfulness that they glorify God (15:8). It is the disciples who continue the mission of Jesus (see Jn 20: 22-23).

Today's Good News

The Christian life is practical. In loving our spouses and families, we profess that God is love. In reaching out to the hurting and oppressed, we announce that God is the champion of the poor. In promoting honesty in our local governments, we proclaim that God is the Lord of justice. In comforting the sorrowful, we state that God is the source of consolation.

Each of these and similar actions spring from our baptism. To enjoy the title of *Christian* means to realize the consequences of the title. Only those who are willing to live out the implications of baptism truly merit the title. Hence, the genuine Christian is the active Christian.

Points for Reflection and Discussion

1. Today's gospel parable paints a vivid picture. Imagine yourself a branch on the vine. How do you feel? Have you ever felt "cut off" from God? Describe the feeling.

_____

_____

_____

_____

_____

2. Paul (Saul) needed Barnabas to smooth his way into the Jerusalem community. Have you ever felt unwelcome—an outsider—within a Christian community? How did (or can) you ultimately earn their trust?

_____

_____

_____

_____

_____

Themes

Community
    M5, Your Prayer Life
Ministry
    M3, Your Special Gifts

Reading 1, Acts of the Apostles 10:25-26, 34-35,44-48

On Peter's arrival Cornelius met him, and falling at his feet, worshiped him. But Peter made him get up, saying, "Stand up; I am only a mortal."

Then Peter began to speak to them: "I truly understand that God shows no partiality, but in every nation anyone who fears him and does what is right is acceptable to him."

While Peter was still speaking, the Holy Spirit fell upon all who heard the word. The circumcised believers who had come with Peter were astounded that the gift of the Holy Spirit had been poured out even on the Gentiles, for they heard them speaking in tongues and extolling God. Then Peter said, "Can anyone withhold the water for baptizing these people who have received the Holy Spirit just as we have?" So he ordered them to be baptized in the name of Jesus Christ. Then they invited him to stay for several days.

Psalm 98:1,2-3,3-4

Reading 2, 1 John 4:7-10

Beloved, let us love one another, because love is from God; everyone who loves is born of God and knows God. Whoever does not love does not know God, for God is love. God's love was revealed among us in this way: God sent his only Son into the world so that we might live through him. In this is love, not that we loved God but that he loved us and sent his Son to be the atoning sacrifice for our sins.

Gospel, John 15:9-17

Jesus said to his disciples:

"As the Father has loved me, so I have loved you; abide in my love. If you keep my commandments, you will abide in my love, just as I have kept my Father's commandments and abide in his love. I have said these things to you so that my joy may be in you, and that your joy may be complete.

"This is my commandment, that you love one another as I have loved you. No one has greater love than this, to lay down one's life for one's friends. You are my friends if you do what I command you. I do not call you servants any longer, because the servant does not know what the master is doing; but I have called you friends, because I have made known to you everything that I have heard from my Father. You did not choose me but I chose you. And I appointed you to go and bear fruit, fruit that will last, so that the Father will give you whatever you ask him in my name. I am giving you these commands so that you may love one another."

A Holy Church

JOHN F. CRAGHAN

How often we yearn to know the mind of God. We would like to ask questions of God and get clear answers. We would prefer to go right to the top and eliminate those in the middle.

Today's readings may seem to frustrate our uniquely private interview. They staunchly maintain that, as believers, *we* are the ones who reflect God's mind and attitude. They state that believers are the ones who reveal God's outlook on reality. Ultimately, they insist that believers share with one another and with others their perception of God and God's values. In these readings, believers speak God's Word.

And Catholic...

In the Cornelius episode (Acts 10:1—11:18), Luke hammers home the conviction that the Christian community is for everyone—that Gentiles need not become Jews in order to enter this community. To that end, he narrates the account of the first Gentile convert to Christianity, namely, Cornelius. It is hardly an accident that Peter launches this catholic (universal) mission.

In addressing his audience, Peter announces the substance of his vision (see Acts 10:1-23). "...God has shown me that I should not call anyone profane or unclean" (10:28). Appealing to the Hebrew Scriptures (Dt 10:17), Peter shows that God is indeed impartial. It is the vision that has led Peter to perceive that "in every nation anyone who fears him (God) and does what is right is acceptable to him" (10:35). The outpouring of the Spirit is proof positive that Peter's perception is correct. Believers speak for God.

And One...

In today's second reading, the author of First John concentrates on the bond that unites God with believers—love. Love is the criterion for knowing God (4:7). God is love (4:8), so love must characterize God's family (4:11). The Son has life from the Father and the believer has this life from the Son (4:9; see also Jn 5:26;6:57). The lifestyle of believers, therefore, is part of God's plan for salvation.

The gospel passage develops the imagery of last week's parable of the vine and the branches (Jn 15:1-6). Like the second reading, the gospel speaks of the love that unites God and the believer (15:9). To "abide" in Jesus' love is to acknowledge that love by responding to his commandments (15:10). This will effect a joy-filled relationship that is linked to Jesus' fidelity to his Father (see Jn 14:31).

And Apostolic...

Jesus' fundamental command is mutual love. This stems from Jesus' love of the disciples, which in turn flows from the Father's love of Jesus. Indeed the specific model of such love is the death of Jesus. But far from being a purely personal acquisition, the love of God looks to others. "You did not choose me but I chose you. And I appointed you to go and bear fruit..." (15:16). For John, believers spread God's Word.

Today's Good News

Genuine Christianity is an exacting religion. It demands the believer not only to understand its creeds but also to reflect them and to act on them in daily life. Within the context of community, the believer is linked to Jesus who is linked to the Father. If God is love and Jesus' self-giving is the supreme expression of that love, then modern believers must communicate the depth of that love by the way they live in the world.

In loving spouse, family, and friends, the Christian reveals a dimension of God's love. In loving enemies and foes, the Christian reflects an even deeper insight into God's love. In reaching out to the homeless and distraught, the Christian shares yet another aspect of God's love. In pursuing justice and honesty, the Christian once again offers a perception of God's love. In these and similar instances believers are one with God in this love. Believers *are* God's Word.

Points for Reflection and Discussion

1. How have you experienced being God for another person(s)? Who has been God for you recently?

_____

_____

_____

_____

_____

2. Do you believe non-Christians can be a part of Christ's catholic (universal) Church? Why or why not?

_____

_____

_____

_____

_____

Themes
Unity
    M7, Holiness
Universality
    M8, Evangelization

Reading 1, Acts of the Apostles 1:15-17,20-26

In those days Peter stood up among the believers (together the crowd numbered about one hundred twenty persons) and said, "Friends, the scripture had to be fulfilled, which the Holy Spirit through David foretold concerning Judas, who became a guide for those who arrested Jesus—for he was numbered among us and was allotted his share in this ministry.

"For it is written in the book of Psalms, 'Let his homestead become desolate, and let there be no one to live in it'; and 'Let another take his position of overseer.' So one of the men who have accompanied us during all the time that the Lord Jesus went in and out among us, beginning from the baptism of John until the day when he was taken up from us—one of these must become a witness with us to his resurrection." So they proposed two, Joseph called Barsabbas, who was also known as Justus, and Matthias. Then they prayed and said, "Lord, you know everyone's heart. Show us which one of these two you have chosen to take the place in this ministry and apostleship from which Judas turned aside to go to his own place." And they cast lots for them, and the lot fell on Matthias; and he was added to the eleven apostles.

Psalm 103:1-2,11-12,19-20

Reading 2, 1 John 4:11-16

Beloved, since God loved us so much, we also ought to love one another. No one has ever seen God; if we love one another, God lives in us, and his love is perfected in us. By this we know that we abide in him and he in us, because he has given us of his Spirit. And we have seen and do testify that the Father has sent his Son as the Savior of the world. God abides in those who confess that Jesus is the Son of God, and they abide in God. So we have known and believe the love that God has for us. God is love, and those who abide in love abide in God, and God abides in them.

Gospel, John 17:11-19

Jesus looked up to heaven and prayed:

And now I am no longer in the world, but they are in the world, and I am coming to you. Holy Father, protect them in your name that you have given me, so that they may be one, as we are one. While I was with them, I protected them in your name that you have given me. I guarded them, and not one of them was lost except the one destined to be lost, so that the scripture might be fulfilled. But now I am coming to you, and I speak these things in the world so that they may have my joy made complete in themselves. I have given them your word, and the world

has hated them because they do not belong to the world, just as I do not belong to the world. I am not asking you to take them out of the world, but I ask you to protect them from the evil one. They do not belong to the world, just as I do not belong to the world. Sanctify them in the truth; your word is truth. As you have sent me into the world, so I have sent them into the world. And for their sakes I sanctify myself, so that they also may be sanctified in truth.

Christt Among Us

JOHN F. CRAGHAN

We can easily be hooked on the appeal of the present moment. We note the advances in science and technology. We witness the expansion of human ingenuity in other areas. We feel inclined to revere the present and reject the past. Jesus is out of sight. Is he also out of mind?

Today's readings focus on the tensions between past and present, and while they do not belittle the significance of the present, they powerfully appeal to our sense of continuity. They urge us to see in Jesus not an outdated relic of the first century but a dynamic force for the twentieth century. To recall and develop the legacy of Jesus is to allow his message to impact the present.

In today's passage from Acts, the Eleven were doing more than finding a replacement for Judas. Basically, they were concerned with the question of continuity. The Church of the Acts of the Apostles needed to be rooted in the experience of Jesus. It was the community of the Twelve that recalled and handed on that experience.

Communicated in Truth

After establishing Judas' defection as part of God's plan (Ps 69:6;109:8; see also Ps 41:10), Peter explains the requirements for a successor to his position. This new member must have been in the company of Jesus from the time of his baptism until the time of his Ascension (Acts 1:21-22). In joining the Eleven, Matthias is thus seen, because of his personal experience of Jesus, as a unique communicator of both the Word and the Spirit.

The author of First John sees Jesus as the link between the Father and the disciples. The love of God enfleshed in Jesus is to become enfleshed in all Christians (4:12). The love that God manifested in sending the Son to die reaches perfection in the mutual love of Christians. Such love, therefore, preserves the supreme example of genuine love.

Although "no one has ever seen God" (4:12), Christians know God in Jesus and the Holy Spirit, who enables them to believe Jesus is the Son of God. Further, by witnessing to the fact that the Father has sent Jesus as the Savior of the world, Christians continue the saving work of Jesus under the protection of the Spirit (see Jn 19:35). These Christians "have known and believe the love that God has for us" (4:16). Such knowing is a dynamic force that is made visible in the Christian way of life.

Consecrated in Truth

This portion of the Gospel of John is part of Jesus' high-priestly prayer (Jn 17:1-26). Here the author highlights the predicament of the disciples. Although they do not belong to the "world" (17:14-16), Jesus gives them his Father's Word and sends them into the "world" (17:18) to provoke a faith response. Since the "world" reacts with hatred (17:14), Jesus prays that the Father protect the disciples with the divine Word. Paradoxically, in sharing the mission of Jesus the disciples also share the joy of Jesus (17:13).

Verses 17-19 deal with the consecration of both Jesus and the disciples. It is God's Word ("truth") that consecrates and purifies them (see Jn 15:3) for their mission. In speaking of Jesus' self-consecration, the author may have in mind Jesus' self-giving in death (see Jn 10:17-18). Thus it may be the self-consecration in death that consecrates the disciples for a life of perpetuating the message and mission of Jesus.

Today's Good News

The modern Christian must often raise the question: How is Jesus present in our midst today? Far from being a speculative question, this is a call to action. To state that Jesus does not walk in our midst as he did in Palestine is to imply that in some other way he must walk in the midst of our community. The task incumbent upon the Christian is to manifest the presence of Jesus.

To offer reconciliation to one who has hurt us is to make the forgiving Jesus alive and well. To provide hope for the depressed is to make the healing Jesus viable for today. To improve the lot of the poor is to make the concerned Jesus present in our midst. To enlighten the minds and hearts of people, especially the young, is to make the teaching Jesus at home in our community. To love without counting the cost is to make the self-giving Jesus a member of our family and community. These and countless other ways simply affirm that Jesus is actually neither out of sight nor out of mind.

Points for Reflection and Discussion

1. How have you made Jesus present in our world this week?

_____

_____

_____

_____

2. Have you ever found joy in the rejection of others? Can you explain that paradox?

_____

_____

_____

_____

Themes

Jesus
    M5, Your Prayer Life
Mission
    M8, Evangelization
Vocation
    M2, The Laity: Called To Build God's Kingdom

Reading 1, Acts of the Apostles 2:1-11

When the day of Pentecost had come, they were all together in one place. And suddenly from heaven there came a sound like the rush of a violent wind, and it filled the entire house where they were sitting. Divided tongues, as of fire, appeared among them, and a tongue rested on each of them. All of them were filled with the Holy Spirit and began to speak in other languages, as the Spirit gave them ability.

Now there were devout Jews from every nation under heaven living in Jerusalem. And at this sound the crowd gathered and was bewildered, because each one heard them speaking in the native language of each. Amazed and astonished, they asked, "Are not all these who are speaking Galileans? And how is it that we hear, each of us, in our own native language? Parthians, Medes, Elamites, and residents of Mesopotamia, Judea and Cappadocia, Pontus and Asia, Phrygia and Pamphylia, Egypt and the parts of Libya belonging to Cyrene, and visitors from Rome, both Jews and proselytes, Cretans and Arabs—in our own languages we hear them speaking about God's deeds of power."

Psalm 104:1,24,29-30,31,34

Reading 2, 1 Corinthians 12:3-7,12-13

No one speaking by the Spirit of God ever says "Let Jesus be cursed!" and no one can say "Jesus is Lord" except by the Holy Spirit.

Now there are varieties of gifts, but the same Spirit; and there are varieties of services, but the same Lord; and there are varieties of activities, but it is the same God who activates all of them in everyone. To each is given the manifestation of the Spirit for the common good.

For just as the body is one and has many members, and all the members of the body, though many, are one body, so it is with Christ. For in the one Spirit we were all baptized into one body—Jews or Greeks, slaves or free— and we were all made to drink of one Spirit.

Gospel, John 20:19-23

When it was evening on that day, the first day of the week, and the doors of the house where the disciples had met were locked for fear of the Jews, Jesus came and stood among them and said, "Peace be with you." After he said this, he showed them his hands and his side. Then the disciples rejoiced when they saw the Lord.

Jesus said to them again, "Peace be with you. As the Father has sent me, so I send you." When he had said this, he breathed on them and said to them, "Receive the Holy Spirit. If you forgive the sins of any, they are forgiven them; if you retain the sins of any, they are retained."

The Spirit Of Community

JOHN F. CRAGHAN

We can experience a glow of satisfaction when we survey a community's gifts. We remember those raw talents that have been developed over the years. We recall the pain that eventually resulted in perfecting our gifts. Nothing we have or do is ours alone—our personal gifts, our personal achievements, our personal talents. They all gather together in what we call community.

Today's readings highlight the role of the Spirit in community. They see the movement of the Spirit in people, which results in gifts and talents. They go on to note that the Spirit's movement is not to end in individuals. Rather, it is to have a ripple effect so that all our gifts and talents promote the common good. These texts clearly attest that the Spirit forms community.

To the Ends of the Earth

Luke structures his Gospel and Acts of the Apostles around a geographical axis: Galilee to Jerusalem to the ends of the earth. Thus in Luke, Jesus travels an inescapable route from Galilee to Jerusalem (see Lk 9:51) and experiences passion, death, and resurrection in the holy city. In Acts, the movement is from Jerusalem to Rome where Paul freely preaches about the Lord Jesus Christ (see Acts 28:30-31). In this structure, Pentecost signals the start of the universal mission of the Church. It is a mission that overcomes human obstacles and has the Spirit as its driving force.

Today's selection from Acts brings together two Hebrew passages. The fire and the great sound refer to the making of the covenant on Mount Sinai (see Ex 19:16,18). The international list of Jews and catechumens is linked to the Tower of Babel (see Gn 11:7,9); but at Pentecost the outcome is unity, not confusion. The Spirit-filled disciples receive the gift of the Spirit and immediately begin to share that gift by speaking to the mixed audience. From the many differences, a community is formed.

Unity in Diversity

Paul's Corinth was a divided community whose chief characteristic was cliquishness. It was a community bent on rugged individualism. All recipients of the gifts of the Spirit flaunted their acquisitions, seeing them as purely personal endowments. In this disintegration, Paul's only course of action was a plea for community.

In the face of diversity of gifts, works, and ministries, Paul stresses unity. In the face of individualism, Paul emphasizes community. "To each is given the manifestation of the Spirit for the common good" (1 Cor 12:7).

In the face of multiplicity of members, Paul underlines community. Thus the "many members" all comprise "one body" in which the chief characteristic is the use of different gifts and talents for the common good.

Peace Be With You

In John's Gospel, Pentecost (as well as the Ascension) occurs on Easter Sunday. In today's scene, the author anticipates the gift of the Spirit by having Jesus address the disciples with "peace." Jesus then initiates the mission by modeling it on his own relationship with the Father. The disciples are commissioned to continue Jesus' mission by bringing life to all believers (see Jn 6: 39-40).

Jesus breathes upon them. This gesture is reminiscent of Genesis 2:7 and thus suggests a new creation. The reception of the Spirit empowers the disciples to forgive or retain sins. Because the author of John stresses that all sin is basically a refusal to believe in Jesus, the Spirit-filled disciples will force people to decide for or against Jesus.

Today's Good News

When we raise the issue of gifts and talents, we somehow tend to limit them to professional people in show business, sports, music, and so forth. While we legitimately admire these people, our perspective should be broader. Patience, understanding, and consolation are gifts we all possess. Wherever one uses such gifts for the community, the Spirit is obviously present and working.

The one who helps develop the skill of a person with disabilities is like the disciples at Luke's Pentecost. He or she brings about unity in the face of confusion. The one who offers to teach in the parish school of religion and similar programs is like the ideal disciple in Paul's Corinth. He or she manifests the Spirit for the common good. The one who consoles a distraught sister or brother in the wake of death or serious illness is like the disciples in John's Gospel. He or she breathes the Spirit to bond faith in Jesus. In these and countless other instances, Spirit means community.

Points for Reflection and Discussion

1. Isn't it wonderful to be a "part" of a "body" that is so big, and so diverse? How do you feel when you think about the concept of unity in diversity *as it applies to the Church?*

_____

_____

_____

_____

_____

2. Do you ever feel the Spirit working through you? Share an experience of Spirit in your life.

_____

_____

_____

_____

_____

Themes

Church
    M2, The Laity: Called To Build God's Kingdom
Holy Spirit
    M3, Your Special Gifts

Reading 1, Deuteronomy 4:32-34,39-40

Moses said to the people:

"Ask now about former ages, long before your own, ever since the day that God created human beings on the earth; ask from one end of heaven to the other: has anything so great as this ever happened or has its like ever been heard of? Has any people ever heard the voice of a god speaking out of a fire, as you have heard, and lived? Or has any god ever attempted to go and take a nation for himself from the midst of another nation, by trials, by signs and wonders, by war, by a mighty hand and an outstretched arm, and by terrifying displays of power, as the Lord your God did for you in Egypt before your very eyes? So acknowledge today and take to heart that the Lord is God in heaven above and on the earth beneath; there is no other. Keep his statutes and his commandments, which I am commanding you today for your own well-being and that of your descendants after you, so that you may long remain in the land that the Lord your God is giving you for all time."

Psalm 33:4-5,6,9,18-19,20,22

Reading 2, Romans 8:14-17

All who are led by the Spirit of God are children of God. For you did not receive a spirit of slavery to fall back into fear, but you have received a spirit of adoption. When we cry, "Abba! Father!" it is that very Spirit bearing witness with our spirit that we are children of God, and if children, then heirs, heirs of God and joint heirs with Christ—if, in fact, we suffer with him so that we may also be glorified with him.

Gospel, Matthew 28:16-20

Now the eleven disciples went to Galilee, to the mountain to which Jesus had directed them. When they saw him, they worshiped him; but some doubted.

And Jesus came and said to them, "All authority in heaven and on earth has been given to me. Go therefore and make disciples of all nations, baptizing them in the name of the Father and of the Son and of the Holy Spirit, and teaching them to obey everything that I have commanded you. And remember, I am with you always, to the end of the age."

Upholding the Family Name

JOHN F. CRAGHAN

We usually take a certain pride in our family name. It sums up our forebears and their/our history. It conjures up the efforts of parents and others to provide for the family in every possible way. As a result, we seek to enhance that name, not tarnish it. Implicitly at least, we live so as to bring honor to the name.

Today's readings focus on family legacies. They maintain that entrance into a particular family involves certain obligations. They show that it is not enough to merely bandy about the family name. They urge all believers to act upon the name and so bring honor to the family. Upholding the family name calls for a specific kind of family living.

The Family of God

The first part of today's passage from Deuteronomy is a brief study in the biblical theme of election, or call. Here Moses asks Israel to review her history, looking back to the moment of creation and then to more recent events. The latter include the Exodus, in which God defeated the Egyptians with plagues and other mighty signs. They also involve the covenant on Sinai where God spoke from the midst of fire. This rapid review of history necessarily leads to the conclusion that God dearly loves Israel, the family of God. They are truly "chosen."

The author of Deuteronomy is quick to link Israel's election as God's family to a sense of honor. Israel is to respond to the obligations of the covenant, to acknowledge no other gods—only Yahweh is to be worshiped. In addition, Israel is to obey Yahweh's statutes and commandments. This is a lifestyle worthy of the family name.

Adoption Into the Name

In his Letter to the Romans, Paul defines a Christian as one who is led by the Spirit. Paul quickly adds that Christians are not slaves; neither are they God's natural sons and daughters. They are, rather, God's adopted children—a status that stems from God's gratuitous love. Owing to this status they can address God as Jesus did, by crying out *"Abba!"* (8:15). This Aramaic word means *father*, but in a most intimate way; it is more closely akin to *daddy*.

Paul goes on to connect the Christians' membership in God's family with their everyday lifestyle. Being heirs of God, with Christ, they are called to act on behalf of the family. Paul describes their action as suffering with Christ. It is that kind of family loyalty that will eventually lead to glorification with Christ. For Paul, upholding the family name calls for a specific kind of family living.

Baptism in the Name

In the final scene from Matthew's Gospel, Jesus announces his exaltation, "All authority in heaven and on earth has been given to me" (28:18). Then he commissions the Eleven, perhaps after the manner of a prophetic commission (see Ex 3:7-17;4:1-16). This commission involves three stages: making disciples, baptizing, and teaching (Mt 28:19-20). Finally Jesus reassures the Eleven of his abiding presence.

According to Matthew, the disciples enjoy a unique and intimate relationship with Jesus. Like the Hebrew prophets, they are members of God's council (see Is 40:1-11). They both share in Jesus' decisions and communicate their experience of Jesus to all nations. Their task, however, will involve temptations. To deal with such temptations, Jesus assures the disciples of his abiding presence (see "*Emmanuel*," meaning *God with us*, in Mt 1:23). Faithful execution of Jesus' mandate will clearly demonstrate their loyalty to him. Upholding the family name calls for a specific kind of family living.

Today's Good News

Baptism is an awesome responsibility. By being baptized *in the name* of the Father and of the Son and of the Holy Spirit, we become unique and intimate members of God's family. Baptism also implies that we gain new sisters and brothers; they too are members of the family. In addition, baptism includes a close bond with the non-baptized because we assume the obligation of making them family members as well.

In our daily lives we either choose or reject our family name. By reaching out to the dejected and discouraged, we opt for the family name; by not showing concern for the weak and helpless, we opt out of the family name. By loving those who are difficult to love, we enhance the family name; by despising those who are worthy of our love, we disparage the family name. Our lifestyle is ultimately a test of our family honor and esteem. Upholding the family name calls for a specific kind of family living.

Points for Reflection and Discussion

1. Family names carry family histories: joys and sorrows, pride and shame. What are your greatest joys and sources of pride as you think about being a member of the family of God? What are your deepest sorrows and sources of shame?

_____

_____

_____

_____

2. Reflect upon Jesus' reassuring words from today's gospel: "Remember I am with you always, to the end of the age." Are those words relevant and significant in your lifestyle?

_____

_____

_____

_____

Themes
Call
    Q1, Journey of Faith
    M1, Conversion: A Lifelong Process
Family
    M4, Family Life
Name
    Q9, Who's Who in the Church
    M3, Your Special Gifts

Reading 1, Exodus 24:3-8

Moses came and told the people all the words of the Lord and all the ordinances; and all the people answered with one voice, and said, "All the words that the Lord has spoken we will do." And Moses wrote down all the words of the Lord. He rose early in the morning, and built an altar at the foot of the mountain, and set up twelve pillars, corresponding to the twelve tribes of Israel. He sent young men of the people of Israel, who offered burnt offerings and sacrificed oxen as offerings of well-being to the Lord. Moses took half of the blood and put it in basins, and half of the blood he dashed against the altar. Then he took the book of the covenant, and read it in the hearing of the people; and they said, "All that the Lord has spoken we will do, and we will be obedient." Moses took the blood and dashed it on the people, and said, "See the blood of the covenant that the Lord has made with you in accordance with all these words."

Psalm 116:12-13,15-16,17-18

Reading 2, Hebrews 9:11-15

When Christ came as a high priest of the good things that have come, then through the greater and perfect tent (not made with hands, that is, not of this creation), he entered once for all into the Holy Place, not with the blood of goats and calves, but with his own blood, thus obtaining eternal redemption. For if the blood of goats and bulls, with the sprinkling of the ashes of a heifer, sanctifies those who have been defiled so that their flesh is purified, how much more will the blood of Christ, who through the eternal Spirit offered himself without blemish to God, purify our conscience from dead works to worship the living God!

For this reason he is the mediator of a new covenant, so that those who are called may receive the promised eternal inheritance, because a death has occurred that redeems them from the transgressions under the first covenant.

Gospel, Mark 14:12-16,22-26

On the first day of Unleavened Bread, when the Passover lamb is sacrificed, his disciples said to him, "Where do you want us to go and make the preparations for you to eat the Passover?" So he sent two of his disciples, saying to them, "Go into the city, and a man carrying a jar of water will meet you; follow him, and wherever he enters, say to the owner of the house, 'The Teacher asks, Where is my guest room where I may eat the Passover with my disciples?' He will show you a large room upstairs, furnished and ready. Make preparations for us there." So the disciples set out and went to the city, and found everything as he had told them; and they prepared the Passover meal.

While they were eating, he took a loaf of bread, and after blessing it he broke it, gave it to them, and said, "Take; this is my body." Then he took a cup, and after giving thanks he gave it to them, and all of them drank from it. He said to them, "This is my blood of the covenant, which is poured out for many. Truly I tell you, I will never again drink of the fruit of the vine until that day when I drink it new in the kingdom of God."

When they had sung the hymn, they went out to the Mount of Olives.

Our Common Bond

JOHN F. CRAGHAN

Blood bond is a term that means *common bond*. As members of a family, we share a common bond. Ideally at least, we recognize family relationships that, in turn, imply family loyalty, often translated as "blood is thicker than water." We feel that we *must* reach out to our blood relatives because we share a common history and common origins. When we fail to live out the implications of our common bond, we acknowledge that to some extent we have failed the family.

Today's readings dwell on the meaning of blood and the family obligations that result from blood bonds. They powerfully suggest that one must accompany the other. To share a common history is to live a common life. A blood bond is a common bond.

In the first reading, Moses has returned from the mountain and reports God's demands to the people for entering a covenant relationship. After their assent, Moses writes down God's terms and has an altar and twelve pillars erected in order to symbolize and ritualize this bond. In addition to whole burnt offerings (holocausts) there are also communion sacrifices. To share a meal is to share a common destiny.

The rite Moses celebrates symbolizes the irrevocable linking of God (the altar) and the people. In the Hebrew Scriptures blood symbolizes life. It is significant that Moses first reads the terms of the covenant and only then sprinkles the people with blood. Thus the blood implies Israel's willingness to adhere to the covenant obligations. The end result is the creation of a new family—a family that shares the same blood and hence the same life as Yahweh. Their blood bond is a common bond.

The Blood of the Lamb

According to the Hebrew Scriptures the only day on which the high priest could enter the Holy of Holies of the Jerusalem Temple was the Day of Atonement *(Yom Kippur)*. Here blood played a key role. The high priest atoned for his own sins and those of his household by using the blood of a young bull. He atoned for the sins of the people by using the blood of a goat. By sprinkling the blood of both animals in the Holy of Holies, the high priest kept alive the bond between God and Israel.

According to the Letter to the Hebrews, Good Friday is the *ultimate* Day of Atonement. Jesus completed the sacrifice of the cross by returning to the heavenly sphere. Whereas the blood of animals made the high priest's entrance possible, it is Jesus' own blood that makes his entrance into the heavenly sanctuary possible. Accordingly, Jesus' sacrifice effects a cleansing from dead works. In turn, Christians are to join in a perpetual liturgy by worshiping God in their everyday lives. Their blood bond is a common bond.

It is not clear whether or not the Last Supper was a Passover meal. While the first part of today's gospel supposes a Passover meal, the second part does not. In any event, the gospel links Jesus' death with Israel's great feast of liberation in which the blood on the doorposts and lintels prevented the deaths of the firstborn in the tenth plague (see Ex 12:11-14). The liberation from Egypt is now the death of God's firstborn, which ushers in a new type of liberation.

In the Last Supper meal, Mark speaks of both covenant and sacrifice. The broken pieces of bread symbolize the disciples' sharing in Jesus' self-offering. "My blood of the covenant" (14:24) refers to Exodus 24:8 (the first reading). By drinking the cup, the disciples enter into a covenant relationship with Jesus. They share a new source of life. They also share the destiny of Jesus, the offering of themselves for "many" (14:24), meaning *all*. Their blood bond is a common bond.

Today's Good News

Eucharist is a precarious experience. By its very nature it implies a bond, not only with our God but also with one another. In sharing the bread and the wine, we share a new life. We also share the joys and sorrows, the happiness and despair of the family community. We cannot have it otherwise. Far from merely relating us to our God, Eucharist necessarily binds us to one another. Eucharist without the family community is a distortion of Eucharist.

By taking part in Eucharist, we implicitly acknowledge that we have a larger family, more sisters and brothers. Their destinies are necessarily intertwined with our own. In reality, we live out the obligations of this family bond in our everyday lives, after we have gone out from our places of worship. By providing one another support, understanding, patience, sustenance, or whatever else is needed, we confess that we cannot, we *must not* go it alone. After all, our blood bond is a common bond.

Points for Reflection and Discussion

1. The blood bond is, in essence, a blood oath to fidelity-unto-death. We are called to give the lifegiving gift of our blood for the common good. Reflect on the importance of your blood, both for your own life and for the lives of your brothers and sisters in your common family of God.

_____

_____

_____

_____

2. Christians find their spiritual source of lifegiving blood in the Eucharist. Share your hunger and thirst for the Eucharist communion.

_____

_____

_____

_____

Themes

Covenant
   Q2, What Do Catholics Believe?
   M4, Family Life
Eucharist
   Q3, What is the Meaning of the Mass?
   M7, Holiness
Liturgy
   Q12, Catholics and Church
   M5, Your Prayer Life

Reading 1, Deuteronomy 5:12-15

Observe the sabbath day and keep it holy, as the Lord your God commanded you. Six days you shall labor and do all your work. But the seventh day is a sabbath to the Lord your God; you shall not do any work—you, or your son or your daughter, or your male or female slave, or your ox or your donkey, or any of your livestock, or the resident alien in your towns, so that your male and female slave may rest as well as you. Remember that you were a slave in the land of Egypt, and the Lord your God brought you out from there with a mighty hand and an outstretched arm; therefore the Lord your God commanded you to keep the sabbath day.

Psalm 81:2-3,4-5,5,6-7,9-10 (NRSV)

Reading 2, 2 Corinthians 4:6-11

It is the God who said, "Let light shine out of darkness," who has shone in our hearts to give the light of the knowledge of the glory of God in the face of Jesus Christ. But we have this treasure in clay jars, so that it may be made clear that this extraordinary power belongs to God and does not come from us. We are afflicted in every way, but not crushed; perplexed, but not driven to despair; persecuted, but not forsaken; struck down, but not destroyed; always carrying in the body the death of Jesus, so that the life of Jesus may also be made visible in our bodies. For while we live, we are always being given up to death for Jesus' sake, so that the life of Jesus may be made visible in our mortal flesh.

Gospel, Mark 2:23—3:6

One sabbath Jesus was going through the grainfields; and as they made their way his disciples began to pluck heads of grain. The Pharisees said to him, "Look, why are they doing what is not lawful on the sabbath?" And he said to them, "Have you never read what David did when he and his companions were hungry and in need of food? He entered the house of God, when Abiathar was high priest, and ate the bread of the Presence, which it is not lawful for any but the priests to eat, and he gave some to his companions." Then he said to them, "The sabbath was made for humankind, and not humankind for the sabbath; so the Son of Man is lord even of the sabbath."

Again he entered the synagogue, and a man was there who had a withered hand. They watched him to see whether he would cure him on the sabbath, so that they might accuse him. And he said to the man who had the withered hand, "Come forward." Then he said to them, "Is it lawful to do good or to do harm on the sabbath, to save life or to kill?" But they were silent. He looked around at them with anger; he was grieved at their hardness of heart and said to the man, "Stretch out your hand." He stretched it out, and his hand was restored. The Pharisees went out and immediately conspired with the Herodians against him, how to destroy him.

Keeping Holy the Sabbath

Elsie Hainz McGrath

Keeping holy the Sabbath is a difficult thing to do, even for those of us who faithfully attend Sunday Mass. After all, we have only so many hours in the day in which to accomplish a myriad of tasks. We sometimes presume that having kept our Sunday "obligation" at Church we have kept "holy" the sabbath. Today's readings show us the error of our ways.

The reading from Deuteronomy establishes the law concerning this holiest of days. God took time to rest (see Gn 2:2). God's people must do the same. But not only God's people—all God's creatures need the refreshment and renewal that a day of rest brings, including foreigners, slaves, and beasts of burden. The people are reminded that they were themselves once slaves, and were it not for God's "mighty hand" and "outstretched arm" (5:15) they would still be slaves. In fact, the overarching reason they are commanded to observe this holy day of rest is because of what God has done for them. They are to "remember" (5:15).

Psalm 81 remembers. The people celebrate their "statute for Israel, an ordinance of the God of Jacob" (81:4), who freed them from slavery and called them to rest from their labor (see Ex 1:14;6:6).

Earthen Vessels

In part of today's second reading (2 Cor 4:8-9), Paul uses the term "we" to illustrate his own experiences in the ministry of Jesus; it would seem this whole section is autobiographical. But Paul is addressing the people of Corinth, so it can be presumed that he is speaking of the whole community of persons who profess to follow Christ, those formed by God from the earthen clay to be light and nourishment for the world—made in the image and likeness of God and called to personify Christ the Lord. "For it is...God who...has shone in our hearts to give the light of the knowledge of the glory of God in the face of Jesus Christ. But we have this treasure in clay jars, so that it may be made clear that this extraordinary power belongs to God and does not come from us" (4:6-7).

In the embodiment of our Savior, being light and nourishment for the world, we are afflicted, perplexed, persecuted, and struck down because "we are always being given up to death for Jesus' sake" (4:11). We earthen vessels will not be constrained, driven to despair, abandoned, or destroyed because we hold this treasure—"the life of Jesus"—and it is to be "made visible in our mortal flesh" (4:11).

Lord of the Sabbath

Mark's Gospel picks up on the theme of Sabbath. Here we find that the Law, which was given to the people in our first reading, has been abused. Having made the Law of God over—into a law that deprived people of refreshment and renewal by making excessive restrictive demands upon them—the Pharisees have defeated the whole purpose of the Law. Jesus explains that "the sabbath was made for humankind, not humankind for the sabbath" (2:27). In other words, the people are to find refreshment and renewal on the Sabbath by resting from their labors and remembering what God has done for them.

To prove his point, Jesus refers the Pharisees back to David and the story of how "he entered the house of God...and ate the bread of the Presence, which it is not lawful for any but the priests to eat, and he gave some to his companions" (2:26; see 1 Sm 21:2-7). He brought this up because the disciples were plucking the heads off the grain as they made their way through a field and the Pharisees called their actions "not lawful" (2:24). The story of David did nothing to change their minds, however, and next we find Jesus in the synagogue. It is the Sabbath. Jesus asks a hypothetical question: "Is it lawful to do good or to do harm on the sabbath, to save life or to kill?" (3:4). They remain silent, an action that both angers and grieves him. It also moves him to heal the withered hand of a man who is in the synagogue.

The Pharisees' reaction to this act on the part of Jesus is to quickly confer with Herod's government officials concerning how they can ultimately put him to death. God's Law of the Sabbath has been superceded by rules and regulations that defeat the purpose of the Law.

Today's Good News

No matter how good our liturgy may be on any given Sunday, does that celebration alone serve to fulfill God's Law concerning keeping holy the Sabbath? How do we spend the rest of the day in refreshment and renewal? How do we remember and celebrate what God has done for us? How do we embody Christ for others?

Today's first reading reminds us of the reason why God gave us the Law of the Sabbath—to rest in imitation of God and to remember what God has done for us. The other readings offer examples of celebration, ministry, and healing. Perhaps our time of rest and remembrance is not best spent in a myriad of "duties" or in strenuous "recreation." Perhaps refreshment and renewal are more readily found in prayer and in service, within ourselves and within others.

Points for Reflection and Discussion

1. Society forces many of us to "work" on our "day of rest." How do you deal with these restrictions on the purpose for God's Law in your life?

_____

_____

_____

_____

_____

2. The Sabbath should be the holiest of all "holy days." What can you do to make the day more "holy" for yourself?

_____

_____

_____

_____

_____

Themes

Law
    Q2, What Do Catholics Believe?
    M6, Discernment
Rest
    Q11, Catholic Practices
    M5, Your Prayer Life
Sabbath
    Q3, What is the Meaning of the Mass?
    M7, Holiness

Reading 1, Genesis 3:9-15

[After Adam had eaten of the tree:]

The Lord God called to the man, and said to him, "Where are you?" He said, "I heard the sound of you in the garden, and I was afraid, because I was naked; and I hid myself." He said, "Who told you that you were naked? Have you eaten from the tree of which I commanded you not to eat?" The man said, "The woman whom you gave to be with me, she gave me fruit from the tree, and I ate." Then the Lord God said to the woman, "What is this that you have done?" The woman said, "The serpent tricked me, and I ate." The Lord God said to the serpent, "Because you have done this, cursed are you among all animals and among all wild creatures; upon your belly you shall go, and dust you shall eat all the days of your life. I will put enmity between you and the woman, and between your offspring and hers; he will strike your head, and you will strike his heel."

Psalm 130:1-2,3-4,5-6,7-8

Reading 2, 2 Corinthians 4:13—5:1

Just as we have the same spirit of faith that is in accordance with scripture—"I believed, and so I spoke"—we also believe, and so we speak, because we know that the one who raised the Lord Jesus will raise us also with Jesus, and will bring us with you into his presence. Yes, everything is for your sake, so that grace, as it extends to more and more people, may increase thanksgiving, to the glory of God.

So we do not lose heart. Even though our outer nature is wasting away, our inner nature is being renewed day by day. For this slight momentary affliction is preparing us for an eternal weight of glory beyond all measure, because we look not at what can be seen but at what cannot be seen; for what can be seen is temporary, but what cannot be seen is eternal.

For we know that if the earthly tent we live in is destroyed, we have a building from God, a house not made with hands, eternal in the heavens.

Gospel, Mark 3:19-35 (NRSV)

Jesus came home [with his disciples], and the crowd came together again, so that they could not even eat. When his family heard it, they went out to restrain him, for people were saying, "He has gone out of his mind." And the scribes who came down from Jerusalem said, "He has Beelzebul, and by the ruler of the demons he casts out demons." And he called them to him, and spoke to them in parables, "How can Satan cast out Satan? If a kingdom is divided against itself, that kingdom cannot stand. And if a house is divided against itself, that house will not be able to stand. And if Satan has risen up against himself and is divided, he cannot stand, but his end has come. But no one can enter a strong man's house and plunder his property without first tying up the strong man; then indeed the house can be plundered.

"Truly I tell you, people will be forgiven for their sins and whatever blasphemies they utter; but whoever blasphemes against the Holy Spirit can never have forgiveness, but is guilty of an eternal sin"—for they had said, "He has an unclean spirit."

Then his mother and his brothers came; and standing outside, they sent to him and called him. A crowd was sitting around him; and they said to him, "Your mother and your brothers and sisters are outside, asking for you." And he replied, "Who are my mother and my brothers?" And looking at those who sat around him, he said, "Here are my mother and my brothers! Whoever does the will of God is my brother and sister and mother."

Of Sin and Salvation

ELSIE HAINZ MCGRATH

The fall from grace that began with the sin of Adam and Eve has been the subject of countless interpretations throughout the ages. The objective of these interpretations is usually the same: to determine exactly what kind of sin led to our undoing. Was it pride or arrogance or faithlessness? It was certainly the first among many—the continuing sins of humankind, as chronicled within the generations from Adam to Noah and from the flood to the Tower of Babel (Gn 3—11), all of which serve to lead us to a realization that we are proud and arrogant and faithless. We are also sexually perverse and murderers and thieves. And we will die.

Today's first reading introduces us to guilt—that instinctive feeling that we have done the wrong thing—and to the typically human ways of dealing with guilt: hide, slough off responsibility, blame somebody else. The people of Israel learned that they were a sinful people, but also that their God was a merciful God.

Out of the Depths

The psalm of lamentation that we recite today is a penitential lament. It acknowledges the sinfulness of the person, who cries to God "out of the depths" (Ps 130:1). The depths are the waters of chaos; the psalmist implies that he is drowning in sin. It was the end of life, separation from living relationships—even relationship with God. But a glimmer of hope remains, because God listens to a cry from the depths and is full of mercy.

The psalmist's lament becomes Paul's thanksgiving because, as he tells the Corinthian community, "we know that if the earthly tent we live in is destroyed, we have a building from God, a house not made with hands, eternal in the heavens" (2 Cor 5:1). While the psalmist *hoped* for redemption, Paul *knows* redemption is at hand. "We do not lose heart," says Paul (4:16). Not even death can separate us from the love of God, because "the one who raised the Lord Jesus will raise us also with Jesus, and will bring us with you into his presence" (4:14).

Coming Home

The scene in Mark's Gospel is an unhappy homecoming. Apparently the family meal is being disrupted by crowds of people clamoring to see Jesus. Members of the family attempt to discredit him for the sake of their own comfort, and they are joined by scribes from Jerusalem who claim that he "has Beelzebul" and "casts out demons" (3:22). Jesus responds with a question, "How can Satan cast out Satan?" (3:23), and a parable to show the inconsistencies in their accusation that he drives out demons. Then he addresses their first accusation: "...whoever blasphemes against the Holy Spirit can never have forgiveness, but is guilty of an eternal sin" (3:29). This sin is eternal because it attributes the work of the Holy Spirit to the power of evil. This sinner turns irrevocably away from God.

The story continues with the news that Jesus' mother and siblings are waiting for him outside. Apparently the house was so crowded by this time that they could not make their way inside. Jesus' response sounds harsh to us, but it isn't a rebuke of his mother and sisters and brothers at all. If we remember the beginning of today's story, where Jesus' relatives placed themselves in opposition to his words and works, the ending is more clear. *Family* is *everyone* who "does the will of God" (3:35). Jesus doesn't *exclude* his blood relatives; he *includes* those who aren't blood related. *We* are members of his family too!

Today's Good News

What better news is there than that we are members of Jesus' family? We can rejoice in being so closely related to our Savior. We can rejoice in his straightforward and consoling words: "Truly I tell you, people will be forgiven for their sins and whatever blasphemies they utter" (Mk 3:28).

But in our rejoicing we must not lose sight of his next words: "but whoever blasphemes against the Holy Spirit can never have forgiveness, but is guilty of an eternal sin" (3:29). Those without hope do not envision victory over evil. They need to hear the Good News lest they fall into that sin. Is there anyone we know who is outside in the cold (either literally or figuratively)? What can we do to bring them into the family fold?

Points for Reflection and Discussion

1. Is there someone in your immediate family who has shunned the family of God? What can (will) you do about it?

_____

_____

_____

_____

2. Have you abdicated responsibility for a personal shortcoming in the past weeks? Have you made amends for it?

_____

_____

_____

_____

Themes
Family
   Q6, The Saints
   M4, Family Life
Forgiveness
   Q10, Catholics and Prayer
   M5, Your Prayer Life
Sin
   Q2, What Do Catholics Believe?
   M7, Holiness

Reading 1, Ezekiel 17:22-24

Thus says the Lord God:

I myself will take a sprig from the lofty top of a cedar; I will set it out. I will break off a tender one from the topmost of its young twigs; I myself will plant it on a high and lofty mountain. On the mountain height of Israel I will plant it, in order that it may produce boughs and bear fruit, and become a noble cedar. Under it every kind of bird will live; in the shade of its branches will nest winged creatures of every kind. All the trees of the field shall know that I am the Lord. I bring low the high tree, I make high the low tree; I dry up the green tree and make the dry tree flourish. I the Lord have spoken; I will accomplish it.

Psalm 92:1-2,12-13,14-15 (NRSV)

Reading 2, 2 Corinthians 5:6-10

We are always confident; even though we know that while we are at home in the body we are away from the Lord—for we walk by faith, not by sight. Yes, we do have confidence, and we would rather be away from the body and at home with the Lord. So whether we are at home or away, we make it our aim to please him. For all of us must appear before the judgment seat of Christ, so that each may receive recompense for what has been done in the body, whether good or evil.

Gospel, Mark 4:26-34

Jesus said [to the crowd]:

"The kingdom of God is as if someone would scatter seed on the ground, and would sleep and rise night and day, and the seed would sprout and grow, he does not know how. The earth produces of itself, first the stalk, then the head, then the full grain in the head. But when the grain is ripe, at once he goes in with his sickle, because the harvest has come."

He also said, "With what can we compare the kingdom of God, or what parable will we use for it? It is like a mustard seed, which, when sown upon the ground, is the smallest of all the seeds on earth; yet when it is sown it grows up and becomes the greatest of all shrubs, and puts forth large branches, so that the birds of the air can make nests in its shade." With many such parables he spoke the word to them, as they were able to hear it; he did not speak to them except in parables, but he explained everything in private to his disciples.

Giving God a Chance

JOHN F. CRAGHAN

In our technological world the computer is supreme. In an instant we can gather seemingly limitless information. On the basis of such information we are able to make reasonable predictions. We can thus forecast both growth and failure. We may, however, run the risk of focusing only on ourselves. We may conclude that we are the sole determiners of hope and happiness. We may find it ever more difficult to give God a chance.

Today's readings are on the subject of growth. While they do not disparage human involvement, they strike a blow for divine providence. They see God not as an impersonal, aloof spectator but as a personal, interested collaborator. They see life not as a power struggle to attain fame and fortune but as a challenging enterprise to acknowledge gifts and graces. They urge the worshiping community to give God a chance.

David Reigns

During the exile in the sixth century B.C., a group of Ezekiel's disciples spoke to the issue of despair overwhelming their community. It was the time when the Temple in Jerusalem lay gutted, a period in which no Davidic king occupied the throne. To counteract the gloom, the disciples announced the restoration of God's people under a king from David's line. As elsewhere (see Ez 34:23-24), they offered no precise formula or timetable for the restoration.

The crest of the cedar is David's house (see Ez 17:4; also Jer 22:6,23). Once again Yahweh will intervene and revive the Davidic dynasty in Israel. This toppled dynasty will regain its former eminence, even to the point of protecting vassal nations ("the shade of its branches," Ez 17:23). Yahweh will reverse the fortunes of the mighty and the lowly ("high/low, green/dry"). Indeed all the trees of the field will not fail to recognize these astounding developments. Owing to God's immutable Word, the promise will become a reality. The message is clearly to give God a chance.

Psalm 92 is a psalm of declarative praise extolling God's providence. It acquired a significant place in the Jewish Sabbath liturgy as the people rested with God on the seventh day. It marked a time, therefore, when God had conquered the forces of evil and met the needs of the people. In this context, praise seemed the only proper response: "It is good to give thanks to the Lord, to sing praises to your name, O Most High..." (92:1).

In verses 13-16 the psalmist spells out God's blessings on the just. He compares them to fertile trees (the palm and the cedar). What is noteworthy is that their fertility is continual. Even in their old age they will still bear fruit (92:15). The psalmist includes God's providence in the litany of blessings. Fear is thereby impossible, since Israel's God is the very foundation ("rock") of order. This audience clearly endorses giving God a chance.

Seeds of Life

In the parable of the seed growing of itself, Mark contrasts the relative inactivity of the farmer and the assurance of the harvest. Growth will come—it is only at harvesttime that the farmer reappears. Since the harvest symbolizes the last judgment (see Jl 4:13), it is likely that the parable addressed a burning issue. It sought to respond to those who questioned the slow progress of God's kingdom.

The parable of the mustard seed addressed another critical point—patience in the face of the relatively small beginnings of the kingdom. While Mark 4:31 stresses the smallness of the mustard seed, verse 32 underlines its phenomenal growth. Hence, even though the beginnings are rather negligible, God can effect considerable growth. So too, although the start of the kingdom with Jesus' preaching is somewhat inconspicuous, God will still bring about astounding developments. Here the plea is: Give God a chance.

Today's Good News

Today's biblical passages should force us to reassess and evaluate those segments of our lives where we tend to exercise sole control. Whether in our business, family, or social roles, we are challenged to ask: Is it possible to make God a partner? This question leads to another: Do I see other humans as things or persons? To treat humans as things is unbridled arrogance—we can never nurture them and thus expect growth. But to treat humans as persons is hope-filled realism—we can encourage them and stimulate growth. In the latter case we allow God a free hand; we give God a chance.

Points for Reflection and Discussion

1. Today's readings call us to hope. Essentially, people with hope are called optimists, *while those who view persons and situations as hopeless are termed* pessimists. *Christians must* be optimists—a people of hope. *What does that mean to you?*

_____

_____

_____

_____

2. Do you ever "give God a chance" only as a last-ditch effort, because nothing you have tried has worked?

_____

_____

_____

_____

Themes

Growth
  Q1, Journey of Faith
  M1, Conversion: A Lifelong Process
Hope
  Q2, What Do Catholics Believe?
  M6, Discernment
Praise
  Q10, Catholics and Prayer
  M5, Your Prayer Life

Reading 1, Job 38:1,8-11

The Lord answered Job out of the whirlwind:
"Who shut in the sea with doors when it burst out from the womb?—when I made the clouds its garment, and thick darkness its swaddling band, and prescribed bounds for it, and set bars and doors, and said, 'Thus far shall you come, and no farther, and here shall your proud waves be stopped'?"

Psalm 107:23-24,25-26,28-29,30-31

Reading 2, 2 Corinthians 5:14-17

The love of Christ urges us on, because we are convinced that one has died for all; therefore all have died. And he died for all, so that those who live might live no longer for themselves, but for him who died and was raised for them.

From now on, therefore, we regard no one from a human point of view; even though we once knew Christ from a human point of view, we know him no longer in that way. So if anyone is in Christ, there is a new creation: everything old has passed away; see, everything has become new!

Gospel, Mark 4:35-41

On that day, when evening had come, Jesus said to [the disciples], "Let us go across to the other side." And leaving the crowd behind, they took him with them in the boat, just as he was. Other boats were with him. A great windstorm arose, and the waves beat into the boat, so that the boat was already being swamped. But he was in the stern, asleep on the cushion; and they woke him up and said to him, "Teacher, do you not care that we are perishing?" He woke up and rebuked the wind, and said to the sea, "Peace! Be still!" Then the wind ceased, and there was a dead calm. He said to them, "Why are you afraid? Have you still no faith?" And they were filled with great awe and said to one another, "Who then is this, that even the wind and the sea obey him?"

Power and Service

JOHN F. CRAGHAN

Think of those people who have risen from the ranks into positions of power. By dint of unflagging efforts they finally make it to the top. While we applaud their success, we still raise the question: How will they use their newly acquired power? Will they use it to consolidate and advance their own personal interests, or will they use it to benefit others? Can power mean service?

While today's readings emphasize the role of power, they perceive that power within the framework of service. They see God's control of chaos as a clear demonstration of divine concern and care for beleaguered believers. They maintain that power must ultimately take the form of loving involvement, of service.

Why Me?

In the first reading, Job's request to have God speak and somehow resolve the problem of Job's pitiable condition is seemingly granted. But, in fact, God takes the offensive and asks provocative questions of Job. Ironically, God's cross-examination will not answer any of Job's questions. They are simply the wrong questions.

The author first depicts the sea as a helpless infant in need of divine solicitude, with clouds as garments and thick darkness as swaddling bands. Conversely, Job is next shown the unruly nature of this creation—its tendency to reassert its chaotic strength, to burst forth and cripple humans. But God's power precludes this possibility, even if Job is unable to comprehend it. The implied question is: If Job cannot understand God's providence for the sea and the powers of nature, how will he ever grasp God's care for humans? In other words, God's power means service.

Psalm 107 is a thanksgiving psalm. It speaks of a variety of dangers that confront believers: travel by land (107:4-5); imprisonment (107:10-12); sickness (107:17-18); and travel by sea (107:23-27). In these desperate situations the people cry out, God intervenes, and finally the people acknowledge their indebtedness for the divine intervention. Today's selection from this psalm contrasts God's strength with the seemingly invincible sea. God is completely in charge. Though God raises up the winds that bring treacherous waves, God remains concerned about the people, and the radical transformation of the storm into a gentle breeze dramatizes God's response to the peoples' plight. God's power means service.

Who Can This Be?

Mark's miracle story consists of many of the same kinds of images. First the scene is set (4:35-36). The contrast presented is between the storm and Jesus' restful sleep (4:37-38). The disciples are frightened and a divine imperative is issued (4:38-39). The story concludes with Jesus' statement about the disciples' lack of trust (4:40), followed by their attitude of amazement over his great feat (4:41).

Though Jesus performs a work that the Hebrew Scriptures regularly ascribe to God (see the first reading and the responsorial psalm), Mark is undoubtedly addressing another agenda. He is focusing on the needs of his post-resurrection community. This community experiences chaos in the form of the Lord's absence and the daily trials of Christian life; so in the story, Jesus seems to be sleeping, unperturbed, and hence not involved. His question—"Why are you afraid? Have you still no faith?" (4:40)—teaches the later community that a lack of faith is not the proper response. Jesus continues to abide with them. His demonstration of power during the storm assures them that he is not really asleep—and that power means service.

Today's Good News

Who are the people wielding the power and how are they using it? We spontaneously think of elected officials and chief executive officers. In many of these cases, brute power is all too evident. But perhaps we would be well advised to dwell on those less evident holders of power. Parents, teachers, government employees, clergy, and so forth come to mind. Their positions give them genuine power over others. The self-sacrifice of parents for their family, the extra efforts of teachers for their students, the additional patience of government employees for their public, the increased understanding of clergy for their people...all these, and many more, unequivocally show that true power means service.

Points for Reflection and Discussion

1. Have you ever abused a position of power—in the workplace or in your family? Have you ever been abused by someone who exercised power over you?

_____

_____

_____

_____

2. Biblical images of water are abundantly diverse, moving from death to life. Why do you suppose water is the primary component in both chaos and calm?

_____

_____

_____

_____

Themes

Power
    Q5, How Do Catholics Interpret the Bible?
    M2, The Laity: Called To Build God's Kingdom
Service
    Q6, The Saints
    M3, Your Special Gifts
Water
    Q11, Catholic Practices
    M1, Conversion: A Lifelong Process

Reading 1, Wisdom 1:13-15;2:23-24

God did not make death and he does not delight in the death of the living. For he created all things so that they might exist; the generative forces of the world are wholesome, and there is no destructive poison in them, and the dominion of Hades is not on earth. For righteousness is immortal.

For God created us for incorruption, and made us in the image of his own eternity, but through the devil's envy death entered the world, and those who belong to his company experience it.

Psalm 30:1,3,4-5,10-11,12 (NRSV)

Reading 2, 2 Corinthians 8:7,9,13-15

Now as you excel in everything—in faith, in speech, in knowledge, in utmost eagerness, and in our love for you— so we want you to excel also in this generous undertaking.

For you know the generous act of our Lord Jesus Christ, that though he was rich, yet for your sakes he became poor, so that by his poverty you might become rich. I do not mean that there should be relief for others and pressure on you, but it is a question of a fair balance between your present abundance and their need, so that their abundance may be for your need, in order that there may be a fair balance. As it is written, "The one who had much did not have too much, and the one who had little did not have too little."

Gospel, Mark 5:21-43

When Jesus had crossed again in the boat to the other side, a great crowd gathered around him; and he was by the sea. Then one of the leaders of the synagogue named Jairus came and, when he saw him, fell at his feet and begged him repeatedly, "My little daughter is at the point of death. Come and lay your hands on her, so that she may be made well, and live." So he went with him. And a large crowd followed him and pressed in on him.

Now there was a woman who had been suffering from hemorrhages for twelve years. She had endured much under many physicians, and had spent all that she had; and she was no better, but rather grew worse. She had heard about Jesus, and came up behind him in the crowd and touched his cloak, for she said, "If I but touch his clothes, I will be made well." Immediately her hemorrhage stopped; and she felt in her body that she was healed of her disease. Immediately aware that power had gone forth from him, Jesus turned about in the crowd and said, "Who touched my clothes?" And his disciples said to him, "You see the crowd pressing in on you; how can you say, 'Who touched

me?' " He looked all around to see who had done it. But the woman, knowing what had happened to her, came in fear and trembling, fell down before him, and told him the whole truth. He said to her, "Daughter, your faith has made you well; go in peace, and be healed of your disease."

While he was still speaking, some people came from the leader's house to say, "Your daughter is dead. Why trouble the teacher any further?" But overhearing what they said, Jesus said to the leader of the synagogue, "Do not fear, only believe." He allowed no one to follow him except Peter, James, and John, the brother of James. When they came to the house of the leader of the synagogue, he saw a commotion, people weeping and wailing loudly. When he had entered, he said to them, "Why do you make a commotion and weep? The child is not dead but sleeping." And they laughed at him.

Then he put them all outside, and took the child's father and mother and those who were with him, and went in where the child was. He took her by the hand and said to her, "Talitha cum," which means, "Little girl, get up!" And immediately the girl got up and began to walk about (she was twelve years of age). At this they were overcome with amazement. He strictly ordered them that no one should know this, and told them to give her something to eat.

The In Crowd

JOHN F. CRAGHAN

No one really wants to stand out from the crowd. We enjoy being part of the group. We relish the feeling of peer support, the comfort of getting along with everyone. We know that to reject the party line is to be ostracized. We realize that to be different is to be alone, to march to the tune of a different drummer is to stand out from the crowd.

Today's readings respond to the typically human concerns of being different. They see God, not as an impersonal energy but as an involved partner who invites humans to engage in the demanding enterprise of believing. They see the believer, not as a community reject but as a dynamic individual who accepts this difficult invitation. In the face of so many conflicting values they maintain that faith is the only party line.

A Party Line

The Book of Wisdom addresses the believer's task of being different. It speaks to Jews living in the cosmopolitan setting of Alexandria in Egypt in the first century B.C. It acknowledges their predicament—fidelity to the God of Israel in the midst of a sophisticated pagan environment. Nonetheless it challenges them to continue to adhere in faith to the God who once called Israel out of Egypt.

The author develops the concept of faith by using life-and-death imagery. Here death is not merely the cessation of the vital functions—it is a loss of intimacy with God and God's party line. Hence the author understands the Garden of Eden story in a fresh way. Those who join the party of the devil (or the snake) experience this loss of intimacy. On the other hand, those who cling to God's party enjoy a very special relationship through the divine gift of imperishable life. To recognize God's sovereignty (see Wis 15:3) is indeed to be different, but it is such recognition that makes immortality possible. Here faith is the only party line.

Today's psalm is a thanksgiving that praises God for delivering the psalmist from suffering and distress. The psalmist cries out for help and experiences divine liberation. God heals him and brings him up from the nether world. The psalmist captures his unique sense of deliverance in a special way—the ability to dance again (30:12).

The liturgy omits verses 7-8, wherein the psalmist explains the reason for his demise. He was too overconfident that he would never be disturbed. In rejecting God, he implicitly accepted a world view where personal security made God dispensable. As a result of his suffering and distress, however, he has regained his relationship with God. He now believes that faith is the only party line.

Arise!

In the gospel account, Mark too underlines the primacy of faith. He mentions that Jairus falls at Jesus' feet and makes an earnest appeal for his daughter, showing his audience a synagogue official who believes in Jesus' power, at least before the point of death. When Jairus receives word that the child is dead, he is challenged to believe on a higher level: that Jesus can raise the dead. While the people proclaim the presence of death by their wailing and crying, Jesus implicitly prepares Jairus to announce the presence of life.

Mark has shaped the story to address the needs of his community. Jairus' request, "Come and lay your hands on her so that she may be made well, and live" (5:23), means for the post-resurrection community, "that she may be saved and enjoy eternal life." Indeed Jesus uses the vocabulary of his own Resurrection toward the end of the episode: "get up!" (egeirein, meaning resurrection from the dead, Mk 5:41; see also Mk 16:6). Mark's use of this story urges his community to believe that faith in Jesus can indeed conquer death despite the opposition of the crowd. Faith is the only party line.

Today's Good News

Places such as Alexandria and Galilee may change but the ongoing task of believers does not. We are daily bombarded with a variety of views such as: only pleasure will satisfy us; pursuit of self is the only really fulfilling enterprise; impatience is weakness; genuine charity is outmoded; and on and on. Each day we are invited to pursue the more popular stance, to join the crowd. Today's readings are a challenge to dare to be different. Ultimately, our response to that challenge is a choice between heaven and hell, between life and death. For Christians, faith is the only party line.

Points for Reflection and Discussion

1. The touch of Jesus brought Jairus' daughter to life; it brought the woman with the hemorrhage to health. Do you believe in the healing power of touch? Have you experienced it?

_____

_____

_____

_____

2. Have you ever had to make a difficult choice between being a part of the crowd or being an outsider—different, rejected? Talk about it.

_____

_____

_____

_____

Themes
Death
    Q1, Journey of Faith
    M1, Conversion: A Lifelong Process
Life
    Q11, Catholic Practices
    M3, Your Special Gifts
Popularity
    Q6, The Saints
    M2, The Laity: Called To Build God's Kingdom

Reading 1, Ezekiel 2:2-5

A spirit entered into me and set me on my feet; and I heard him speaking to me. He said to me: Mortal, I am sending you to the people of Israel, to a nation of rebels who have rebelled against me; they and their ancestors have transgressed against me to this very day. The descendants are impudent and stubborn. I am sending you to them, and you shall say to them, "Thus says the Lord God." Whether they hear or refuse to hear (for they are a rebellious house), they shall know that there has been a prophet among them.

Psalm 123:1-2,2,3-4

Reading 2, 2 Corinthians 12:7-10

Consider the exceptional character of the revelations. Therefore, to keep me from being too elated, a thorn was given me in the flesh, a messenger of Satan to torment me, to keep me from being too elated. Three times I appealed to the Lord about this, that it would leave me, but he said to me, "My grace is sufficient for you, for power is made perfect in weakness." So, I will boast all the more gladly of my weaknesses, so that the power of Christ may dwell in me.

Therefore I am content with weaknesses, insults, hardships, persecutions, and calamities for the sake of Christ; for whenever I am weak, then I am strong.

Gospel, Mark 6:1-6

Jesus left that place and came to his hometown, and his disciples followed him. On the sabbath he began to teach in the synagogue, and many who heard him were astounded. They said, "Where did this man get all this? What is this wisdom that has been given to him? What deeds of power are being done by his hands! Is not this the carpenter, the son of Mary and brother of James and Joses and Judas and Simon, and are not his sisters here with us?" And they took offense at him. Then Jesus said to them, "Prophets are not without honor, except in their hometown, and among their own kin, and in their own house." And he could do no deed of power there, except that he laid his hands on a few sick people and cured them. And he was amazed at their unbelief. Then he went about among the villages teaching.

Strength In Weakness

JOHN F. CRAGHAN

We all admire strength. We look for it in our athletes, our financial planners, our politicians, and our armed forces. On the other hand, we are not really prepared to deal with weakness. In our athletes, weakness means poorer performance; in our financial planners, loss of revenue from dissatisfied customers; in our politicians, possible loss of office; and in our armed forces, possible humiliating defeats. While weakness is all too blatant, we don't seem ready to handle it.

Today's readings are a study in weakness. They propose for our consideration three individuals who experienced significant weakness in the exercise of their mission. Ironically they hold up their achievements as a basis for hoping. In the face of a strength-intoxicated society, these biblical selections argue that weakness can mean strength.

The passage from Ezekiel is part of his vocation scene. In the year 593 B.C., God appeared to Ezekiel in the land of exile and called upon him to prophesy. Ezekiel felt God's dynamic presence ("spirit") but at the same time he became acutely aware of the opposition of his countrymen: "rebels...impudent and stubborn" (2:3,4). Given such an audience, it is hardly surprising that the prophet felt discouraged. At the conclusion of the call scene, Ezekiel records: "I came to the exiles at Tel-abib, who lived by the river Chebar. And I sat there among them, stunned, for seven days" (3:15).

The rest of this prophetic book reveals a spokesperson who pantomimes God's message and performs bizarre symbolic actions. He first attacks the people for their infidelities. Nevertheless, when news of the fall of Jerusalem reaches the exiles, he offers them a message of hope. The biblical record ultimately discloses a resilient person in the service of his people. Here weakness can mean strength.

The Flesh and the Devil

In this section of his Letter to the Corinthians, Paul has just finished speaking about his visions and revelations. He pushes on to discuss other personal experiences with his God. "A thorn was given me in the flesh, a messenger of Satan to torment me, to keep me from being too elated" (12:7). While this may refer to a grave illness (see Lk 13:16), it more probably implies persecution at the hands of his own people (see Ez 28:24). In these circumstances he earnestly asked God to remove the affliction.

God's response was not to remove the problem but to assure Paul of his ongoing support. "He said to me, 'My grace is sufficient for you, for power is made perfect in weakness'" (12:9). This experience was the catalyst for Paul's understanding of the interrelationship of weakness and strength. The weaker the person, the greater the display of God's power. "I will boast all the more gladly of my weaknesses, so that the power of Christ may dwell in me" (12:9). Paul insists that weakness can mean strength.

Homecoming

In 4:35—5:43, Mark exploited Jesus' power and acceptance by a series of great feats. Now, however, when Jesus returns to his hometown, the people reject him. They sense a glaring discrepancy between his family tree and his teaching/miracles. They are prompted to ask: "Is not this the carpenter?" (6:3). Jesus' reaction is one of both discouragement and astonishment: "Prophets are not without honor except in their hometown..." (6:4). Apart from curing a few sick, he works no miracles; the lack of faith is all too distressing.

Previously Mark had noted the growing opposition to Jesus by the Jewish authorities (2:1—3:6) and his own family (3:20-35). In this synagogue scene, Mark is probably foreshadowing the final rejection on Good Friday (15:6-15). The last word, however, is neither weakness nor defeat. Looking up at the dead body of Jesus, the centurion proclaims: "Truly this man was God's Son!" (15:39). The message to the women at the tomb, "He has been raised" (16:6), also testifies that weakness can become strength.

Today's Good News

We witness many forms of weakness in our daily lives. We are challenged to transform weakness into strength. The married couples who recognize the problems in their relationship can begin to solve them. Those dependent on drugs or alcohol who acknowledge their addiction can start on the road to rehabilitation. Leaders who realize their mistakes can undertake strategies for improvement. These examples may be multiplied time and again. They ultimately suggest that weakness need not be the final word. After all, God is able to use our faults as well as our assets. Weakness can become strength.

Points for Reflection and Discussion

1. Have you ever experienced acceptance among strangers and rejection at home? Can you imagine Jesus' feelings of amazement at his neighbors' lack of faith? What else do you suppose Jesus felt?

_____

_____

_____

_____

2. Much has been made of Paul's "thorn in the flesh" statement, but it is not known with certainty what he was referring to. What do you see as your "thorn in the flesh"?

_____

_____

_____

_____

_____

Themes
Opposition
    Q1, Journey of Faith
    M2, The Laity: Called To Build God's Kingdom
Strength
    Q10, Catholics and Prayer
    M3, Your Special Gifts
    M8, Evangelization
Weakness
    Q11, Catholic Practices
    M6, Discernment

Reading 1, Amos 7:12-15

Amaziah said to Amos, "O seer, go, flee away to the land of Judah, earn your bread there, and prophesy there; but never again prophesy at Bethel, for it is the king's sanctuary, and it is a temple of the kingdom." Then Amos answered Amaziah, "I am no prophet, nor a prophet's son; but I am a herdsman, and a dresser of sycamore trees, and the Lord took me from following the flock, and the Lord said to me, 'Go, prophesy to my people Israel.' "

Psalm 85:8-9,10-11,12-13 (NRSV)

Reading 2, Ephesians 1:3-14

Blessed be the God and Father of our Lord Jesus Christ, who has blessed us in Christ with every spiritual blessing in the heavenly places, just as he chose us in Christ before the foundation of the world to be holy and blameless before him in love. He destined us for adoption as his children through Jesus Christ, according to the good pleasure of his will, to the praise of his glorious grace that he freely bestowed on us in the Beloved.

In him we have redemption through his blood, the forgiveness of our trespasses, according to the riches of his grace that he lavished on us. With all wisdom and insight he has made known to us the mystery of his will, according to his good pleasure that he set forth in Christ, as a plan for the fullness of time, to gather up all things in him, things in heaven and things on earth.

In Christ we have also obtained an inheritance, having been destined according to the purpose of him who accomplishes all things according to his counsel and will, so that we, who were the first to set our hope on Christ, might live for the praise of his glory. In him you also, when you had heard the word of truth, the gospel of your salvation, and had believed in him, were marked with the seal of the promised Holy Spirit; this is the pledge of our inheritance toward redemption as God's own people, to the praise of his glory.

Gospel, Mark 6:7-13

Jesus called the twelve and began to send them out two by two, and gave them authority over the unclean spirits. He ordered them to take nothing for their journey except a staff; no bread, no bag, no money in their belts; but to wear sandals and not to put on two tunics. He said to them, "Wherever you enter a house, stay there until you leave the place. If any place will not welcome you and they refuse to hear you, as you leave, shake off the dust that is on your feet as a testimony against them." So they went out and proclaimed that all should repent. They cast out many demons, and anointed with oil many who were sick and cured them.

Chosen To Serve

JOHN F. CRAGHAN

For some reason we humans love contests. We relish sports contests, beauty contests, job contests, and on and on. We admire those who survive the cut and are finally chosen. Usually we don't anticipate that these lucky people will have any obligations to us. We generally expect that their personal selection will mean their personal advancement.

Today's readings take a decidedly different view of selection. They see the chosen within the context of community. They see the winners within the context of the larger society. They regard the victors, not as those who have already achieved something for themselves but as those who will yet have to achieve something for others. They urge that when selected one must serve.

Around the year 760 B.C., the Lord chose a shepherd and dresser of sycamores from the Judaean town of Tekoa. He prevailed upon Amos to leave his traditional occupation and proceed to the northern city of Bethel with its prestigious sanctuary. In today's passage, Amos defends himself before Amaziah, the priest of Bethel, by stating with powerful simplicity that the Lord called him and said: "Go, prophesy to my people Israel" (7:15).

Amos' selection meant commitment to the Lord's cause. Although the northern kingdom of Israel was enjoying great prosperity and expansion, the poor were getting poorer. The wealthy few sold the poor person for a pair of sandals (2:6), while they themselves guzzled wine from basins and feasted on the choicest meat (6:4,6). Against this deplorable background, the prophet had to announce the inexorable end of the northern kingdom: "The end has come upon my people Israel" (8:2). Although Amos' task was most unpleasant, its execution clearly demonstrates that when selected one must serve.

Chosen to Praise

The author of Ephesians begins with a hymn of praise to God for inaugurating the plan of salvation. That plan starts in heaven but impacts earth. God chose God's people before the world began with a purpose in mind, namely, genuine Christian living. Their selection commissions them "to the praise of his glorious grace that he freely bestowed on us in the Beloved" (1:6).

Selection also implies liberation. Owing to the self-giving of Christ, believers are set free. Indeed they are privileged to be called into God's council chambers.

They thereby listen to God's mystery—the plan of salvation—and participate in divine deliberations. This liberation dimension of the selection process also empowers Christians to provide hope for a divided world, to bring creation out of chaos. To that extent, the text implies that when selected one must serve.

Chosen to Heal

In creating today's gospel scene, Mark envisions missionary work outside of Palestine. Nonetheless he is careful to connect such missionary enterprises with the teaching experience of Jesus. Just as Mark earlier linked rejection of Jesus with the call of the Twelve, he now joins the rejection at Nazareth with the mission of the Twelve (see Mk 3:6,13-19;6:1-6). Mark thus sees the teaching/work of the Twelve as an extension of the teaching/work of Jesus.

The missionary charge of the Twelve focuses on the needs of the community. Disparaging provisions for every emergency and rejecting the best accommodations, the missionaries resolutely pursue the proclamation of a complete and radical change ("repent"). They continue Jesus' victory over the forces of evil by expelling demons. They advance Jesus' program by anointing the sick and working cures. At the same time the missionaries will experience rejection as Jesus did. Hence they are instructed to shake the dust from their feet, in other words, to remove the last vestige of contact with a pagan atmosphere. Clearly, when selected one must serve.

Today's Good News

The selection process of the Christian begins at baptism. While the sacrament makes one a member of God's elite, it also commissions one to think and act in terms of service to the community. To be sure, service can and does take many forms. We think, for example, of those who console the sorrowing, who educate the uninstructed, who encourage the despairing, who welcome the homeless, who love the unloved. These and other forms of reaching out are ultimately grounded in being chosen. By its very nature, selection means service. When selected one must serve.

Points for Reflection and Discussion

1. Why do you suppose Jesus sent the Twelve out "two by two"?

_____

_____

_____

_____

_____

2. Think about being chosen to serve. How does that make you feel?

_____

_____

_____

_____

Themes

Chosen
    Q2, What Do Catholics Believe?
    M2, The Laity: Called To Build God's Kingdom
Discipleship
    Q1, Journey of Faith
    M3, Your Special Gifts
Service
    Q12, Catholics and Church
    M8, Evangelization

Reading 1, Jeremiah 23:1-6

Woe to the shepherds who destroy and scatter the sheep of my pasture! says the Lord. Therefore thus says the Lord, the God of Israel, concerning the shepherds who shepherd my people: It is you who have scattered my flock, and have driven them away, and you have not attended to them. So I will attend to you for your evil doings, says the Lord. Then I myself will gather the remnant of my flock out of all the lands where I have driven them, and I will bring them back to their fold, and they shall be fruitful and multiply. I will raise up shepherds over them who will shepherd them, and they shall not fear any longer, or be dismayed, nor shall any be missing, says the Lord.

The days are surely coming, says the Lord, when I will raise up for David a righteous Branch, and he shall reign as king and deal wisely, and shall execute justice and righteousness in the land. In his days Judah will be saved and Israel will live in safety. And this is the name by which he will be called: "The Lord is our righteousness."

Psalm 23:1-3,3-4,5,6

Reading 2, Ephesians 2:13-18

In Christ Jesus you who once were far off have been brought near by the blood of Christ. For he is our peace; in his flesh he has made both groups into one and has broken down the dividing wall, that is, the hostility between us. He has abolished the law with its commandments and ordinances, that he might create in himself one new humanity in place of the two, thus making peace, and might reconcile both groups to God in one body through the cross, thus putting to death that hostility through it. So he came and proclaimed peace to you who were far off and peace to those who were near; for through him both of us have access in one Spirit to the Father.

Gospel, Mark 6:30-34

The apostles gathered around Jesus, and told him all that they had done and taught. He said to them, "Come away to a deserted place all by yourselves and rest a while." For many were coming and going, and they had no leisure even to eat. And they went away in the boat to a deserted place by themselves. Now many saw them going and recognized them, and they hurried there on foot from all the towns and arrived ahead of them.

As he went ashore, he saw a great crowd; and he had compassion for them, because they were like sheep without a shepherd; and he began to teach them many things.

Shepherding

JOHN F. CRAGHAN

We seem somehow prone to see the world and react to it only insofar as it benefits "me, myself, and I." Our vision is thus myopic; we make ourselves the criterion of relationships. We may occasionally reach out to others, but all too often only on the condition that we will reap considerable personal advantages. With this kind of attitude people are reduced to things that will satisfy our needs and our pleasures.

Today's readings take a decidedly different approach to the question of relationships—a pastoral approach, like that of a shepherd. They unfold a world in which personal growth derives from communal concern. They hold before our eyes the identification of the shepherd in terms of the sheep. They also challenge us to reassess our own sense of relationships. Will we be a pastoral people, a people who shepherds?

Shepherd was a traditional title for a *king* in the ancient Near East. By its very nature it conjured up the ideal relationship between heads of state and subjects. It suggested an attitude of providing and caring. By and large the kings of Israel and Judah did not meet the legitimate demands of their people. The verbs "scattered," "driven away," and "not attended to" (Jer 23:2) reflect this dimension of neglect.

The editors responsible for bringing together and updating Jeremiah's vision of kingship (see Jer 21:11— 23:6) paint a picture of pastoral concern on Yahweh's part. Into this grievous situation, Yahweh intervenes: "I myself will gather the remnant of my flock...and I will bring them back to their fold" (Jer 23:3); and "I will raise up shepherds over them..." (23:4). Yahweh will finally raise up a Davidic king who "shall...reign wisely" and "shall execute justice and righteousness in the land" (23:5). Here there is indeed a positive answer to the peoples' dilemma. A shepherd will lead them, and the shepherd's name will be "the Lord is our righteousness" (23:6).

By choosing several concrete verbs, the author of the twenty-third psalm evokes the entire gamut of pastoral concern: This Shepherd gives repose, leads, refreshes, guides. "Pastures" and "waters" catch up the character of Yahweh as provider and sustainer. With rod and staff, the Shepherd defends the sheep against wild animals and urges on those who stray. It is hardly surprising that these sheep are without fear.

The author also links Yahweh's shepherding with the dynamism of the "name" (23:3). It is fidelity to the name, hence fidelity to the covenant relationship, that demands such exclusive attention to the sheep; Yahweh the Shepherd feels compelled to carry out the obligations of shepherd/pastor.

Come Away

The gospel episode is Mark's prelude to the feeding of the five thousand (6:35-44). The missionaries have returned from their first "pastoral" experience and are recounting their activities to Jesus. Jesus sees that, especially given the crowds, they are in need of solitude and sleep. This scene sets the stage for the further use of shepherd/royal imagery in the feeding of the five thousand (see Ez 34:13-15).

Mark also seems to link Jesus' compassion to Yahweh's care of the Israelites during the desert wandering. "Sheep without a shepherd" (6:34) reminds the reader of Moses' prayer for a successor: "Let the Lord...appoint someone over the congregation...who shall lead them out and bring them in, so that the congregation of the Lord may not be like sheep without a shepherd" (Nm 27:16-17). The mention of "a deserted place" (Mk 6:32) may reinforce the wilderness background. It is clear that Jesus, having perceived the need, immediately prepares to respond by teaching—and subsequently by feeding. Jesus has indeed answered the question: He will pastor, he will shepherd.

Today's Good News

The shepherd imagery may or may not appeal to us. In any event the needs of others must appeal to us. In baptism the Christian both draws strength from the community and is directed to allay the weaknesses of the community. At liturgies, especially, we gather as a community sworn to provide for one another. In that sense we are all pastors—shepherds who give repose, lead, refresh, and guide in countless different situations. Today's readings challenge us to provide pastures and waters for others in our technological computerized world. Ultimately we face the question: Will we be a pastoral people, a people who shepherds?

Points for Reflection and Discussion

1. Contrasts appear in today's readings: On the one hand, it is important for those who shepherd to seek their own refreshment in quiet repast and repose; on the other hand, when the sheep need their shepherd, the shepherd relinquishes repast and repose on their account. Is there an answer to this dilemma for those who would be a pastoral people? How have you handled similar conflict in your life?

_____

_____

_____

_____

2. Reread and reflect upon Psalm 23. How does it make you feel?

_____

_____

_____

_____

Themes

Leadership
   Q9, Who's Who in the Church
   M3, Your Special Gifts
Ministry
   Q11, Catholic Practices
   M6, Discernment
Refreshment
   Q10, Catholics and Prayer
   M5, Your Prayer Life

Reading 1, 2 Kings 4:42-44

A man came from Baal-shalishah, bringing food from the first fruits to the man of God: twenty loaves of barley and fresh ears of grain in his sack. Elisha said, "Give it to the people and let them eat." But his servant said, "How can I set this before a hundred people?" So he repeated, "Give it to the people and let them eat, for thus says the Lord, 'They shall eat and have some left.' " He set it before them, they ate, and had some left, according to the word of the Lord.

Psalm 145:10-11,15-16,17-18

Reading 2, Ephesians 4:1-6

I..., the prisoner in the Lord, beg you to lead a life worthy of the calling to which you have been called, with all humility and gentleness, with patience, bearing with one another in love, making every effort to maintain the unity of the Spirit in the bond of peace. There is one body and one Spirit, just as you were called to the one hope of your calling, one Lord, one faith, one baptism, one God and Father of all, who is above all and through all and in all.

Gospel, John 6:1-15

Jesus went to the other side of the Sea of Galilee, also called the Sea of Tiberias. A large crowd kept following him, because they saw the signs that he was doing for the sick. Jesus went up the mountain and sat down there with his disciples. Now the Passover, the festival of the Jews, was near. When he looked up and saw a large crowd coming toward him, Jesus said to Philip, "Where are we to buy bread for these people to eat?" He said this to test him, for he himself knew what he was going to do. Philip answered him, "Six months' wages would not buy enough bread for each of them to get a little."

One of his disciples, Andrew, Simon Peter's brother, said to him, "There is a boy here who has five barley loaves and two fish. But what are they among so many people?" Jesus said, "Make the people sit down." Now there was a great deal of grass in the place; so they sat down, about five thousand in all. Then Jesus took the loaves, and when he had given thanks, he distributed them to those who were seated; so also the fish, as much as they wanted. When they were satisfied, he told his disciples, "Gather up the fragments left over, so that nothing may be lost." So they gathered them up, and from the fragments of the five barley loaves, left by those who had eaten, they filled twelve baskets.

When the people saw the sign that he had done, they began to say, "This is indeed the prophet who is to come into the world." When Jesus realized that they were about to come and take him by force to make him king, he withdrew again to the mountain by himself.

Sign Language

JOHN F. CRAGHAN

Every day we experience a variety of signs: signs of affection from loved ones, tokens of thanks from the grateful, pats on the back from well-wishers, and so forth. There is a danger that we will accept all of these signs but never search out their deeper meaning. Somehow we find it too difficult, or too much of a bother, to analyze signs and uncover their basic message. We choose to take them for granted and leave the drudgery of interpretation to psychologists and social scientists.

Today's readings urge us to take a different stance toward signs. They see signs not as neutral objective phenomena but as personal demonstrations of God's concern for us. They maintain that signs by their very nature should evoke a sense of awe, gratitude, and praise. They demand that we put aside our take-it-for-granted attitude and begin to make serious inquiries about the significance of signs in our lives. They hold that signs reflect our God's involvement.

Elisha was a great prophetic figure of the ninth century B.C. who is presented as the successor of the mighty Elijah (see 2 Kgs 2:1-18). Whereas Elijah was a solitary figure, Elisha was the colorful leader of a prophetic guild. Given the latter's dynamic personality, it is not surprising that his disciples handed down accounts of the great moments in the prophet's life. Indeed, many of these accounts are miracle stories.

Today's story underlies Elisha's devotion to his band. It also, however, points to a higher reality—the fidelity of God to God's word. With a group of one hundred men, twenty barley loaves seem rather paltry. The seemingly small supply and the overwhelming number of diners are set in the context of a prediction-fulfillment story. "For thus says the Lord" (2 Kgs 4:43) gives way to "according to the word of the Lord" (4:44). The leftovers demonstrate Elisha's concern and God's fidelity to God's word. Such signs reflect God's involvement.

With Open Hands

Psalm 145 is a hymn of descriptive praise. All of creation and the Israelite community are invited to extol Yahweh: "All your works shall give thanks to you, O Lord, and all your faithful shall bless you" (145:10). This call to praise presupposes that God's actions on behalf of creation and humanity are not discrete objective events but individual and personal exhibitions of profound love.

In today's selection the psalmist stresses the hopeful glance of creation as it anticipates food at the proper time (145:15). He also focuses attention on God's hand (145:16), which is open—a gesture calculated to satisfy the desires of all living things. This leads to the perception that Yahweh is not a divine architect removed from the world of worries: "The Lord is near to all who call on him in truth" (145:18). This call to praise acknowledges that signs reflect our God's involvement.

Faith Food

While Matthew, Mark, and Luke all reflect the eucharistic symbolism of the multiplication of the loaves and fishes (Mt 14:13-21; Mk 6:32-44; Lk 9:10-17), it is John who exploits the scene for its sign potential. In John one can perceive the wondrous deeds of Jesus on two levels. On the first level they are miracles, prodigious events. On the second level they are signs that lead to faith. When they do lead to faith, they provoke God's presence as revealed in Jesus.

John presents Jesus against a Mosaic background. Like Moses on Mount Sinai, Jesus is on the mountain (6:3). Like Moses, who was concerned about the availability of food (see Nm 11:22), Jesus must entertain Philip's observation about the money and mouthfuls (6:5,7). Actually a current expectation was that the great catalyst of salvation for the people would be a new Moses, the founder of a new Israel (6:14). Unfortunately the audience sees Jesus' feat as only a miracle; they want to make him king (6:15). They do not see the multiplication of food as a sign; they refuse to understand Jesus as the revealer of God's presence. John tells his readers that signs clearly reflect God's involvement.

Today's Good News

Who are the people we take for granted, those who are our possible "sign" people? Our loved ones, who sustain and support us in trying times, are signs. Our public officials, who demonstrate their concern in ongoing efforts to promote the common good, are signs. These and so many others reveal the presence of a concerned God. Signs truly reflect God's involvement in our lives.

Points for Reflection and Discussion

1. Have you ever been really hungry? Was there a sign of God's presence in the alleviation of your hunger? Have you ever been a sign of God's presence in the alleviation of someone else's hunger?

_____

_____

_____

_____

_____

2. Talk about a sign of God's presence in your life that you have been aware of during the past few weeks.

_____

_____

_____

_____

_____

Themes

Hunger
    Q1, Journey of Faith
    M8, Evangelization
Signs
    Q11, Catholic Practices
    M6, Discernment
Thanksgiving
    Q10, Catholics and Prayer
    M5, Your Prayer Life

Reading 1, Exodus 16:2-4,12-15

The whole congregation of the Israelites complained against Moses and Aaron in the wilderness. The Israelites said to them, "If only we had died by the hand of the Lord in the land of Egypt, when we sat by the fleshpots and ate our fill of bread; for you have brought us out into this wilderness to kill this whole assembly with hunger."

Then the Lord said to Moses, "I am going to rain bread from heaven for you, and each day the people shall go out and gather enough for that day. In that way I will test them, whether they will follow my instruction or not.

"I have heard the complaining of the Israelites; say to them, 'At twilight you shall eat meat, and in the morning you shall have your fill of bread; then you shall know that I am the Lord your God.' "

In the evening quails came up and covered the camp; and in the morning there was a layer of dew around the camp. When the layer of dew lifted, there on the surface of the wilderness was a fine flaky substance, as fine as frost on the ground. When the Israelites saw it, they said to one another, "What is it?" For they did not know what it was. Moses said to them, "It is the bread that the Lord has given you to eat."

Psalm 78:3-4,23-24,25,54

Reading 2, Ephesians 4:17,20-24

This I affirm and insist on in the Lord: you must no longer live as the Gentiles live, in the futility of their minds. That is not the way you learned Christ! For surely you have heard about him and were taught in him, as truth is in Jesus. You were taught to put away your former way of life, your old self, corrupt and deluded by its lusts, and to be renewed in the spirit of your minds, and to clothe yourselves with the new self, created according to the likeness of God in true righteousness and holiness.

Gospel, John 6:24-35

When the crowd saw that neither Jesus nor his disciples were there, they themselves got into the boats and went to Capernaum looking for Jesus.

When they found him on the other side of the sea, they said to him, "Rabbi, when did you come here?" Jesus answered them, "Very truly, I tell you, you are looking for me, not because you saw signs, but because you ate your fill of the loaves. Do not work for the food that perishes, but for the food that endures for eternal life, which the Son of Man will give you. For it is on him that God the Father has set his seal."

Then they said to him, "What must we do to perform the works of God?" Jesus answered them, "This is the work of God, that you believe in him whom he has sent." So they said to him, "What sign are you going to give us then, so that we may see it and believe you? What work are you performing? Our ancestors ate the manna in the wilderness; as it is written, 'He gave them bread from heaven to eat.' "

Then Jesus said to them, "Very truly, I tell you, it was not Moses who gave you the bread from heaven, but it is my Father who gives you the true bread from heaven. For the bread of God is that which comes down from heaven and gives life to the world." They said to him, "Sir, give us this bread always." Jesus said to them, "I am the bread of life. Whoever comes to me will never be hungry, and whoever believes in me will never be thirsty."

Values Systems

JOHN F. CRAGHAN

Daily the media saturates us with instant information. They package this information, eliminating some items and seasoning the remains with their unique viewpoints. In so doing they also present us with a challenge to assess these world, national, and local events. We are consequently called upon to question God's viewpoint in these matters. As believers, we must accept God's values system.

Today's readings confront the issues of values systems. They present scenes in which values systems are in conflict. On the one hand, they show the non-believer's assessment of key events; on the other hand, they show the believer's appraisal of these same events. The lingering question these readings pose is one of choice: Which values system will we go with?

Of Feasts and Famines

This account of the manna and the quail is part of the whole wilderness experience of the Israelites. Some scholars say that manna is the sticky secretion of two insects that live on the tamarisk tree in central Sinai. The quail are birds that come back to the Sinai coast from Europe in the autumn. After such a tiring journey they can be easily caught. Both the manna and the quail, therefore, are clear indications of God's providential care of the "chosen people" during their demanding experience.

In today's account the murmuring motif has been added. The manna and the quail are no longer signs of God's concern. Instead they have become an occasion for grumbling against Moses first, and then against God. The significance of this grumbling is that it questions the validity of the entire Exodus. The participants are challenged to choose: accept Egypt with its abundance of food; or accept the wilderness with its manna and quail. The believer chooses God's values system.

The author of Ephesians speaks of two values systems: those of the pagans and of the Christians. He characterizes the first as empty. In 4:18-19, which do not appear in today's reading, this pagan system is characterized by ignorance and resistance. He adds: "They have lost all sensitivity and have abandoned themselves to licentiousness, greedy to practice every kind of impurity" (4:19). Accordingly, the basic cause of this system's malaise is its firm refusal to recognize and acknowledge the truth.

Borrowing from baptismal liturgy, the author describes the Christian values system in terms of rites of passage. Such a system allows Christians to put off their former pagan values and be plunged into Christ through faith. The result is that they have put on new clothes, which symbolize their radically new way of life. Like humanity in Genesis 2, they are in God's image and are challenged to reflect that image in their journey through life. Once again, the believer accepts God's values system.

The Bread of Life

John also speaks of the two values systems of the believer and the non-believer. Non-believers adopt a values system in which they do not see the real meaning of the multiplication of loaves and fish. To non-believers it is merely a question of perishable food. When confronted with Jesus' challenge of faith, non-believers think that they are merely to believe in some new sign that he will perform—like the manna in the desert. In this values system Jesus is a worker of miracles and nothing more.

For believers, the values system is precisely the opposite. Here Jesus himself is the real heavenly food that the Father will give. Hence he is much more than a great provider of instant nourishment. Alluding to the experience of the Israelites in the desert, Jesus explains that believers (those who come to him) will never again experience hunger or thirst. In this values system Jesus is indeed the Bread of Life. It is the choice believers must make.

Today's Good News

Seated before their television sets, Christians are exposed to a variety of views concerning respect for human life, the use of violence, involvement in the affairs of other nations, and so forth. To be sure, not many issues are black and white, but when the smoke has cleared, Christians are challenged to respond with their votes, their letters, their words, and their actions. What is ultimately at stake is the acceptance or rejection of particular values. Today's readings powerfully remind us that believers choose God's values system.

Points for Reflection and Discussion

1. What are a few of your values in life? Are there values you used to hold that you have discarded?

_____

_____

_____

_____

2. Thinking of the images in today's readings, reflect upon the "daily bread" we pray for in the Lord's Prayer. What does the phrase "Give us this day our daily bread" mean in your life?

_____

_____

_____

_____

Themes
Bread
    Q3, What is the Meaning of the Mass?
    M5, Your Prayer Life
Life
    M7, Holiness
Values
    Q12, Catholics and Church
    M6, Discernment

Reading 1, 1 Kings 19:4-8

Elijah went a day's journey into the wilderness, and came and sat down under a solitary broom tree. He asked that he might die: "It is enough; now, O Lord, take away my life, for I am no better than my ancestors." Then he lay down under the broom tree and fell asleep. Suddenly an angel touched him and said to him, "Get up and eat." He looked, and there at his head was a cake baked on hot stones, and a jar of water. He ate and drank, and lay down again. The angel of the Lord came a second time, touched him, and said, "Get up and eat, otherwise the journey will be too much for you." He got up, and ate and drank; then he went in the strength of that food forty days and forty nights to Horeb the mount of God.

Psalm 34:1-2,3-4,5-6,7-8 (NRSV)

Reading 2, Ephesians 4:30—5:2

Do not grieve the Holy Spirit of God, with which you were marked with a seal for the day of redemption. Put away from you all bitterness and wrath and anger and wrangling and slander, together with all malice, and be kind to one another, tenderhearted, forgiving one another, as God in Christ has forgiven you.

Therefore be imitators of God, as beloved children, and live in love, as Christ loved us and gave himself up for us, a fragrant offering and sacrifice to God.

Gospel, John 6:41-51

The Jews began to complain about him because he said, "I am the bread that came down from heaven." They were saying, "Is not this Jesus, the son of Joseph, whose father and mother we know? How can he now say, 'I have come down from heaven'?"

Jesus answered them, "Do not complain among yourselves. No one can come to me unless drawn by the Father who sent me; and I will raise that person up on the last day. It is written in the prophets, 'And they shall all be taught by God.' Everyone who has heard and learned from the Father comes to me. Not that anyone has seen the Father except the one who is from God; he has seen the Father. Very truly, I tell you, whoever believes has eternal life. I am the bread of life. Your ancestors ate the manna in the wilderness, and they died. This is the bread that comes down from heaven, so that one may eat of it and not die. I am the living bread that came down from heaven. Whoever eats of this bread will live forever; and the bread that I will give for the life of the world is my flesh."

The Origin of the Species

JOHN F. CRAGHAN

It is not unusual for people to speculate about their backgrounds. They look at their name, their physical characteristics, their birth environment, and they ask about ancestry, roots, family origins. They seem convinced that, somehow, they are inexorably linked to those origins. They conclude that in knowing about their origins they will come to know more about themselves. It is a question of roots.

Today's readings focus—at least implicitly—on origins. They appear to suggest that roots indeed tend to condition our way of thinking and acting. In the context of today's liturgy, they challenge believers to look to their backgrounds and inquire about how those backgrounds should impact daily living.

Around the middle of the ninth century B.C., Elijah, the Israelite prophet, clashed with Jezebel, the Israelite queen. Since Elijah had defeated her pagan prophets on Mount Carmel, Jezebel was now determined to be rid of him. Sensing the queen's ire, Elijah chose to flee, and consequently went back to his roots on Mount Horeb (Mount Sinai). While on his way, God provided, just as God had earlier provided for the people of Moses' time, by supplying food and drink. Like Moses, who spent forty days and nights on the mountain (see Ex 24:18; Dt 9:18), Elijah walked forty days and nights to the mountain.

Elijah's destination was not an accidental choice. At Horeb (Sinai), the people of Israel discovered their destiny in becoming God's people. It was the experience of this covenant with God that determined Israel's character and way of life. By returning to Horeb (Sinai), Elijah entered into the experience of his ancestors. Indeed the experience offered the prophet the encouragement and strength to speak out boldly on behalf of Israel's covenant God. It is a question of roots.

Consummate Imitation

In the epistle passage, the author of Ephesians offers a Christian way of life based on God's action in Jesus. To begin with, the author advances an attitude in which injury to our neighbor is injury to the Holy Spirit who dwells within that neighbor. Next is presented a norm for forgiveness: kindness and compassion and forgiveness "as God in Christ has forgiven you" (4:32). Finally he recommends love—but not some vague, indefinite kind of love. The guideline for loving is imitation of Christ: "Therefore be imitators of God, as beloved children, and live in love, as Christ loved us and gave himself up for us, a fragrant offering and sacrifice to God" (5:1-2).

In making these recommendations, the author of Ephesians is implicitly urging Christians to reassess their roots. It is a matter of God, Jesus, and the Holy Spirit. Since Christians identify in terms of all three, they must act in a way that reveals such a grandiose pedigree. It is a question of roots.

Living Bread

In the gospel development of the multiplication of loaves and fish, John continues to employ bread as an apt symbol to characterize the person and work of Jesus. In turn, this symbol is designed to reveal the person and work of the Father. In this passage Jesus cites Isaiah 54:13: "They shall all be taught by God" (Jn 6:45). Jesus fulfills this passage by seeing himself as the one who offers everything contained in the religious symbol of bread. As bread sustains life, Jesus will sustain life in all who approach him in faith.

His audience reduces everything to a matter of origins. Jesus seems to possess merely human credentials—he is Joseph's son. Fittingly, Jesus reduces everything to a matter of origins too. Jesus is actually the manifestation of the Father. At the conclusion of the gospel reading, bread is connected to Jesus' redemptive death—"the bread that I will give for the life of the world is my flesh" (6:51). To acknowledge Jesus as the living bread is to acknowledge him as the ultimate expression of the Father's love in his death-glorification.

Today's Good News

Why do we do the things we do? Why do we reach out to the homeless and helpless? Do we perceive our God's image in them? Why do we refuse to resort to violence in settling conflicts? Do we hear the message of the Prince of Peace? Why do we uphold our neighbor's reputation? Do we find in him or her a brother or sister of Christ? We can multiply these daily scenes and repeat the upsetting question "why?" Hopefully it is a question of roots.

Points for Reflection and Discussion

1. How much do you know about your roots? Has knowledge of family origins affected your own life in any way? What if you could trace your roots all the way back to Jesus? How would such a genealogy affect your life?

_____

_____

_____

_____

_____

2. Do you truly believe Jesus is present in the Eucharist? How does your answer make you feel?

_____

_____

_____

_____

_____

Themes
Eucharist
  Q3, What is the Meaning of the Mass?
  M5, Your Prayer Life
Roots
  Q2, What Do Catholics Believe?
  M1, Conversion: A Lifelong Process
Trinity
  Q5, How Do Catholics Interpret the Bible?
  M7, Holiness

Reading 1, Proverbs 9:1-6

Wisdom has built her house, she has hewn her seven pillars. She has slaughtered her animals, she has mixed her wine, she has also set her table. She has sent out her servant girls, she calls from the highest places in the town, "You that are simple, turn in here!" To those without sense she says, "Come, eat of my bread and drink of the wine I have mixed. Lay aside immaturity, and live, and walk in the way of insight."

Psalm 34:1-2,9-10,11-12,13-14 (NRSV)

Reading 2, Ephesians 5:15-20

Be careful how you live, not as unwise people but as wise, making the most of the time, because the days are evil. So do not be foolish, but understand what the will of the Lord is. Do not get drunk with wine, for that is debauchery; but be filled with the Spirit, as you sing psalms and hymns and spiritual songs among yourselves, singing and making melody to the Lord in your hearts, giving thanks to God the Father at all times and for everything in the name of our Lord Jesus Christ.

Gospel, John 6:51-58

[Jesus said to the crowds:] "I am the living bread that came down from heaven. Whoever eats of this bread will live forever; and the bread that I will give for the life of the world is my flesh."

The Jews then disputed among themselves, saying, "How can this man give us his flesh to eat?" So Jesus said to them, "Very truly, I tell you, unless you eat the flesh of the Son of Man and drink his blood, you have no life in you. Those who eat my flesh and drink my blood have eternal life, and I will raise them up on the last day; for my flesh is true food and my blood is true drink. Those who eat my flesh and drink my blood abide in me, and I in them. Just as the living Father sent me, and I live because of the Father, so whoever eats me will live because of me. This is the bread that came down from heaven, not like that which your ancestors ate, and they died. But the one who eats this bread will live forever."

Fully Alive

JOHN F. CRAGHAN

"That's living!" How often we use this phrase for those who have made it big in their professions and are now enjoying their benefits. "Now that's a wise person!" is another oft-used expression—one that points to shrewdness and experience, but not necessarily to the living of life to its fullest. We seem to create division—we separate the fully alive from the wise. Why can we not admit that the truly wise really know how to live?

Today's readings link living and wisdom. They urge an assessment of our often implicit tendency to separate the fully alive from the wise. They show that the truly wise know how to live or, conversely, that those who really know how to live are genuinely wise.

The Wisdom Woman

Israel's exile demonstrated that a purely human wisdom self-destructed. "Fear of the Lord" was absolutely essential. Building upon this premise, the author of Proverbs teaches that wisdom, that delicate art of steering a path through life, requires a trustworthy guide. To this end we are introduced to the Wisdom Woman, God's special creation. As the personification of wisdom, she says: "...whoever finds me finds life and obtains favor from the Lord" (Prv 8:35).

In today's passage the Wisdom Woman is a hostess. As such, she welcomes those lacking wisdom to grace her table and sample her food and drink. In abandoning their foolishness, her guests will truly live. Biblically, *life* calls up more than success and the passing of time. It connotes such a sense of community with God that living becomes celebration. Indeed the truly wise know how to live.

Wise Living

The author of Ephesians clearly adopts the vocabulary of wisdom. All are to live "not as unwise people but as wise" (5:15). They are not to continue in ignorance, but to discern the Lord's will (5:17). They are to make "the most of the time because the days are evil" (5:16). Hence the situation is not merely a crisis; it is a faith opportunity.

The author links this wisdom approach to daily living. The faithful are to avoid drunkenness, which leads to debauchery. Instead of being filled with wine, they should be filled with God's Spirit, and this experience of the Spirit will impact their conduct. They will address one another in a more spiritual way and they will praise the Lord. They will especially give "thanks to God the Father always and for everything in the name of our Lord Jesus Christ" (5:20).

Life Eternal

In the gospel passage a nearly imperceptible move is made: from bread as symbol to bread as sacrament. The focus is now on eating Jesus' flesh and drinking his blood. No doubt the separate mention of flesh and blood emphasizes the conviction that believers receive the living Jesus in the celebration of Eucharist. To share in the Eucharist is ultimately to share in the life of Father, Son, and Spirit (see Jn 15:26).

In the prologue of the Gospel of John, Jesus appears as the Word. Like the Wisdom Woman, he is wisdom personified. He reflects God's glory and light. He also provokes decisions, however, and in today's passage he challenges his audience to accept him as the Living Bread. The *wise*—those who accept him as such—will share in the fullness of *life* that Jesus derives from God the Father. Those who are truly wise know how to live.

Today's Good News

Eucharist is communion in the very person of Jesus—in his flesh and blood and in his life. To eat and drink with Jesus and the community is to rise and serve Jesus and the community. Bread and wine move in the direction of wise living. Eucharist clearly teaches that the truly wise know how to live.

Points for Reflection and Discussion

1. It is said that most people never live up to more than ten percent of their potential. Based upon that assessment, try to imagine what a fully alive person might experience. Talk about it.

---

2. Do you know anyone you consider to be truly wise? Talk about that person.

Themes

Living
   Q1, Journey of Faith
   M1, Conversion: A Lifelong Process
Sacrament
   Q11, Catholic Practices
   M5, Your Prayer Life
Wisdom
   Q12, Catholics and Church
   M7, Holiness

Reading 1, Joshua 24:1-2,15-17,18

Joshua gathered all the tribes of Israel to Shechem, and summoned the elders, the heads, the judges, and the officers of Israel; and they presented themselves before God. And Joshua said to all the people, "If you are unwilling to serve the Lord, choose this day whom you will serve, whether the gods your ancestors served in the region beyond the River or the gods of the Amorites in whose land you are living; but as for me and my household, we will serve the Lord."

Then the people answered, "Far be it from us that we should forsake the Lord to serve other gods; for it is the Lord our God who brought us and our ancestors up from the land of Egypt, out of the house of slavery, and who did those great signs in our sight. He protected us along all the way that we went, and among all the peoples through whom we passed. Therefore we also will serve the Lord, for he is our God."

Psalm 34:1-2,15-16,17-18,19-20,21-22 (NRSV)

Reading 2, Ephesians 5:21-32

Be subject to one another out of reverence for Christ.

Wives, be subject to your husbands as you are to the Lord. For the husband is the head of the wife just as Christ is the head of the church, the body of which he is the Savior. Just as the church is subject to Christ, so also wives ought to be, in everything, to their husbands.

Husbands, love your wives, just as Christ loved the church and gave himself up for her, in order to make her holy by cleansing her with the washing of water by the word, so as to present the church to himself in splendor, without a spot or wrinkle or anything of the kind—yes, so that she may be holy and without blemish. In the same way, husbands should love their wives as they do their own bodies. He who loves his wife loves himself. For no one ever hates his own body, but he nourishes and tenderly cares for it, just as Christ does for the church, because we are members of his body.

"For this reason a man will leave his father and mother and be joined to his wife, and the two will become one flesh." This is a great mystery, and I am applying it to Christ and the church.

Gospel, John 6:60-69

Many of his disciples...said, "This teaching is difficult; who can accept it?" But Jesus, being aware that his disciples were complaining about it, said to them, "Does this offend you? Then what if you were to see the Son of Man ascending to where he was before? It is the spirit that gives life; the flesh is useless. The words that I have spoken to you are spirit and life. But among you there are some who do not believe." For Jesus knew from the first who were the ones that did not believe, and who was the one that would betray him. And he said, "For this reason I have told you that no one can come to me unless it is granted by the Father." Because of this many of his disciples turned back and no longer went about with him. So Jesus asked the twelve, "Do you also wish to go away?" Simon Peter answered him, "Lord, to whom can we go? You have the words of eternal life. We have come to believe and know that you are the Holy One of God."

Loyalty

JOHN F. CRAGHAN

Loyalty is a word we use rather freely. We know that spouses promise to be loyal to each other, but constant fighting seems to question that loyalty. We are aware that friends pledge to be loyal to each other, but gossip and bickering appear to doubt that loyalty. We realize that members of parish communities offer loyalty and support to one another, but lack of concern and demonstrations of hostility seem to raise questions about that loyalty.

Today's readings challenge us to reassess our sense of loyalty. They clearly show that loyalty is a reality that we cannot take too lightly. They show that loyalty is a genuine response to those we love, a reality that calls for the greatest sacrifice. According to today's Liturgy of the Word, loyalty is akin to covenant, "a great mystery" (Eph 5:32) of unity.

In the first reading, this final chapter of Joshua recounts the hero's farewell speech to his people. Actually it is a speech that describes covenant-making. At the ancient shrine of Shechem, Joshua gathers together all the tribes of Israel. Finally settled in the Promised Land, these Israelites are now challenged to make the ultimate choice: To whom will they pledge their loyalty?

To be an Israelite means to be faithful to Yahweh. The people recount Yahweh's wholehearted concern for Israel throughout their exodus. This historical review necessarily leads to the conclusion that all other gods must be excluded. It is Yahweh or nothing! Indeed allegiance to another god is a denial that Yahweh is Yahweh. Though Israel's ancestors worshiped other gods, the Israel of Joshua's time promises unflagging devotion to their God.

Subordination

The author of Ephesians employs a domestic code, a list of obligations of the various members of the household, to explain and motivate the duties of a Christian household. The underlying reality in the whole passage is loyalty. It is that attitude that prompts submissiveness and love; to be loyal means to support a person with one's whole heart.

Spouses are to "be subject to one another out of reverence for Christ" (5:21). A wife's model is the Church's loyalty to Christ; a husband's model is Christ's loyalty to the Church. Quite appropriately, the author concludes with Genesis 2:24. To be so joined that "the two will become one flesh" (5:31) is to realize the commitment of covenant (see Dt 11:22). Such loyalty is clearly "a great mystery" (5:32) of unity.

To Whom Shall We Go?

The author of John records the mixed reactions of Jesus' audience to his Bread of Life discourses. The first response is a refusal by many of Jesus' disciples to take his talk seriously. They cannot believe that Jesus is the bread come down from heaven. Clearly they would find it even more difficult "to see the Son of Man ascending to where he was before" (6:62). They decide to break away and no longer remain in his company. They rescind their loyalty to Jesus.

The second response to the discourse is that of the Twelve. Jesus' poignant question is basically a test of their loyalty: "Do you also wish to go away?" (6:67). Peter's reply is to call Jesus "the Holy One of God" (6:69) and to acknowledge that only he has "the words of eternal life" (6:68). The response of the Twelve as articulated by Peter is a response motivated by faith in Jesus. It is also an announcement of profound loyalty. The contrast of the two groups shows that loyalty is "a great mystery" (Eph 5:32) of unity.

Today's Good News

We are called to recall specific moments when we promised loyalty. Wedding days, baptismal days, and similar occasions come easily to mind. Their remembrance evokes questions such as: How loyal have I been to my spouse? How loyal have I been to my faith community? How loyal have I been to my friends? Today's readings are both the challenge and the encouragement to renew those loyalties by dwelling on the value of the person or persons to whom we once promised our commitment. Loyalty = covenant = mystery = unity = today's Good News.

Points for Reflection and Discussion

1. What does the word loyal *mean to you? Do today's readings challenge your definition in any way?*

---

2. The epistle reading on marriage epitomizes the "great mystery" between Christ and his Church. In a nutshell, this is why marriage is sacramental. Reflect on this passage. Share your feelings.

Themes

Covenant
    Q5, How Do Catholics Interpret the Bible?
    M2, The Laity: Called To Build God's Kingdom
Friendship
    Q6, The Saints
    M8, Evangelization
Marriage
    M4, Family Life

Reading 1, Deuteronomy 4:1-2,6-8

Moses said to the people:

Now, Israel, give heed to the statutes and ordinances that I am teaching you to observe, so that you may live to enter and occupy the land that the Lord, the God of your ancestors, is giving you. You must neither add anything to what I command you nor take away anything from it, but keep the commandments of the Lord your God with which I am charging you. You must observe them diligently, for this will show your wisdom and discernment to the peoples, who, when they hear all these statutes, will say, "Surely this great nation is a wise and discerning people!" For what other great nation has a god so near to it as the Lord our God is whenever we call to him? And what other great nation has statutes and ordinances as just as this entire law that I am setting before you today?

Psalm 15:2-3,3-4,5 (NRSV)

Reading 2, James 1:17-18,21-22,27

Every generous act of giving, with every perfect gift, is from above, coming down from the Father of lights, with whom there is no variation or shadow due to change. In fulfillment of his own purpose he gave us birth by the word of truth, so that we would become a kind of first fruits of his creatures.

Welcome with meekness the implanted word that has the power to save your souls. But be doers of the word, and not merely hearers who deceive themselves.

Religion that is pure and undefiled before God, the Father, is this: to care for orphans and widows in their distress, and to keep oneself unstained by the world.

Gospel, Mark 7:1-8,14-15,21-23

When the Pharisees and some of the scribes who had come from Jerusalem gathered around him, they noticed that some of his disciples were eating with defiled hands, that is, without washing them. (For the Pharisees, and all the Jews, do not eat unless they thoroughly wash their hands, thus observing the tradition of the elders; and they do not eat anything from the market unless they wash it; and there are also many other traditions that they observe, the washing of cups, pots, and bronze kettles.) So the Pharisees and the scribes asked him, "Why do your disciples not live according to the tradition of the elders, but eat with defiled hands?" He said to them, "Isaiah prophesied rightly about you hypocrites, as it is written, 'This people honors me with their lips, but their hearts are far from me; in vain do they worship me, teaching human

precepts as doctrines.' You abandon the commandment of God and hold to human tradition."

Then he called the crowd again and said to them, "Listen to me, all of you, and understand: there is nothing outside a person that by going in can defile, but the things that come out are what defile.

"For it is from within, from the human heart, that evil intentions come: fornication, theft, murder, adultery, avarice, wickedness, deceit, licentiousness, envy, slander, pride, folly. All these evil things come from within, and they defile a person."

We Were Made For Service

JOHN F. CRAGHAN

How often we talk a good game but do nothing more. We hear our duties within a parish or the workplace, but somehow never get beyond the listening. We recite our obligations as spouses or as parents, but for some reason never advance beyond the recitation. We study about our Church or our nation, but for whatever reason we remain merely on the study level. We experience an often-growing chasm between duty and fulfillment.

Today's readings powerfully suggest that the genuine believer is a person of action. They endorse a way of life in which the will must result in deeds. They urge a plan for living in which good intentions must give way to concrete accomplishments. They announce an agenda in which the actions to be taken end up as actions already taken. Only *real* service—not *lip* service—will do.

Real Response

Psalm 15 is often classified as an entrance liturgy. It resembles that part of Christian liturgy where the faithful, before moving on to actual worship, first pause and examine their consciences. This awareness of obligations fulfilled or unfulfilled has to precede the ceremonies in the Temple. As such, the psalm implies a link between formal worship and genuine living in everyday affairs.

What is immediately striking is that the psalm emphasizes social not cultic obligations. It is not a question of praying, fasting, or sacrificing. Rather, it is a matter of inter-human relationships. Divine services must reflect human services. Only those who have respected their neighbor, who have caused no harm, who have avoided all usury, and who have rejected all bribes may enter to take part in worship. For the author of Psalm 15 only *real* service—not *lip* service—will do.

To Hear Is to Do

Scholars debate the authorship of the Letter of James. Whoever the author was, it is clear that he uses the Hebrew wisdom style of exhortation and that he categorically rejects a purely speculative Christianity. It can only be a question of a practical Christianity—one that translates the vibrant message of Christ into specific deeds. The believer must indeed welcome God's Word, but then must act on it. Only to listen to it is self-deception. In today's passage the author offers a very concrete way to reduce the Word to action: to provide for the perennial welfare cases of the ancient Near East, the widows and orphans. Only *real* service—not *lip* service—will do.

In the Markan gospel passage, Jesus abolishes the practice of ritual purity and the distinction between clean and unclean foods. (Although only priests were obliged to this washing of hands, the Pharisees extended the practice.) Mark is no doubt envisioning the mission to the Gentiles—Gentiles did not have to become Jews in order to become Christians. To make his point, Jesus quotes Isaiah 29:13 (Mk 7:6-7). Thus Jesus' opponents offer God only lip service and choose to disregard God's law in order to embrace their own human institutions.

Jesus rejects the Pharisees' and scribes' notion of sin. For Jesus, sin is the human spirit gone wrong, not a failure to distinguish types of food. Jesus' attitude toward sin is consistent with his view regarding the Sabbath—that the institution is for the people, not that the people are for the institution (see Mk 2:27). Merely to observe the letter of the Law and yet refuse to help the suffering is dehumanizing (see Mk 3:4-5); it is also not genuine observance of the Law. Only *real* service—not *lip* service—will do.

Today's Good News

"One of these days" or "we'll get together sometime" or "I should look into that"—these are so often the slogans of lip service. Today's liturgy challenges believers to formulate a plan of concrete action. "Tomorrow" or "We'll get together next Tuesday" or "I will look into that on Wednesday"—these are phrases of real service. To take our duties seriously is to develop a serious timetable. Only *real* service—not *lip* service—will do.

Points for Reflection and Discussion

1. Is there something that needs doing in your life over which you are still procrastinating? Why?

_____

_____

_____

_____

_____

2. Faith and works appear to have always gone hand-in-hand amongst the truly just. Why do you suppose people tend to get engrossed in "the Law" to the detriment of their sisters and brothers?

_____

_____

_____

_____

_____

Themes

Justice
  Q12, Catholics and Church
  M8, Evangelization
Law
  Q11, Catholic Practices
  M6, Discernment
Service
  Q10, Catholics and Prayer
  M2, The Laity: Called To Build God's Kingdom

Reading 1, Isaiah 35:4-7

Say to those who are of a fearful heart, "Be strong, do not fear! Here is your God. He will come with vengeance, with terrible recompense. He will come and save you." Then the eyes of the blind shall be opened, and the ears of the deaf unstopped; then the lame shall leap like a deer, and the tongue of the speechless sing for joy. For waters shall break forth in the wilderness, and streams in the desert; the burning sand shall become a pool, and the thirsty ground springs of water.

Psalm 146:5,6-7,8-9,9-10 (NRSV)

Reading 2, James 2:1-5

My brothers and sisters, do you with your acts of favoritism really believe in our glorious Lord Jesus Christ? For if a person with gold rings and in fine clothes comes into your assembly, and if a poor person in dirty clothes also comes in, and if you take notice of the one wearing the fine clothes and say, "Have a seat here, please," while to the one who is poor you say, "Stand there," or, "Sit at my feet," have you not made distinctions among yourselves, and become judges with evil thoughts?

Listen, my beloved brothers and sisters. Has not God chosen the poor in the world to be rich in faith and to be heirs of the kingdom that he has promised to those who love him?

Gospel, Mark 7:31-37

Jesus returned from the region of Tyre, and went by way of Sidon towards the Sea of Galilee, in the region of the Decapolis. They brought to him a deaf man who had an impediment in his speech; and they begged him to lay his hand on him. He took him aside in private, away from the crowd, and put his fingers into his ears, and he spat and touched his tongue. Then looking up to heaven, he sighed and said to him, "Ephphatha," that is, "Be opened." And immediately his ears were opened, his tongue was released, and he spoke plainly. Then Jesus ordered them to tell no one; but the more he ordered them, the more zealously they proclaimed it. They were astounded beyond measure, saying, "He has done everything well; he even makes the deaf to hear and the mute to speak."

The Strength of Compassion

JOHN F. CRAGHAN

We experience pitiable persons all around our cities. There are many who have not yet reached their plateau in the American dream. There are the derelicts who have sunk to the depths of degradation owing to alcohol and/or drugs. There are the homeless who wander our streets in search of shelter and food. There are the people with AIDS who are fast becoming the American untouchables. To such marginalized we may *react*—with pity—but recognizing their dignity of personhood calls us to *act*—with compassion.

Today's readings offer a concretely clear picture of how believers should respond to the hurting. They endorse a program of compassion. They proclaim an innate sense of concern whereby believers identify with the downtrodden and a strategy of involvement whereby believers find strength in helping. They maintain that compassion is a mark of the strong and the faithful.

It is generally agreed that today's passage from the Hebrew Scriptures is from Second Isaiah, the anonymous prophet of the exile. To the discouraged and bewildered he speaks a message of hope and intervention. In developing this message, he uses imagery of the Exodus. God's people will go home, as they did in the first Exodus. Like the Israelites under Moses, they will experience the miracles of the desert: springs, rivers, pools of water.

The author shows the all-powerful God of Israel (see Is 40:28-31) responding to the felt needs of the people. He singles out four groups who will benefit from Yahweh's compassionate might: the blind, the deaf, the lame, and the speechless. Opened eyes, cleared ears, leaping limbs, and singing mute—these are the images of divine vindication and recompense. Yahweh's identifying with the plight of the despondent exiles shows that compassion is a mark of the strong and the faithful.

Show No Partiality

The author of James is well acquainted with our human tendency to prefer the wealthy and neglect the poor. He cautiously begins his attack on this weakness by asking whether the people "really believe in our glorious Lord Jesus Christ" (2:1). Basically this is a summary of the Christian creed. It confesses that the Jesus who was crucified is the glorified Lord through the Resurrection. Favoritism and prejudice in favor of the wealthy are a rejection of that Christian belief.

The author's example of the rich person and the poor person coming into the assembly suggests that such discrimination was a problem in his community. He implies that it takes the Christian faith mentioned above to focus one's attention on the needs of the poor, not the comfort of the rich. He then adds a theological reason for preferring the poor—they are God's chosen, heirs of the kingdom. "Have you not made distinctions among yourselves, and become judges with evil thoughts?" (2:4) James asks of those who favor the rich. Compassion is a mark of the strong and the faithful.

Ephphatha!

Throughout the Gospel of Mark, Jesus the Son of God *must* reach out to the marginalized of his time: the poor, the women, the tax collectors, the lepers. In today's passage the compassionate Jesus accedes to the wishes of some people who brought him a deaf man with a speech impediment. Two noteworthy features of the cure are Jesus' groaning and the reaction of the crowd. While the latter speaks of the unbounded amazement of the people, the former suggests Jesus' great compassion for the sufferer.

Mark uses this episode as a building block in showing the Church's universal mission. Jesus—God's strong one (see Mk 1:7;3:27)—also has compassion on the Gentiles. To this end Mark notes that Jesus is in Gentile territory, "the region of the Decapolis" (Mk 7:31). On this level, the pagans, who were once deaf and mute toward God, are now able to hear and proclaim the message of God's Son; the ears are opened and speech unlocked. Clearly compassion is a mark of the strong and the faithful.

Today's Good News

We have become insulated against tragedy. The entertainment and news media saturate us; they blur distinctions between fact and fiction. Widespread apathy tends to lead to a presumption that occasional pity is the best reaction we can muster. Today's readings, however, should prompt two other reactions. The first is a genuine emotional outburst, not unlike the groaning of Jesus in the gospel. The second is an equally genuine effort to move from pity to compassion. Both these reactions call for strength on our part. To feel for the hurting and then to suffer with them (com-passion) *must* eventually lead to concrete *action*. Such action is not for the timid and weak. After all, compassion is a mark of the strong and the faithful.

Points for Reflection and Discussion

1. Societal norms seem to hold that compassion is a mark of weakness and stupidity, making the exercise of compassion a very real and concerted effort of strength and faith. Do you know anyone you would identify as "compassionate"? Do you believe that person is strong? faithful?

_____

_____

_____

_____

2. Have you ever been "marginalized"? How did you feel? How did you cope? Talk about it.

_____

_____

_____

_____

_____

Themes

Compassion
   Q12, Catholics and Church
   M8, Evangelization
Marginalized
   Q9, Who's Who in the Church
   M7, Holiness
Prejudice
   Q1, Journey of Faith
   M1, Conversion: A Lifelong Process

Reading 1, Isaiah 50:4-9

[The Lord God] wakens my ear to listen as those who are taught. The Lord God has opened my ear, and I was not rebellious, I did not turn backward. I gave my back to those who struck me, and my cheeks to those who pulled out the beard; I did not hide my face from insult and spitting. The Lord God helps me; therefore I have not been disgraced; therefore I have set my face like flint, and I know that I shall not be put to shame; he who vindicates me is near. Who will contend with me? Let us stand up together. Who are my adversaries? Let them confront me. It is the Lord God who helps me; who will declare me guilty?

Psalm 116:1-2,3-4,5-6,8-9

Reading 2, James 2:14-18

What good is it, my brothers and sisters, if you say you have faith but do not have works? Can faith save you? If a brother or sister is naked and lacks daily food, and one of you says to them, "Go in peace; keep warm and eat your fill," and yet you do not supply their bodily needs, what is the good of that? So faith by itself, if it has no works, is dead.

But someone will say, "You have faith and I have works." Show me your faith apart from your works, and I by my works will show you my faith.

Gospel, Mark 8:27-35

Jesus went on with his disciples to the villages of Caesarea Philippi; and on the way he asked his disciples, "Who do people say that I am?" And they answered him, "John the Baptist; and others, Elijah; and still others, one of the prophets." He asked them, "But who do you say that I am?" Peter answered him, "You are the Messiah." And he sternly ordered them not to tell anyone about him.

Then he began to teach them that the Son of Man must undergo great suffering, and be rejected by the elders, the chief priests, and the scribes, and be killed, and after three days rise again. He said all this quite openly. And Peter took him aside and began to rebuke him. But turning and looking at his disciples, he rebuked Peter and said, "Get behind me, Satan! For you are setting your mind not on divine things but on human things."

He called the crowd with his disciples, and said to them, "If any want to become my followers, let them deny themselves and take up their cross and follow me. For those who want to save their life will lose it, and those who lose their life for my sake, and for the sake of the gospel, will save it."

Lost And Found

JOHN F. CRAGHAN

We constantly are asked to raise the question: Who is the real me? In response we attempt to develop our self-image. We look to our self-fulfillment and self-realization. But perhaps that is the real problem. We may tend to focus on ourselves to such an extent that we end up as navel gazers. It is extremely difficult to endorse the scriptural line: To find oneself is to lose oneself.

Today's readings consider the crucial issue of identity, but they differ from the contemporary approach described above by diverting our attention to the world of others. They see the whole question of identity is linked to service to others. They maintain that to immerse oneself in the problems of others is to discover oneself. Here to find oneself is to lose oneself.

A Suffering Servant

The first reading is part of the third Suffering Servant passage (Is 50:4-11). Against the background of the end of exile in Babylon the poem reveals a servant who is open to God's Word. Unlike his unwilling audience, this disciple trusts in Yahweh and relies on his God. His steadfastness is met with frequent humiliations (striking, pulling of beard, insults, spitting). Nonetheless he refuses to react to violence with violence.

The servant's determination to preach God's Word to an unbending audience shows that he has identified himself in terms of his hearers' needs. He willingly sustains all the ignominy because he sees himself as an instrument of Yahweh for the exilic community. Their plight has become his plight. Though they refuse to connect their sins with the punishment of exile, this servant will not cease to proclaim his message. Implicitly at least he reveals that to find oneself is to lose oneself.

The author of James contrasts living faith and dead faith. He holds that within the area of everyday life Christians implement their living faith. He teaches that to accept God's revelation (to believe) is ultimately to open ourselves up to God's world of concerns. Consequently, to wish a person good luck without also addressing his or her needs is a powerful image of lifeless faith. To the objection that some specialize in faith and others in good works, the author counters that such is not the case; rather, faith is the very basis of good works (see Gal 5:6). In other words, to find oneself is to lose oneself.

The Way of the Cross

This gospel passage ends the first half of Mark's Gospel and begins the second half. It unequivocally endorses the suggestion found in so many of Mark's earlier scenes: Jesus is the Messiah. At the same time it prepares for the passion and death by qualifying Jesus' messiahship: He will be a suffering Messiah. While Peter clearly confesses that Jesus is the Messiah, he cannot accept the qualification of suffering and death as the road to glory. In so doing he plays the part of God's opponent or prosecuting attorney (Satan). Peter argues on the basis of purely human categories, not God's plan.

Mark uses Peter's misunderstanding as an occasion for teaching about the nature of Christian discipleship. To be a disciple means to deny oneself (not simply to deny *something* to oneself) and take up one's cross. To save one's life is paradoxically to lose one's life. Indeed to follow Jesus is to forget oneself—a forgetting that stands in the shadow of Calvary. To find oneself is to lose oneself.

Today's Good News

The modern believer does not have to look very far to uncover countless opportunities for Christian discipleship. One can conveniently begin right at home. As a married person, do I make my spouse's concern my concern? As a parent, do I see my family's problems as my problems as well? As a member of a local community, do I recognize the community's need is my need too? As a parishioner in a particular faith community, do I accept the parish's priorities as my personal priorities? These are indeed startling questions. At the same time they may provide a more accurate barometer of our identity search: I know the real me to the extent that I am involved in the world of concerns. To find oneself is to lose oneself.

Points for Reflection and Discussion

1. Have you ever experienced unjust persecution? How did you react? How did you feel?

_____

_____

_____

_____

2. Imagine you are Peter, first identifying Jesus as "Messiah" and nearly as quickly being called "Satan" by your Messiah. Can you relate his experience of belief/denial to a similar one in your own life?

_____

_____

_____

_____

_____

Themes

Discipleship
   Q7, Mary
   M2, The Laity: Called To Build God's Kingdom
Identity
   Q1, Journey of Faith
   M1, Conversion: A Lifelong Process
Suffering
   Q10, Catholics and Prayer
   M6, Discernment

Reading 1, Wisdom 2:12,17-20

[The wicked say] Let us lie in wait for the righteous man, because he is inconvenient to us and opposes our actions; he reproaches us for sins against the law, and accuses us of sins against our training. Let us see if his words are true, and let us test what will happen at the end of his life; for if the righteous man is God's child, he will help him, and will deliver him from the hand of his adversaries. Let us test him with insult and torture, so that we may find out how gentle he is, and make trial of his forebearance. Let us condemn him to a shameful death, for, according to what he says, he will be protected.

Psalm 54:1-2,3,4,6 (NRSV)

Reading 2, James 3:16—4:3

Where there is envy and selfish ambition, there will also be disorder and wickedness of every kind. But the wisdom from above is first pure, then peaceable, gentle, willing to yield, full of mercy and good fruits, without a trace of partiality or hypocrisy. And a harvest of righteousness is sown in peace for those who make peace.

Those conflicts and disputes among you, where do they come from? Do they not come from your cravings that are at war within you? You want something and do not have it; so you commit murder. And you covet something and cannot obtain it; so you engage in disputes and conflicts. You do not have, because you do not ask. You ask and do not receive, because you ask wrongly, in order to spend what you get on your pleasures.

Gospel, Mark 9:30-37

[Jesus and his disciples] went on from there and passed through Galilee. He did not want anyone to know it; for he was teaching his disciples, saying to them, "The Son of Man is to be betrayed into human hands, and they will kill him, and three days after being killed, he will rise again." But they did not understand what he was saying and were afraid to ask him.

Then they came to Capernaum; and when he was in the house he asked them, "What were you arguing about on the way?" But they were silent, for on the way they had argued with one another who was the greatest. He sat down, called the twelve, and said to them, "Whoever wants to be first must be last of all and servant of all." Then he took a little child and put it among them; and taking it in his arms, he said to them, "Whoever welcomes one such child in my name welcomes me, and whoever welcomes me welcomes not me but the one who sent me."

Imitation Of Life

JOHN F. CRAGHAN

Whose lifestyle should we imitate? Who will be our role model? The media regularly supply answers to these very profound questions. Usually they hold out for our emulation the lifestyles of the rich and the famous—those who have made it big in business or athletics or entertainment. Often their lives tend to leave something to be desired. They command our attention, but not necessarily our respect.

Today's readings also offer an answer to the questions raised above. They hold up for our emulation people who are renowned for their wisdom. Such people see fidelity and service as a lifestyle that is truly rewarding and satisfying, though difficult. Faithfulness to principles and openness to others characterize their model of wisdom. Today's readings urge imitation of the lifestyles of the truly wise, not of the rich and the famous.

Around the middle of the first century B.C., the author of the Book of Wisdom sought to provide role models for his Jewish community in Hellenistic Egypt. In so doing, he contrasted the "just" Jew and the "wicked" Jew. Drawing upon the Book of Isaiah (see chapters 52—66), he vividly described the attacks of the wicked on the just. Their purpose was to determine whether or not the way of the just was really wise: "Let us see if his words are true, and let us test what will happen at the end of his life" (Wis 2:17).

The reason for the vicious reprisals against the just man is that his lifestyle is a condemnation of the wicked. As the wicked so aptly put it, "he...opposes our actions; he reproaches us for sins against the law, and accuses us of sins against our training" (2:12). By clinging to the word of his God, this just man proclaims a message of fidelity and, as chapter three shows, he is vindicated—he really does not die since he shares community with the God of Israel. The author of Wisdom was clearly advocating imitation of the lifestyles of the truly wise, not those of the rich and the famous.

In the second reading, the author of James cites some of the qualities of genuine wisdom: pure, peaceable, gentle, yielding, merciful, fruitful, impartial, and sincere. He then points out some of the causes of unrest in his community. Even in prayer, those who promote discord in the community fail: "You ask and do not receive, because you ask wrongly, in order to spend what you get on your pleasures" (4:3). In opposition to conflict and envy, a truly Christian wisdom is ultimately dedication to others. It is precisely this type of wisdom that ushers in a harvest of peace. It is worthy of imitation.

Becoming a Child of Jesus

This gospel passage is primarily Mark's second passion prediction. It follows the same pattern as that found in last Sunday's gospel: prediction (9:31), misunderstanding (9:32-33), and instruction on the nature of discipleship (9:34-37). For Mark, such scenes contain all the basic ingredients of Christian wisdom. To follow Jesus is to imitate his lifestyle.

Jesus responds to the question of leadership in the community by linking together two startling scenarios: "Whoever wants to be first must be last of all and servant of all" (9:35; see Mt 20:27-28). Further: "Whoever welcomes one such child in my name welcomes me, and whoever welcomes me welcomes not me but the one who sent me" (Mk 9:36-37; see Mt 10:40;18:4-5; Lk 9:46-48; Jn 13:20). Since children in both Greco-Roman and Jewish societies had no value and were subject to the authority of the head of the household, this child was an apt symbol for powerlessness and total reliance on others. The teaching for Mark's community: Welcome the powerless and the disenfranchised, and imitate them. They are the truly wise, not the rich and the famous.

Today's Good News

In all communities we have those who are committed to principle, to promoting peace, and to welcoming the powerless. Though we may know of them, we must candidly admit that they probably don't get the recognition they surely deserve. They more likely, in fact, are denigrated as foolish and as losers. Today we are urged to make these examples our role models. The readings demand that we continue our eucharistic celebration beyond these church doors, so that fidelity, peace, and service may become hallmarks of our lives as well. We need to recognize the wisdom of the just, and a most effective form of recognition is imitation. In this way we will endorse the views of the authors of Wisdom, James, and Mark: Imitate the lifestyles of the truly wise, not those of the rich and the famous.

Points for Reflection and Discussion

1. Where are you confronted by injustice in your daily life? What is your response?

_____

_____

_____

_____

2. The disciples did not understand when Jesus told them about his death and resurrection, and they "were afraid to ask him" (Mk 9:32). Have you ever not understood and been afraid to question your God? What were the results?

_____

_____

_____

_____

Themes

Justice
  Q6, The Saints
  M8, Evangelization
Leadership
  Q9, Who's Who in The Church
  M2, The Laity: Called To Build God's Kingdom
Wisdom
  Q10, Catholics and Prayer
  M7, Holiness

Reading 1, Numbers 11:25-29

The Lord came down in the cloud and spoke to Moses, and took some of the spirit that was on him and put it on the seventy elders; and when the spirit rested upon them, they prophesied.

Two men remained in the camp, one named Eldad, and the other named Medad, and the spirit rested on them; they were among those registered, but they had not gone out to the tent, and so they prophesied in the camp. And a young man ran and told Moses, "Eldad and Medad are prophesying in the camp." And Joshua son of Nun, the assistant of Moses, one of his chosen men, said, "My lord Moses, stop them!" But Moses said to him, "Are you jealous for my sake? Would that all the Lord's people were prophets, and that the Lord would put his spirit on them!"

Psalm 19:7,9,11-12,13 (NRSV)

Reading 2, James 5:1-6

Come now, you rich people, weep and wail for the miseries that are coming to you. Your riches have rotted, and your clothes are moth-eaten. Your gold and silver have rusted, and their rust will be evidence against you, and it will eat your flesh like fire. You have laid up treasure for the last days. Listen! The wages of the laborers who mowed your fields, which you kept back by fraud, cry out, and the cries of the harvesters have reached the ears of the Lord of hosts. You have lived on the earth in luxury and in pleasure; you have fattened your hearts in a day of slaughter. You have condemned and murdered the righteous one, who does not resist you.

Gospel, Mark 9:38-43,45,47-48

John said to Jesus, "Teacher, we saw someone casting out demons in your name, and we tried to stop him, because he was not following us." But Jesus said, "Do not stop him; for no one who does a deed of power in my name will be able soon afterward to speak evil of me. Whoever is not against us is for us. For truly I tell you, whoever gives you a cup of water to drink because you bear the name of Christ will by no means lose the reward.

"If any of you put a stumbling block before one of these little ones who believe in me, it would be better for you if a great millstone were hung around your neck and you were thrown into the sea. If your hand causes you to stumble, cut it off; it is better for you to enter life maimed than to have two hands and to go to hell, to the unquenchable fire. And if your foot causes you to stumble, cut it off; it is better for you to enter life lame than to have two feet and to be thrown into hell. And if your eye causes you to stumble, tear it out; it is better for you to enter the kingdom of God with one eye than to have two eyes and to be thrown into hell, where their worm never dies, and the fire is never quenched."

Judge Ye Not...

JOHN F. CRAGHAN

Almost instinctively we make judgments about others. In a spirit of elitism we may conclude that others are not worthy of our club or community. With a sense of exclusivism we may decide that others do not measure up to our norms or rules. With such attitudes of superiority we reduce subjective individuals or groups of persons to little more than objective things—unworthy of decent human treatment. Setting ourselves up as judges, it becomes impossible to employ God as our model for judging.

Today's readings are a timely appeal to see God, not ourselves, as the criterion for judging. They urge believers to consider the radical ability of our God to give to others. They persuade us to reflect on the boundless capacity of our God to empower others. They compel us to look to the limitless graciousness of our God to respect others. In these passages believers make God the norm for judging.

Moses had earlier complained to God that he could not adequately provide for Israel in the desert by himself (see Nm 11:14-17). To alleviate the situation, God promised to confer Moses' prophetic spirit on seventy elders of Israel. Most likely this account reflects later problems of the Israelite community. To resolve such problems, those responsible for the account read them back into the time of Moses and thus justified their actions.

In this story two men, Eldad and Medad, were not present in the camp when God conferred some of Moses' spirit on the seventy elders. Nonetheless these two also received the Spirit and began to prophesy. Essentially the passage answers the question of God's power. God had gifted Moses with the Spirit, and now God gifts seventy others with the same Spirit. God even gifts two who were not with the assembly. Who is "worthy," and under what circumstances, is simply not within our limited knowledge to judge.

That Ye Be Not Judged!

The author of James maintains that the rich have treated their employees as objects. In effect, the wealthy have judged their workers according to their own perceptions, thereby denigrating them to the level of things. The author decries their sin. Since they have withheld the wages of their farmhands, they will see their silver and gold corrode and their garments fall prey to the ravaging moth. The wealthy have not realized that the Lord is the God of the poor who hears their cry and takes action against the guilty. These perpetrators, who have even stooped to murder, are negative examples of the conviction that believers make God the norm for judging.

In today's gospel passage, Mark has brought together a series of sayings of Jesus to buttress the second passion prediction (Mk 9:31-37). In the first saying (Mk 9:39-40), Jesus rejects the elitism of the disciples. An outsider who expels demons through Jesus' name does not detract from Jesus' power or position. In the second saying (Mk 9:41), anyone who gives the disciples a drink of water, precisely because they belong to Christ, will not be neglected. Hence no one may look down on a person who takes Jesus with all due seriousness. In the third saying (Mk 9:42), Jesus returns to the theme of the little ones (Mk 9:36-37). They are the ones who totally depend on God. As a result, no one has the right to lead them astray. Here the millstone captures the iniquity of such an act.

In all these sayings, Mark teaches that the disciples must dismiss their narrow vision and accept Jesus' perceptions. The "outsider" exorcist, the giver of a drink of water, and the simple believer must each be assessed according to Jesus' criteria. Believers make God the norm for judging.

Today's Good News

Constricted judgments are alive and well—both outside and inside our Church. We can easily note the merging position of women in our Church and in society at large. Why should we suppress our God's capacity to give regardless of sex? We can reflect on all minorities. Why should we limit our God's graciousness to empower them to take prominent offices in our communities? We can also observe the talents and gifts of our neighbors. Why should we restrain our God's liberty to endow those who don't seem to possess our privileges and status? These examples can be multiplied without any difficulty. These situations can indeed become an occasion for implementing the focus of today's readings: Believers make God the norm for judging.

Points for Reflection and Discussion

1. Have you ever judged a person "unworthy" to do something that later proved to have been done well?

_____

_____

_____

_____

_____

2. Is there a particular talent you would like to develop for the good of others? Have you prayed about it?

_____

_____

_____

_____

_____

Themes

Judgment
    M6, Discernment
Personhood
    M3, Your Special Gifts
Spirit
    M7, Holiness

Reading 1, Genesis 2:18-24

The Lord God said, "It is not good that the man should be alone; I will make him a helper as his partner." So out of the ground the Lord God formed every animal of the field and every bird of the air, and brought them to the man to see what he would call them; and whatever the man called every living creature, that was its name. The man gave names to all cattle, and to the birds of the air, and to every animal of the field; but for the man there was not found a helper as his partner.

So the Lord God caused a deep sleep to fall upon the man, and he slept; then he took one of his ribs and closed up its place with flesh. And the rib that the Lord God had taken from the man he made into a woman and brought her to the man. Then the man said, "This at last is bone of my bones and flesh of my flesh; this one shall be called Woman, for out of Man this one was taken." Therefore a man leaves his father and his mother and clings to his wife, and they become one flesh.

Psalm 128:1-2,3,4-5,6

Reading 2, Hebrews 2:9-11

We do see Jesus, who for a little while was made lower than the angels, now crowned with glory and honor because of the suffering of death, so that by the grace of God he might taste death for everyone. It was fitting that God, for whom and through whom all things exist, in bringing many children to glory, should make the pioneer of their salvation perfect through sufferings. For the one who sanctifies and those who are sanctified all have one Father. For this reason Jesus is not ashamed to call them brothers and sisters.

Gospel, Mark 10:2-16

Some Pharisees came, and to test Jesus they asked, "Is it lawful for a man to divorce his wife?" He answered them, "What did Moses command you?" They said, "Moses allowed a man to write a certificate of dismissal and to divorce her." But Jesus said to them, "Because of your hardness of heart he wrote this commandment for you. But from the beginning of creation, 'God made them male and female. For this reason a man shall leave his father and mother and be joined to his wife, and the two shall become one flesh.' So they are no longer two, but one flesh. Therefore what God has joined together, let no one separate." Then in the house the disciples asked him again about this matter. He said to them, "Whoever divorces his wife and marries another commits adultery against her;

and if she divorces her husband and marries another, she commits adultery."

People were bringing little children to him in order that he might touch them; and the disciples spoke sternly to them. But when Jesus saw this, he was indignant and said to them, "Let the little children come to me; do not stop them; for it is to such as these that the kingdom of God belongs. Truly I tell you, whoever does not receive the kingdom of God as a little child will never enter it." And he took them up in his arms, laid his hands on them, and blessed them.

Created In God's Image

JOHN F. CRAGHAN

In our society we readily observe a lack of mutual trust among friends, floundering confidence within families, the failure of many marriages. While there are no easy solutions to these complex breakdowns, we can conclude that for one reason or another commitments are not kept and loyalty wanes.

Today's readings jolt us into reassessing our sense of loyalty. They reveal that the very foundation of marriage is mutual commitment, that marriage partners must reach out to each other. They also indicate that relationships, in order to succeed, must be grounded in mutual respect and esteem. They maintain that loyalty is still number one.

Male and Female

The Genesis account is a tenth-century B.C. tradition of creation. In it the Yahwist author insists on the mutual bond uniting husband and wife. God provides the man with companionship in the form of animals and birds. While exercising authority over all these, shown by his naming of them, the man still was lonely. While the man is in a deep sleep (God's revelation in a state of unconsciousness), the perfect complement is brought forth. In creating woman, God has made creation complete.

The expression "bone of my bones and flesh of my flesh" is a formula of abiding mutual loyalty (see 2 Sm 5:1-3). It implies fidelity through thick (bone) and thin (flesh). The author enhances this mutual bond by using the word *cling* (Gn 2:24). *To cling* or *to hold fast* connotes shared concerns and mutual commitment (see Dt 11:22). Our creation story thus highlights faithful relationships in the natural scheme of things human.

Psalm 128 is a wisdom psalm that underlines the consequences of loyalty. Truly happy are all who are faithful to Yahweh ("fears the Lord and walks in his ways," 128:1). According to the psalmist, this fidelity brings in its wake blessings such as fertility of land and marriage-bed. It is significant that such bounty is not a purely individual affair. The blessing of the God-fearing redounds to the prosperity of Jerusalem (128:5) and the peace of Israel (128:6). As a result, the fidelity of this one relationship impacts the good of the nation. Loyalty is still number one.

Two Become One

In this Markan question of divorce, the scribes quote Deuteronomy 24:1-4 in which Moses allowed a man to divorce his wife. In response, Jesus remarks that Moses' reason for permitting divorce was the stubbornness of the people. (Because in Jewish law a woman could not divorce her husband, Mark's verse 12 reflects his Gentile Christian audience.) By citing both Genesis 1 (Mk 10:6; Gn 1:27) and Genesis 2 (Mk 10:7-8; Gn 2:24), Jesus points out that the people failed to attain the high demands of these creation texts. They did not live out the consequences of the marital community: mutual support and loyalty.

Jesus does not focus on the permissiveness of Moses. He, rather, directs attention to the real issue: What does God intend? Clearly, the divine intent is that husband and wife reflect the zenith of God's creative energy; thus not even the authority of Moses sets aside God's grand design in the scheme of things human. Loyalty is still number one.

Today's Good News

Instead of dwelling on the all too apparent lack of loyalty in our community, both ecclesial and civil, we might do well to emphasize some of those qualities that promote and encourage loyalty. Husbands and wives should appreciate ongoing commitment and dedication. When one spouse regularly fulfills the demands of support and concern, the other spouse should duly recognize it. Children should be received by parents as God's blessing on the faithful marital relationship; they should be welcomed by all as faithful representatives of God's kingdom (Mk 10:14-15). Family members should acknowledge consistent efforts to provide for their community. When one member continues to contribute to the common good, the other members should offer words of congratulation and appreciation. Friends should take due note of unflagging generosity and thoughtfulness. One friend should make it a point to show gratitude for the other's graciousness. By these and similar actions we show that loyalty is still number one.

Points for Reflection and Discussion

1. Family values are the focus of today's readings. How do God's family values differ from those of the contemporary society? How do they differ from your own?

_____

_____

_____

_____

_____

2. Reflect upon the "entrance requirements" for membership in God's kingdom. What does this mean in terms of how society treats its children? What does it mean in terms of your treatment of children (yours and/or others')?

_____

_____

_____

_____

_____

Themes

Family, Marriage, Relationships
    C7, The Sacrament of Marriage
    C12, Catholics and Church
    M4, Family Life

Reading 1, Wisdom 7:7-11

I prayed, and understanding was given me; I called on God, and the spirit of wisdom came to me. I preferred her to scepters and thrones, and I accounted wealth as nothing in comparison with her. Neither did I liken to her any priceless gem, because all gold is but a little sand in her sight, and silver will be accounted as clay before her. I loved her more than health and beauty, and I chose to have her rather than light, because her radiance never ceases. All good things came to me along with her, and in her hands uncounted wealth.

Psalm 90:12-13,14-15,16-17

Reading 2, Hebrews 4:12-13

Indeed, the word of God is living and active, sharper than any two-edged sword, piercing until it divides soul from spirit, joints from marrow; it is able to judge the thoughts and intentions of the heart. And before him no creature is hidden, but all are naked and laid bare to the eyes of the one to whom we must render an account.

Gospel, Mark 10:17-30

As Jesus was setting out on a journey, a man ran up and knelt before him, and asked him, "Good Teacher, what must I do to inherit eternal life?" Jesus said to him, "Why do you call me good? No one is good but God alone. You know the commandments: 'You shall not murder; You shall not commit adultery; You shall not steal; You shall not bear false witness; You shall not defraud; Honor your father and mother.'"

He said to him, "Teacher, I have kept all these since my youth." Jesus, looking at him, loved him and said, "You lack one thing; go, sell what you own, and give the money to the poor, and you will have treasure in heaven; then come, follow me." When he heard this, he was shocked and went away grieving, for he had many possessions. Then Jesus looked around and said to his disciples, "How hard it will be for those who have wealth to enter the kingdom of God!" And the disciples were perplexed at these words. But Jesus said to them again, "Children, how hard it is to enter the kingdom of God! It is easier for a camel to go through the eye of a needle than for someone who is rich to enter the kingdom of God."

They were greatly astounded and said to one another, "Then who can be saved?" Jesus looked at them and said, "For mortals it is impossible, but not for God; for God all things are possible."

Peter began to say to him, "Look, we have left everything and followed you." Jesus said, "Truly I tell you,

there is no one who has left house or brothers or sisters or mother or father or children or fields, for my sake and for the sake of the good news, who will not receive a hundredfold now in this age—houses, brothers and sisters, mothers and children, and fields with persecutions—and in the age to come eternal life."

One For All

JOHN F. CRAGHAN

The word *wisdom* often conjures up years of study and dedication whereby a person becomes an acknowledged expert in a specific field. For some reason we see such wisdom as a personal acquisition and triumph. The expertise glorifies the expert—the individual person has made it! How strange it would seem if this wisdom automatically became the birthright of the community.

Today's readings all address the topic of wisdom. They never regard wisdom as a purely personal attainment. They understand it as a gift that must benefit the community. Expertise is always centrifugal, moving out from the one to the many. Wisdom is the birthright of the community.

Wisdom of Heart

In first-century B.C. Hellenistic Egypt, the author of the Book of Wisdom mythologized a wise and benevolent king as the exemplar of human perfection. Although he portrayed Solomon at prayer, he was not thinking of the historical son of David but of the ideal king. For such a ruler, wisdom must be preferred to wealth, health, beauty—even kingship itself.

This ideal king is to employ his wisdom for the benefit of the people. He is wise to the extent that his subjects receive just and equitable government. To promote the common good is to exercise this gift of wisdom. Far from being a purely personal acquisition, such wisdom is radically communal. It is the birthright of the community.

The psalm is a communal lament. The people meditate on the value of human life. They first contrast human duration and divine eternity (90:1-6); they next reflect on God's anger because of human sinfulness (90:7-11). In today's passage they ask God for the ability to cope in life.

"A wise heart" (90:12) has to do with living in a way that subtly balances relationships with God and others. It emphasizes the harmony between God and the community. Wisdom means that the community experiences God's gracious presence (90:15-16); it implies that

God both sees and acknowledges the work of our hands by giving it fullness (90:17). God's own wisdom inherently becomes the birthright of the community.

Wisdom of Poverty

Mark's Gospel continually depicts a Jesus who is recognized for his wisdom. The man in today's story seeks his expertise regarding everlasting life. Jesus first refers to the commandments, a form of wisdom in which one looks to the common good. The man, however, has already attained that level of wisdom. He looks for more.

Jesus' second reply is a more demanding form of wisdom. Wealth can be an obstacle that prevents one from reaching this higher level of wisdom. Everlasting life means giving up everything that detracts from following Jesus. To sell one's possessions and give to the poor is a liberating experience that stresses service to the community.

Today's Good News

The wise occupy a variety of positions. We can readily think of parents. They have acquired wisdom by coping in life. They share that wisdom by instructing and guiding their family. Teachers as a group come easily to mind. They demonstrate their wisdom by reaching out to struggling students—often after school hours. Counselors also serve as examples of the wise. They employ their talents when they seek to help others help themselves—especially when they receive no fringe benefits. Our legal community is a significant group. They offer their wisdom whenever they aid victims of injustice—particularly when their fee is minimal or nothing. There are many other people of wisdom. In the final analysis, they are the people who see their expertise as a gift to be shared with all. Wisdom is a birthright of the community.

Points for Reflection and Discussion

1. God's wisdom is folly to those of the world. How have you communicated God's wisdom to skeptics? Who has communicated God's wisdom to you?

_____

_____

_____

_____

2. The Letter to the Hebrews says the "word of God is living and active" (4:12). How has God's Word been living and active in your life today?

_____

_____

_____

_____

Themes

Community
    Q3, What is the Meaning of the Mass?
    M2, The Laity: Called To Build God's Kingdom
Gifts
    Q6, The Saints
    M3, Your Special Gifts
Wisdom
    Q10, Catholics and Prayer
    M6, Discernment

Reading 1, Isaiah 53:10-11

It was the will of the Lord to crush him with pain. When you make his life an offering for sin, he shall see his offspring, and shall prolong his days; through him the will of the Lord shall prosper. Out of his anguish he shall see light; he shall find satisfaction through his knowledge. The righteous one, my servant, shall make many righteous, and he shall bear their iniquities.

Psalm 33:4-5,18-19,20,22

Reading 2, Hebrews 4:14-16

Since...we have a great high priest who has passed through the heavens, Jesus, the Son of God, let us hold fast to our confession. For we do not have a high priest who is unable to sympathize with our weaknesses, but we have one who in every respect has been tested as we are, yet without sin. Let us therefore approach the throne of grace with boldness, so that we may receive mercy and find grace to help in time of need.

Gospel, Mark 10:35-45

James and John, the sons of Zebedee, came forward to him and said to him, "Teacher, we want you to do for us whatever we ask of you." And he said to them, "What is it you want me to do for you?" And they said to him, "Grant us to sit, one at your right hand and one at your left, in your glory." But Jesus said to them, "You do not know what you are asking. Are you able to drink the cup that I drink, or be baptized with the baptism that I am baptized with?" They replied, "We are able." Then Jesus said to them, "The cup that I drink you will drink; and with the baptism with which I am baptized, you will be baptized; but to sit at my right hand or at my left is not mine to grant, but it is for those for whom it has been prepared." When the ten heard this, they began to be angry with James and John. So Jesus called them and said to them, "You know that among the Gentiles those whom they recognize as their rulers lord it over them, and their great ones are tyrants over them. But it is not so among you; but whoever wishes to become great among you must be your servant, and whoever wishes to be first among you must be slave of all. For the Son of Man came not to be served but to serve, and to give his life a ransom for many."

Privilege and Obligation

JOHN F. CRAGHAN

We tend to identify status with all those who enjoy power and prestige. Regardless of their contributions to humanity these are the people who have made it to the top—hence these are the people whom we seek to imitate. For some reason we are happy to focus on the privilege of status—we chose not to think of the obligation of status.

Today's readings take a decidedly different approach to the question of status. They understand leadership and power positions only within the framework of service. They appreciate individual attainments only insofar as others also attain something. They reserve their accolades for those who choose to meet the needs of others. Herein the servant has both the privilege and the obligation of status.

A Servant Song

Around 540 B.C., an anonymous prophet (Second Isaiah) beseeches his exiled community, in Babylon, to respond to God's call to return home to Israel. In this poem he speaks of the Servant as himself and all those who are willing to share in this new but daring enterprise. As the full poem indicates (Is 52:13—53:12), it is a challenge that involves the utmost dedication.

If the opening half-verse is part of the text, it is Yahweh's pleasure to make the Servant an object of abuse. In the language of sacrifice, the Servant is an offering for sin. By accepting this call, the Servant suffers on behalf of all the people, the outcome being that he will effect the people's reinstatement with God. Through his experience of pain and suffering, he will restore all ("many") to a living relationship with God. Though guiltless, the Servant will bear their guilt. It is both his privilege and his obligation to do so.

The author of Hebrews does not use the title *servant* for Jesus; his title of *high priest* is seemingly more worthy of status. He does, however, paint a portrait in which Jesus' self-giving becomes both the model and the source of encouragement for the author's audience. Paradoxically, while the author speaks of Jesus' divinity, he does not disparage his humanity. His lowliness is linked to his exaltation.

Neither is this letter writer ashamed to speak of Jesus' temptations. Indeed these experiences reveal that he is a high priest who can empathize with his people. Believers can approach God more confidently because of his experiences. Earlier the author puts it this way: "Because he himself was tested through what he suffered, he is able to help those who are being tested" (2:18). Jesus' suffering led to his perfection—a perfection that results in eternal salvation (5:8-10). His privilege of status as high priest carries ominous obligations.

Table Etiquette

This scene in Mark follows upon the third prediction of the passion (Mk 10:32-34). Jesus' prediction of his fate leads to misunderstanding on the part of the disciples (10:35-41). James and John seek positions of honor when Jesus enters upon his glory. This misunderstanding gives way to further instruction on the nature of Christian discipleship (10:42-45), as in reply Jesus points out that real honor is bound up with suffering. For example, "the cup" (10:38-39) is nothing less than the passion (see Mk 14:36).

Jesus speaks about the exercise of power that "the Gentiles...and their great ones" (10:42) evidence. They make their status felt. By contrast, those who aspire to greatness in Jesus' kingdom must be servants. This is expressed in the life-and-death style of Jesus himself: to serve, not to be served—the privilege and the obligation of status.

Today's Good News

Most of us enjoy power or rank of one sort or another: We are parents or clergy or teachers or whatever. But do we really assess our performance in terms of our children, our parish, our students, or whomever? Today's readings demand we assess our position only in terms of service rendered to others. The patience, understanding, gentleness, and love we show in our positions of power become the barometer of our true status. It is both our privilege and our obligation to serve.

Points for Reflection and Discussion

1. Being servant to others has always been counter-cultural to "success." How well do you serve? Who has been an example of servant for you?

_____

_____

_____

_____

2. Have you had experiences of being "crushed in infirmity"? Have such experiences ultimately led you to closer walks with God? Do you believe that God "tests" us? Why or why not?

_____

_____

_____

_____

_____

Themes
Servant
    Q9, Who's Who in the Church
    M2, The Laity: Called To Build God's Kingdom
Status
    Q7, Mary
    M3, Your Special Gifts
Suffering
    Q6, The Saints
    M8, Evangelization

Reading 1, Jeremiah 31:7-9

Thus says the Lord: Sing aloud with gladness for Jacob, and raise shouts for the chief of the nations; proclaim, give praise, and say, "Save, O Lord, your people, the remnant of Israel." See, I am going to bring them from the land of the north, and gather them from the farthest parts of the earth, among them the blind and the lame, those with child and those in labor, together; a great company, they shall return here. With weeping they shall come, and with consolations I will lead them back, I will let them walk by brooks of water, in a straight path in which they shall not stumble; for I have become a father to Israel, and Ephraim is my firstborn.

Psalm 126:1-2,2-3,4-5,6

Reading 2, Hebrews 5:1-6

Every high priest chosen from among mortals is put in charge of things pertaining to God on their behalf, to offer gifts and sacrifices for sins. He is able to deal gently with the ignorant and wayward, since he himself is subject to weakness; and because of this he must offer sacrifice for his own sins as well as for those of the people. And one does not presume to take this honor, but takes it only when called by God, just as Aaron was. So also Christ did not glorify himself in becoming a high priest, but was appointed by the one who said to him, "You are my Son, today I have begotten you"; as he says also in another place, "You are a priest forever, according to the order of Melchizedek."

Gospel, Mark 10:46-52

As Jesus and his disciples and a large crowd were leaving Jericho, Bartimaeus son of Timaeus, a blind beggar, was sitting by the roadside. When he heard that it was Jesus of Nazareth, he began to shout out and say, "Jesus, Son of David, have mercy on me!" Many sternly ordered him to be quiet, but he cried out even more loudly, "Son of David, have mercy on me!" Jesus stood still and said, "Call him here." And they called the blind man, saying to him, "Take heart; get up, he is calling you." So throwing off his cloak, he sprang up and came to Jesus. Then Jesus said to him, "What do you want me to do for you?" The blind man said to him, "My teacher, let me see again." Jesus said to him, "Go; your faith has made you well." Immediately he regained his sight and followed him on the way.

The Eyes Of Faith

JOHN F. CRAGHAN

We all experience times of despair and disillusionment. Death of a loved one, loss of a job, falling out of love, crippling disease—these are but a few of those times when the world around us turns into darkness. We grope, we fidget, we ultimately give up—our only friend is the dark gloom, the empty desolation.

Today's readings deal with crises in the lives of God's people. They reveal those times when Israel's God seems aloof and unconcerned. Yet they proceed to unfold a God who is dynamically present despite the depressing circumstances. They speak of a God who pierces the darkness and offers the ability to hope. They maintain that hope is the capacity to see anew.

The reading from Jeremiah probably stems from the early part of that prophet's career. He addresses the northern tribes of Israel, whose families had experienced the fall of their kingdom and their subsequent exile in 722 B.C. The survivors are indeed a remnant, but they are not neglected. Jeremiah consoles the people with a reminder that Yahweh is their father and the northern kingdom of Israel is Yahweh's firstborn.

Basically the prophet's message is an appeal to hope again, to realize that things can be different. Hence he exhorts his audience to shout with joy and exult, for Yahweh had indeed delivered them. This God will be personally involved by gathering up all of the exiles, including the blind, the lame, the mothers, and the pregnant women. Jeremiah offers a pointed contrast: the tearful departure versus the joyous return. After the manner of the first Exodus, Yahweh will provide a level road with abundant supplies of water. Jeremiah offers hope—the capacity to see anew.

The Lord Has Done Great Things For Us

Psalm 126 is a communal lament that catches up the despair and subsequent joy of the victims of the Babylonian exile. Yahweh's action in reclaiming these exiles seemed so incredible it was like a dream. Nonetheless God offered the capacity to laugh and rejoice once again. This radical change of events provoked the enemy into remarking: "The Lord has done great things for them" (126:2). God's people concur: "The Lord had done great things for us" (126:3).

Israel recalled this experience whenever they pilgrimaged to Jerusalem. Yahweh's earlier intervention became their catalyst for hope in later crises. They could anticipate abundant waters in their arid condition. Though their sowing began in tears, it would end in joy. Though their seed seemed meager, it would produce an abundant harvest. The psalmist reminds Israel of their capacity to see anew, to hope in the Lord who had done great things for them.

Mark, the evangelist, frames his central message of the passion as the condition for glory with two stories: that of the unnamed blind man of Bethsaida (8:22-26) and that of Bartimaeus, the blind man of Jericho. This second account is strategically located. It follows that "blind" ambition of James and John with the misunderstanding of the other ten (10:35-45) and introduces the transition to Jesus' ministry in Jerusalem (11:1).

Mark sees genuine discipleship as the ability to hope for glory in and through suffering. Hence the true disciple is the one who can *see* the exaltation of Jesus in and through his passion and death. Those with such hope must persevere—they must continue to call out like Bartimaeus despite all obstacles. In addition, they must relentlessly pursue Jesus on his way to the cross, the condition for glory. Clearly, hope is the capacity to see anew.

Today's Good News

Those who wear glasses for the first time begin to realize the sights they previously missed. Traffic signs and reading material, even people, come into sharper focus. Christian faith is not unlike this experience. It is the capacity to look at depression and despair from a new perspective. It is the awareness that our God is involved in our problems and is waiting for us to reach out. Hope sees beyond the obvious pain and frustration; it discovers a God who cares. Hope is the capacity to see anew.

Points for Reflection and Discussion

1. Is there an area of "blindness" in your life? What can you do in order to "see" your way through it?

_____

_____

_____

_____

_____

2. It is said that "hope springs eternal" in the lives of God's people. Jeremiah restored hope to the remnant by reminding them that things would get better. Do you know anyone for whom hope seems to have run out? Can you offer sustaining hope?

_____

_____

_____

_____

_____

Themes
Faith
    Q1, Journey of Faith
    M6, Discernment
Healing
    Q11, Catholic Practices
    M5, Your Prayer Life
Hope
    Q12, Catholics and Church
    M7, Holiness

Reading 1, Deuteronomy 6:2-6

Moses told the people:

Fear the Lord your God all the days of your life, and keep all his decrees and his commandments that I am commanding you, so that your days may be long. Hear therefore, O Israel, and observe them diligently, so that it may go well with you, and so that you may multiply greatly in a land flowing with milk and honey, as the Lord, the God of your ancestors, has promised you. Hear, O Israel: The Lord is our God, the Lord alone. You shall love the Lord your God with all your heart, and with all your soul, and with all your might. Keep these words that I am commanding you today in your heart.

Psalm 18:2,2-3,46,50 (NRSV)

Reading 2, Hebrews 7:23-28

The former priests were many in number, because they were prevented by death from continuing in office; but he holds his priesthood permanently, because he continues forever. Consequently he is able for all time to save those who approach God through him, since he always lives to make intercession for them. For it was fitting that we should have such a high priest, holy, blameless, undefiled, separated from sinners, and exalted above the heavens. Unlike the other high priests, he has no need to offer sacrifices day after day, first for his own sins, and then for those of the people; this he did once for all when he offered himself. For the law appoints as high priests those who are subject to weakness, but the word of the oath, which came later than the law, appoints a Son who has been made perfect forever.

Gospel, Mark 12:28-34

One of the scribes asked Jesus, "Which commandment is the first of all?" Jesus answered, "The first is, 'Hear, O Israel: the Lord our God, the Lord is one; you shall love the Lord your God with all your heart, and with all your soul, and with all your mind, and with all your strength.' The second is this, 'You shall love your neighbor as yourself.' There is no other commandment greater than these." Then the scribe said to him, "You are right, Teacher; you have truly said that 'he is one, and besides him there is no other'; and 'to love him with all the heart, and with all the understanding, and with all the strength,' and 'to love one's neighbor as oneself,'—this is much more important than all whole burnt offerings and sacrifices." When Jesus saw that he answered wisely, he said to him, "You are not far from the kingdom of God." After that no one dared to ask him any question.

Hear, O Israel

JOHN F. CRAGHAN

Love is certainly one of the most abused words in our language. It can suggest pure emotion devoid of feeling. It can imply using another person without any respect, or grabbing self-gratification at the expense of others. It can, in other words, mean pursuit of self at the cost of pain and hurt to others.

Today's readings take a decidedly different approach to love and its meaning. They understand love within the context of concern. They maintain that to use the word *love* means to embark on a plan of action on behalf of others. They reveal that love is a precarious undertaking since it implies the obligation to demonstrate love by appropriate action. Love is never passive, never abusive, never self-serving.

Heart, Soul, and Strength

The Book of Deuteronomy is Israel's covenant expression par excellence. Drawing from the treaties of the ancient Near East, this book understands Yahweh as a sovereign and Israel as a vassal. After a historical prologue recounting the sovereign's generosity to the vassal, there is a general stipulation; this is the overall attitude toward the sovereign that is then spelled out in specific obligations. Such an attitude is the Great Commandment—it catches up the spirit and content of all the concrete duties.

In addition to "fear" (6:2), today's passage mentions "love" (6:5) of the sovereign Lord. In the treaty language of the ancient Near East *to love* means *to obey*. "With all your heart, and with all your soul, and with all your might" (6:5) are also part and parcel of the diplomatic language of the time. What this formulation implies is Yahweh's exclusive claim on Israel. It is a claim, however, that reveals itself in concrete actions. Love is active and caring and selfless.

A Rock of Refuge

Psalm 18 is a royal psalm of thanksgiving. It has a reasonable claim to being rooted in the actual experience of David when God dramatically intervened to save him from his enemies (see 2 Sm 22). Against this background, the psalm's intent is to praise Yahweh for such a concrete demonstration of support and concern.

Today's passage is a commentary on the meaning of love (although the Hebrew words are different from those of the first reading). In the opening verse, "I love you" more literally means "I have pity on you." It derives from the Hebrew word for *womb* and, as such, has all the connotations of feminine compassion. Here Yahweh addresses Israel. Israel responds with a variety of divine titles: rock, fortress, shield, and so forth (18:3). Yahweh clearly merits such praise because of intervention on behalf of the king: "I shall be saved from my enemies" (18:3). Significantly, the liturgical passage concludes with the last verse of the psalm (verse 51). This recalls God's promise to David (see 2 Sm 7) to protect and help him. Hence Yahweh's covenantal loyalty ("steadfast love") takes the form of physical aid. This is love in action.

The Greatest Commandment

In Mark, the Great Commandment reappears under two names: the first of all the commandments (12:28) and the greatest commandment (12:31). Out of the 248 positive commands and 365 negative prohibitions of the Torah, Jesus selects but two (Dt 6:4-5 and Lv 19:18). These two, love of God and love of neighbor, give meaning to all the others.

Mark is not content with making this scene an abstract exercise. He has already pointed out how Jesus incorporated this twofold love into his lifestyle. For example, he loved his neighbor by reaching out to those despised by others (see Mk 2:16-17;10:14). He loved his Father by accepting his Father's will, and would continue to do so even unto suffering and death (see Mk 14:36). This is selfless and caring love in action.

Today's Good News

Perhaps we can best begin to live up to the Great Commandment by asking ourselves: Whom have I promised to love? We should immediately think of spouses, children, family, friends, neighbors, colleagues. Today's biblical passages then raise this demanding question: How have I shown my love to these people? More often then not, we begin to fail in little things: lack of signs of affection, lack of respect, lack of encouragement, lack of a helping hand and a cheerful face. Today's readings offer us the occasion to recall our promise to love and to renew our resolve to love—concretely and specifically. The world needs—and the Lord demands—selfless and caring love in action.

Points for Reflection and Discussion

1. Think of someone in your life whom you have great difficulty loving. Ask God to grant you the grace to love this person. Ask those with whom you are gathered to join you in prayer for this intention.

_____

_____

_____

_____

2. The psalm depicts God's love for Israel in terms of military might. Do you believe such a show of strength ever fairly represents love in action, given that love must also be caring and selfless?

_____

_____

_____

_____

Themes

Forgiveness
    Q1, Journey of Faith
    M1, Conversion: A Lifelong Process
Love
    Q10, Catholics and Prayer
    M7, Holiness
Neighbors
    Q12, Catholics and Church
    M4, Family Life

Reading 1, 1 Kings 17:10-16

Elijah set out and went to Zarephath. When he came to the gate of the town, a widow was there gathering sticks; he called to her and said, "Bring me a little water in a vessel, so that I may drink." As she was going to bring it, he called to her and said, "Bring me a morsel of bread in your hand." But she said, "As the Lord your God lives, I have nothing baked, only a handful of meal in a jar, and a little oil in a jug; I am now gathering a couple of sticks, so that I may go home and prepare it for myself and my son, that we may eat it, and die." Elijah said to her, "Do not be afraid; go and do as you have said; but first make me a little cake of it and bring it to me, and afterwards make something for yourself and your son. For thus says the Lord the God of Israel: The jar of meal will not be emptied and the jug of oil will not fail until the day that the Lord sends rain on the earth." She went and did as Elijah said, so that she as well as he and her household ate for many days. The jar of meal was not emptied, neither did the jug of oil fail, according to the word of the Lord that he spoke by Elijah.

Psalm 146:6-7,8-9,9-10

Reading 2, Hebrews 9:24-28

Christ did not enter a sanctuary made by human hands, a mere copy of the true one, but he entered into heaven itself, now to appear in the presence of God on our behalf. Nor was it to offer himself again and again, as the high priest enters the Holy Place year after year with blood that is not his own; for then he would have had to suffer again and again since the foundation of the world. But as it is, he has appeared once for all at the end of the age to remove sin by the sacrifice of himself. And just as it is appointed for mortals to die once, and after that the judgment, so Christ, having been offered once to bear the sins of many, will appear a second time, not to deal with sin, but to save those who are eagerly waiting for him.

Gospel, Mark 12:38-44

As he taught, Jesus said, "Beware of the scribes, who like to walk around in long robes, and to be greeted with respect in the marketplaces, and to have the best seats in the synagogues and places of honor at banquets! They devour widows' houses and for the sake of appearance say long prayers. They will receive the greater condemnation."

He sat down opposite the treasury, and watched the crowd putting money into the treasury. Many rich people put in large sums. A poor widow came and put in two small copper coins, which are worth a penny. Then he

called his disciples and said to them, "Truly I tell you, this poor widow has put in more than all those who are contributing to the treasury. For all of them have contributed out of their abundance; but she out of her poverty has put in everything she had, all she had to live on."

Regarding Strength

JOHN F. CRAGHAN

"The survival of the fittest" is alive and well in our midst. Many of us seem to think that we must develop our strengths by focusing only on our own needs and priorities. We thus conclude that the only genuine weakness is not to promote our strengths and thus survive. As a result, those less fortunate than we do not—indeed cannot—enter our world of concern. By definition, to help the weak is to diminish our strength.

Today's readings are 180 degrees removed from "the survival of the fittest." These passages dwell on those most in need of help and attention. They are not simply objective and emotionless statements about the ills afflicting the less fortunate. They are, rather, a call to action. In the context of today's liturgy they clearly maintain that strength lies in helping the weak.

A Widow's Plight

In the ancient Near East, widows figured among the most dramatic welfare cases. In a male-dominated and male-controlled economy, widows suffered acutely. Their situation was compounded when they had no parental home they could return to, or no children to care for them (see the plight of Naomi in the Book of Ruth). Not infrequently, destitution was the bitter experience of widows.

Elijah was God's spokesperson at a very critical period in the history of the northern kingdom of Israel (ninth-century B.C.). Because of the paganizing tendencies of King Ahab and his Canaanite queen, Jezebel, the prophet predicted a long drought (1 Kgs 17:1). During this drought and subsequent famine, the prophet asks a Sidonian widow—a pagan—for a drink of water and a little cake. Given the acute circumstances, Elijah's request is considerable. The biblical author, however, points out that those who honor the petitions of God's prophets are rewarded. The full jug of oil and jar of flour are testimony to Elijah's compassion and gratitude. In the setting of today's liturgy the passage reveals that strength lies in helping the weak.

Psalm 146 is a hymn of descriptive praise. It depicts God's ongoing role as creator: "...who made heaven and earth, the sea, and all that is in them" (146:6). It is an appeal that reaches to the innermost recesses of the believer: "Praise the Lord, O my soul!....I will praise the Lord as long as I live" (146:1,2). At this point one begins to wonder what motives prompt such praise.

The author diverts attention from such powerful persons as "princes" (146:3). He chooses, instead, to dwell on those who most clearly make a solid case for God's ongoing creation: the oppressed, the hungry, the prisoners, the blind, the bowed down, the strangers (those not enjoying full citizenship in Israel), the orphans, and the widows. The God who continues to care for these kinds of people indeed merits the highest praise. Thus God's strength lies in helping the weak.

A Widow's Mite

In today's gospel passage, Jesus criticizes the scribes (Mk 12:38-40), lay theologians of the day. He calls attention to their pomposity, their penchant for showing off, and their false piety. He also notes that they "devour widows' houses" (verse 40). The avarice of these scribes brings one widow in particular to penury (12:41-44). As Luke makes clearer (see Lk 20:45—21:4), Jesus' message is directed to all the disciples. They are not to exploit the poor, as the scribes have done.

In the larger context of Mark's Gospel, Jesus reaches out to the weak and needy. He associates with the sick, the unclean, the tax collectors, and so forth. Discipleship necessarily becomes a call to service that is solidly based on Jesus' own example. He came not to be served but to serve (see Mk 10:45). Writing against the background of the cross, Mark repeatedly points out that strength lies in helping the weak.

Today's Good News

The list of the weak in Psalm 146 may serve as a point of departure for discovering the needy in our lives. The psalm speaks of the oppressed, the hungry, the prisoners, and so forth. Reflecting on that psalm, we need to inquire into our present-day variety of oppressed, of hungry, of prisoners, and so forth. The minorities, the homeless, the drug and alcohol dependent come to mind. Here the disturbing news is that the God of the psalm will meet the needs of these modern categories only through our efforts. The God "who made heaven and earth" is a God of strength who now defers to us—in our strength—to reach out. Paradoxically, in aiding the weak we become stronger. Indeed we not only survive, we thrive. Strength lies in helping the weak.

Points for Reflection and Discussion

1. A theme of giving goes hand-in-hand with today's stories of strength. The weak widows gave of their sustenance and were given God's own strength. Do you know of people who tithe, and who swear their sustenance never runs out because of it? Do you continue to give only of your excess?

_____

_____

_____

_____

2. In the days of Elijah, widows were lower-class citizens. In the days of Jesus, widows were lower-class citizens. Doesn't it seem ironic, and counter-Christian, to find that widows of today are still lower-class citizens? Is there something you can do to change all that?

_____

_____

_____

_____

Themes

Strength
　　Q7, Mary
　　M6, Discernment
Weakness
　　Q1, Journey of Faith
　　M5, Your Prayer Life
Widowhood
　　Q6, The Saints
　　M4, Family Life

Reading 1, Daniel 12:1-3

At that time Michael, the great prince, the protector of your people, shall arise. There shall be a time of anguish, such as has never occurred since nations first came into existence. But at that time your people shall be delivered, everyone who is found written in the book. Many of those who sleep in the dust of the earth shall awake, some to everlasting life, and some to shame and everlasting contempt. Those who are wise shall shine like the brightness of the sky, and those who lead many to righteousness, like the stars forever and ever.

Psalm 16:5,8,9-10,11

Reading 2, Hebrews 10:11-14,18

Every priest stands day after day at his service, offering again and again the same sacrifices that can never take away sins. But when Christ had offered for all time a single sacrifice for sins, "he sat down at the right hand of God," and since then has been waiting "until his enemies would be made a footstool for his feet." For by a single offering he has perfected for all time those who are sanctified. Where there is forgiveness of these, there is no longer any offering for sin.

Gospel, Mark 13:24-32

Jesus said to his disciples:

In those days, after that suffering, the sun will be darkened, and the moon will not give its light, and the stars will be falling from heaven, and the powers in the heavens will be shaken. Then they will see "the Son of Man coming in clouds" with great power and glory. Then he will send out the angels, and gather his elect from the four winds, from the ends of the earth to the ends of heaven. From the fig tree learn its lesson: as soon as its branch becomes tender and puts forth its leaves, you know that summer is near. So also, when you see these things taking place, you know that he is near, at the very gates. Truly I tell you, this generation will not pass away until all these things have taken place. Heaven and earth will pass away, but my words will not pass away.

But about that day or hour no one knows, neither the angels in heaven, nor the Son, but only the Father.

A God Who Cares

JOHN F. CRAGHAN

People understand their gods in a variety of ways. God may be the divine architect who, having created the world, has let it go off spinning by itself. God may be the celestial administrator who spends each day entering the credits and debits of human progress and failure. God may be the impersonal heavenly CEO who takes no genuine interest in any of us creatures (or employees).

Today's readings provide a totally different picture of God. They reveal a God who is interested in the joys and sorrows of human existence. They speak of a God who, far from being aloof, actually becomes a party to the crises of human life. They tell of a God who makes the problems of humanity God's very own. Our God is a caring God.

A Guardian Angel

This passage from Daniel is part of the book's apocalypse or revelation. Written against the background of the persecution of the Syrian king, Antiochus IV Epiphanes (c. 165 B.C.), this revelation is calculated to offer hope and consolation to the faithful Jewish community. Although the forces of evil seem to have the upper hand at present, in the end the power of good will triumph. This is the heavenly vision that an angel explains to Daniel who, in turn, encourages his beleaguered audience.

In the midst of intense pain and suffering, Michael, Israel's guardian angel, intervenes on behalf of the faithful. These elect, who are written in the book (see Ex 32:32-33), will escape (12:1). Moreover, the dead ("those who sleep") will come back to life; some will have "everlasting life," while others will encounter only "shame and everlasting contempt" (12:2). For the author's community, this is a God who will deliver them, a God who cares.

Psalm 16 is a psalm of confidence. It is clear that the author (David?) has experienced intense pain and frustration, but throughout this ordeal he has clung all the more tenaciously to his God. Though God has appeared all too incomprehensible at times, the psalmist is certain that this God of Israel is deeply concerned with the needs of the people.

God is the psalmist's "portion" and "cup" (see Dt 10:8-9), who has no choice but to provide and protect (16:5). Even in the face of possible death ("Sheol"), the psalmist has no doubt that his God will offer security (16:10). It is the presence of this God (probably limited to this life) that makes existence a celebration (16:11). This is truly a caring God.

Be Watchful!

Mark 13 is often called the "little apocalypse." Like Daniel, chapters 7 through 12, and the Book of Revelation, it focuses on a world of persecution and harassment where the believer is tempted to capitulate (see Mk 13: 9-13). In this farewell speech of Jesus, Mark deals realistically with the problems of his community. He points out two realities. First, Jesus will fulfill the Hebrew texts about the end of time (compare Mk 13:26 with Dn 7:13). Second, the disciples are not to fret about the precise time of the *Parousia* (Jesus' Second Coming, 13:21-23). Only the Father is aware of the precise timetable (13:32).

Jesus expresses the Father's concern for the disciples. Like Daniel's "Son of Man," with unmistakable cosmic signs to herald his arrival, Jesus will return (13:24-26). Then he will exercise his authority as God's ruler. For those who accept him as the Father's envoy there is good news. Jesus will "send out the angels, and gather his elect from the four winds, from the ends of the earth to the ends of heaven" (13:27).

Today's Good News

In the period between Jesus' Ascension and his Second Coming, the tasks of believers are considerable. Disciples of Jesus are called upon to reveal their caring God. The followers who reach out to the homeless, who provide hope for the despairing, who react to violence with nonviolence, who console the dying, and so forth, project a viable image of a concerned and interested God. Otherwise we will have only divine architects, celestial administrators, and impersonal heavenly CEO's. By definition, the God of believers must be a caring God.

Points for Reflection and Discussion

1. Do you find comfort in today's readings, or do they unsettle you? Talk about the implications for your own life in not knowing what will happen, or when.

_____

_____

_____

_____

2. To be watchful means to be involved with (for) others. The more we focus on our own salvation, the further we move from the heritage of our Savior. What can you do right now that will more fully involve you with (for) others?

_____

_____

_____

_____

Themes

Confidence
   Q1, Journey of Faith
   M5, Your Prayer Life
Revelation
   Q10, Catholics and Prayer
   M6, Discernment
Second Coming
   Q2, What Do Catholics Believe?
   M1, Conversion: A Lifelong Process

Reading 1, Daniel 7:13-14

As I watched in the night visions, I saw one like a human being coming with the clouds of heaven. And he came to the Ancient One and was presented before him. To him was given dominion and glory and kingship, that all peoples, nations, and languages should serve him. His dominion is an everlasting dominion that shall not pass away, and his kingship is one that shall never be destroyed.

Psalm 93:1-2,5

Reading 2, Revelation 1:5-8

Jesus Christ [is] the faithful witness, the firstborn of the dead, and the ruler of the kings of the earth. To him who loves us and freed us from our sins by his blood, and made us to be a kingdom, priests serving his God and Father, to him be glory and dominion forever and ever. Amen. Look! He is coming with the clouds; every eye will see him, even those who pierced him; and on his account all the tribes of the earth will wail. So it is to be. Amen.

"I am the Alpha and the Omega," says the Lord God, "who is and who was and who is to come, the Almighty."

Gospel, John 18:33-37

Pilate entered the headquarters again, summoned Jesus, and asked him, "Are you the King of the Jews?" Jesus answered, "Do you ask this on your own, or did others tell you about me?" Pilate replied, "I am not a Jew, am I? Your own nation and the chief priests have handed you over to me. What have you done?"

Jesus answered, "My kingdom is not from this world. If my kingdom were from this world, my followers would be fighting to keep me from being handed over to the Jews. But as it is, my kingdom is not from here." Pilate asked him, "So you are a king?"

Jesus answered, "You say that I am a king. For this I was born, and for this I came into the world, to testify to the truth. Everyone who belongs to the truth listens to my voice."

Christ the King

JOHN F. CRAGHAN

History has taught us that kings and queens always take good care of themselves. But what about service to their people? Here the verdict of history is not so edifying. We know about monarchs who amassed huge fortunes to squander on their pleasures while their subjects went hungry. We are aware of modern leaders who use their political office to enhance their wealth while so many citizens live beneath the poverty level. Royalty and service do not necessarily go hand in hand.

Today's readings introduce us to a different perception of royalty. They see royalty, not as an isolated personal honor, but as an all-embracing communal task. They understand royal office as the obligation to pursue, first and foremost, the common good, not the individual fancies of the incumbent. They regard kingship/queenship as an enterprise in which only those who serve the people are worthy of a crown. Here royalty means service.

One Like a Son of Man

Against the background of the persecution of Antiochus IV Epiphanes (c. 165 B.C.), the author of this passage from Daniel encourages his Jewish audience to remain faithful to their religious convictions. To support them, he introduces the scene of heavenly judgment where God, the Ancient One, projects an image of splendor and awe. According to Daniel 7:17-18 the "one like a human being" is not explicitly identified, although "the holy ones of the Most High shall receive the kingdom" (7:18). It is likely that the "one like a human being" not only represents the persecuted Jews but is also a heavenly power (probably an angel) that supports them.

Given the persecution, the royalty of the faithful Jews is indeed a demanding one. Even in the face of death (see 1 Mc 1:54-63) they are to persevere in their loyalty to the "Ancient One." Although supported by the "one like a human being," they must nevertheless be willing to resist their persecutors. Here royalty means service.

Firstborn of the Dead

The apocalyptic author of Revelation addresses an audience in Asia Minor toward the end of the first Christian century. It is an audience suffering persecution at the hands of the government. Their temptation is to say, "Caesar is Lord," rather than, "Jesus is Lord." To encourage them to persevere in their faith, the author shows that the faithful will eventually be the victors, not the persecutors.

The author implicitly contrasts two kings: Jesus as ruler of the kings of earth, and the pagan king as persecutor. The price of Jesus' royalty is his very life's blood, but his self-giving has made Christians "to be a kingdom, priests serving his God and Father" (1:6). Finally he shows Jesus returning "with the clouds" (1:7; refer back to Dn 7:13). To share in the consolation of their own glorious return, Christians must be willing to imitate the price of Jesus' royalty. Here royalty means service.

King of the Jews

In John 18:28—19:16, kingship and involvement play significant roles. It is clear that Pilate does not wish to get involved in God's Word. He tries to avoid the task of passing judgment and hence vacillates when Jesus questions him about the title of "the King of the Jews." Jesus goes on to state that his kingdom is other-worldly. It is one of truth, concerned with the revelation of God's Word.

In John's Gospel, Jesus goes to his death as a king. The soldiers crown him and mock him (19:2-3) because Pilate has already proclaimed him a king (18:37). "Here is the man!" (19:5) sets up a proclamation of kingship before the assembly. Finally, the crucifixion becomes Jesus' enthronement because his kingship is announced to the international community through a trilingual inscription (19:19-20). In this gospel, royalty means service.

Today's Good News

Baptism makes the believer a royal figure. The question that the follower of Jesus must then raise is: How am I going to exercise my royal prerogatives? Will I oppress my subjects (family, friends, neighbors) by focusing on my own pleasures and fancies? Or will I enhance my subjects by looking to their needs and concerns? Royalty, therefore, is a matter of everyday life. At my job, in my home, in the company of others, I have limitless opportunities to exercise my scepter and crown. Will it be a matter of service or disservice?

Points for Reflection and Discussion

1. How do today's world leaders (presidents, monarchs, bishops, and so forth) represent Christ-like royalty in their dealings with the people they profess to serve? What do you see as your own role in enhancing their service?

_____

_____

_____

_____

2. Have you ever thought of yourself as royalty? Today's readings tell us that we have been made into a kingdom of priests for God. How are you living up to that mandate?

_____

_____

_____

_____

Themes

Christianity
    Q2, What Do Catholics Believe?
    M1, Conversion: A Lifelong Process
Kingship/Queenship
    Q6, The Saints
    M2, The Laity: Called To Build God's Kingdom
Service
    Q12, Catholics and Church
    M3, Your Special Gifts

*Boldface numbers refer to pages
in this book.
Numbers preceded by a letter refer to Handouts:
Q = Inquiry; C = Catechumenate;
L = Lent; M = Mystagogy.*

Example: Anointing...**34-35**, C2, C3, C6. Information on *anointing* may be found in this book on pages 34-35. Further information may be found in the Catechumentate Handouts, numbers 2, 3, and 6.

SUPPLEMENTAL MATERIALS FOR EASTER TRIDUUM AND OCCASIONAL SUNDAYS

These supplemental materials "complete" the total **JOURNEY OF FAITH** program.

Here you will find:

- The *readings* for the *Easter Triduum*
- The *cycle A readings* for the *third, fourth, and fifth Sundays of Lent*
- The *readings* for those occasional *Sundays that supersede ordinary time* readings
- *Scripture commentary* for every set of readings
- *Discussion and/or reflection questions* for every set of readings
- Every set of readings is *cross-referenced to the catechetical handouts*

TABLE OF CONTENTS

Reading 1 (ABC), Gensis 3:9-15,20

The Lord God called to the man, and said to him, "Where are you?" He said, "I heard the sound of you in the garden, and I was afraid, because I was naked; and I hid myself." He said, "Who told you that you were naked? Have you eaten from the tree of which I commanded you not to eat?" The man said, "The woman whom you gave to be with me, she gave me fruit from the tree, and I ate."

Then the Lord God said to the woman, "What is this that you have done?" The woman said, "The serpent tricked me, and I ate." The Lord God said to the serpent, "Because you have done this, cursed are you among all animals and among all wild creatures; upon your belly you shall go, and dust you shall eat all the days of your life. I will put enmity between you and the woman, and between your offspring and hers; he will strike your head, and you will strike his heel."

The man named his wife Eve, because she was the mother of all living.

Psalm 98:1,2-3,3-4 (R verse 2)

Reading 2 (ABC), Ephesians 1:3-6,11-12

Blessed be the God and Father of our Lord Jesus Christ, who has blessed us in Christ with every spiritual blessing in the heavenly places, just as he chose us in Christ before the foundation of the world to be holy and blameless before him in love. He destined us for adoption as his children through Jesus Christ, according to the good pleasure of his will, to the praise of his glorious grace that he freely bestowed on us in the Beloved.

In Christ we have also obtained an inheritance, having been destined according to the purpose of him who accomplishes all things according to his counsel and will, so that we, who were the first to set our hope on Christ, might live for the praise of his glory.

Gospel (ABC), Luke 1:26-38

In the sixth month the angel Gabriel was sent by God to a town in Galilee called Nazareth, to a virgin engaged to a man whose name was Joseph, of the house of David. The virgin's name was Mary. And he came to her and said, "Greetings, favored one! The Lord is with you." But she was much perplexed by his words and pondered what sort of greeting this might be. The angel said to her, "Do not be afraid, Mary, for you have found favor with God. And now, you will conceive in your womb and bear a son, and you will name him Jesus. He will be great, and will be called the Son of the Most High, and the Lord God will give to him the throne of his ancestor David. He will reign over the house of Jacob forever, and of his kingdom there will be no end." Mary said to the angel, "How can this be, since I am a virgin?" The angel said to her, "The Holy Spirit will come upon you, and the power of the Most High will overshadow you; therefore the child to be born will be holy; he will be called Son of God. And now, your relative Elizabeth in her old age has also conceived a son; and this is the sixth month for her who was said to be barren. For nothing will be impossible with God."

Then Mary said, "Here am I, the servant of the Lord; let it be with me according to your word." Then the angel departed from her.

The Mother of All the Living

ELSIE HAINZ MCGRATH

Remember that when "God created humankind in his image…male and female he created them"; God gave them, the male and the female, the richness of the earth and its yield and dominion over all the other living creatures (see Gn 1:27-31). Today the story of the "fall" is presented as the reason why our world is filled with sin and toil and pain and shame. It explains why the good earth does not always yield good food, why folks generally are not fond of reptiles, and even why women are not equal to men. (This strongly suggests that the subordination of women in Israelite society was not intended by God. Note that the serpent and the woman are punished for their sins while the man is simply chastised; the *earth* is punished for the sin of the man!) The conclusion to be reached from this story, of course, is that all the world's imperfections are due to us—human beings—aspiring to be our own god.

Significantly, the man now gives the woman *another* name, Eve, meaning *life*, "but God said, 'You shall not eat of the fruit of the tree that is in the middle of the garden, nor shall you touch it, or you shall *die*' " (3:3). To *live*, as regards eating from the forbidden tree, meant to live *forever*, like God. To *live* as the child of Eve meant merely to live *until you die*, like an earth creature fashioned from dust by the only eternal God. That is the primary theology behind original sin and redemption. If we had not sinned we would not have known death; because we did, we could not live forever until we were saved by a Redeemer.

Children of God

The author of Ephesians reminds us today that we are no longer children of Eve: We are children of God, who has adopted us because of Christ, our Redeemer. Now we are assured of real and eternal *life;* life that we have not earned but that has been earned for us by the sacrifice of Jesus. This is why we bless God, "so that we, who were the first to set our hope on Christ, might live for the praise of his glory."

The gospel gives us the story of the Annunciation: the angel Gabriel announces the impending birth of the Redeemer to his mother, Mary, and she humbly accepts the awesome challenge. This is why Mary is sometimes called "the new Eve." By giving birth to the One who will redeem humankind from death, *she* assumes the role of "mother of all the living." In the same way, Jesus is often referred to as "the new Adam." Through Adam sin and death entered the world, through Jesus salvation and life are restored (see Rom 5:12-16, for example).

The feast we celebrate today is not about sin and death. It is about birth and life: the birth and life of Mary. Specifically, it is about the conception of Mary, believed to be free from the stain of that "original" sin we all inherited in the Garden of Eden because she was predestined to become the Mother of God. As all great truths, this truth is a Mystery, something that cannot be logically and rationally explained but only believed in faith. Also as all great truths, this truth came to be defined as dogma precisely because the Tradition of the Church has believed it for centuries.

Today's gospel tells us that Gabriel addressed Mary not as "Mary" but as "favored one." This name indicates the divine gifts bestowed upon one who has been elected for bearing the Light of the world. "If this election is fundamental for the accomplishment of God's salvific designs for humanity, and if the eternal choice in Christ and the vocation to the dignity of adopted children is the destiny of everyone, then the election of Mary is wholly exceptional and unique. Hence also the singularity and uniqueness of her place in the mystery of Christ." (*Mother of the Redeemer,* Pope John Paul II.)

Today's Good News

Mary's immaculate conception was not what kept her from making bad decisions, any more than our baptisms keep us from sin. We *all* know that baptism, while opening us up to the possibility of salvation, does *not,* in-and-of itself, keep us free from sin! Thus was it Mary's responsibility to choose to be holy and it was wholly *her* choice to take on the responsibility of divine maternity.

Those of us who wish to "be perfect" (Mt 5:48) would do well to emulate Mary. She truly is "one of us" who is yet without sin. She is not so far removed from our world as to be just a plaster statue. Mary lived and loved. She knew pain and fear and heartbreak. She risked divorce from the man she loved, even death from those who thought her guilty of the sin of adultery, when she said those poignant words to Gabriel: "Here am I, the servant of the Lord; let it be with me according to your word." Mary can be our beacon in this world of selfishness and violence and death; she shows us the way to love and service and life.

Points for Reflection and Discussion

1. Say these words to yourself: "Let it be with me *according to your Word." As you say them, think about those things you must immediately change in your life in order to* really *mean them.*

_____

_____

_____

_____

_____

2. How does the society in which we live look at life? How does the contemporary view differ from the view of life we are offered in today's readings?

_____

_____

_____

_____

_____

Themes

Immaculate Conception, Mary
    C9, The People of God
    C10, Who is Jesus Christ?
Life
    C2, The Sacrament of Baptism
    C6, The Sacrament of the Anointing of the Sick
    C15, The Consistent Life Ethic
    C16, The Dignity of Life
Sin
    C5, The Sacrament of Penance

Reading 1 (ABC), Isaiah 9:2-4,6-7

The people who walked in darkness have seen a great light; those who lived in a land of deep darkness—on them light has shined. You have multiplied the nation, you have increased its joy; they rejoice before you as with joy at the harvest, as people exult when dividing plunder. For the yoke of their burden, and the bar across their shoulders, the rod of their oppressor, you have broken as on the day of Midian.

For a child has been born for us, a son given to us; authority rests upon his shoulders; and he is named Wonderful Counselor, Mighty God, Everlasting Father, Prince of Peace. His authority shall grow continually, and there shall be endless peace for the throne of David and his kingdom. He will establish and uphold it with justice and with righteousness from this time onward and forevermore. The zeal of the Lord of hosts will do this.

Psalm 96:1-2,3-4,11-12,13 (*R* Lk 2:11)

Reading 2 (ABC), Titus 2:11-14

The grace of God has appeared, bringing salvation to all, training us to renounce impiety and worldly passions, and in the present age to live lives that are self-controlled, upright, and godly, while we wait for the blessed hope and the manifestation of the glory of our great God and Savior, Jesus Christ. He it is who gave himself for us that he might redeem us from all iniquity and purify for himself a people of his own who are zealous for good deeds.

Gospel (ABC), Luke 2:1-14

In those days a decree went out from Emperor Augustus that all the world should be registered. This was the first registration and was taken while Quirinius was governor of Syria. All went to their own towns to be registered. Joseph also went from the town of Nazareth in Galilee to Judea, to the city of David called Bethlehem, because he was descended from the house and family of David. He went to be registered with Mary, to whom he was engaged and who was expecting a child.

While they were there, the time came for her to deliver her child. And she gave birth to her firstborn son and wrapped him in bands of cloth, and laid him in a manger, because there was no place for them in the inn.

In that region there were shepherds living in the fields, keeping watch over their flock by night. Then an angel of the Lord stood before them, and the glory of the Lord shone around them, and they were terrified. But the angel said to them, "Do not be afraid; for see—I am bringing you good news of great joy for all the people: to you is born this day in the city of David a Savior, who is the Messiah, the Lord. This will be a sign for you: you will find a child wrapped in bands of cloth and lying in a manger." And suddenly there was with the angel a multitude of the heavenly host, praising God and saying, "Glory to God in the highest heaven, and on earth peace among those whom he favors!"

Royal Titles

JOHN F. CRAGHAN

Titled people are committed people. This may strike us as a little odd. In our world we simply assume that people with titles are people with power and prestige. As such, these people expect others to serve them and provide for them. Those serving and providing must be committed to the titled people. To reverse the process is to promote chaos.

The readings we hear tonight fly in the face of our basic assumption. They speak of titled people, i.e., the Davidic king and Jesus, but they also speak of them as committed people. Title-bearers are thus people who take on obligations for others. They are true to their titles only insofar as they are committed to their people.

Wonderful Counselor and Mighty God

Before tonight's reading, Isaiah of Jerusalem spoke of the downfall of the northern kingdom of Israel (see Is 8:22). Only after the gloom and despair of that experience will the Lord raise up an ideal Davidic king who will reunite the tribes of Israel. For the people who walked in darkness, it will indeed be a day of great light and joy comparable to harvest time and the division of spoils after a battle. The yoke symbolizes allegiance to a foreign power, here the neo-Assyrians. The Lord, however, will smash and utterly destroy that yoke after the manner of Gideon's defeat of the Midianites (see Jgs 7:16-25).

Isaiah next describes the ideal Davidic king and his commitment to the people through the use of titles. The king is God's adopted son/child on the day of his coronation (see Ps 2:7). His relationship to the people is captured in throne names or titles like "Everlasting Father" and "Prince of Peace." According to the former, the Davidic king is to lavish paternal love and care on his people. According to the latter, he is to effect peace and prosperity for them. It is, however, only the practice of justice and righteousness that will ensure the well-being of the king's subjects. For Isaiah, titled people are committed people.

God and Savior

In 2:2-10, the author of Titus enumerates the rules for the household, including old men, old and young women, young men, and slaves. In 2:11-14, the author offers a theological basis for the previously-listed duties. This basis is the fact that God has manifested his goodness to all people and calls for a response in the form of a truly Christian life now.

The author uses the title "Savior" for Jesus. While this title was applied to gods, kings, emperors, and so forth in the Greco-Roman world, it takes on very special significance in this letter. Jesus is Savior insofar as he "gave himself for us that he might redeem us...." Jesus' self-giving is epitomized in his suffering and death on behalf of humanity. For the author of Titus, titled people are committed people.

Messiah and Lord

Playing on some Hebrew Testament texts, Luke interprets the significance of Jesus' birth. The manger may refer to Isaiah 1:13. Now, however, Israel recognizes the presence of its Lord who provides for his people. The inn may suggest Jeremiah 14:8, where only the passing traveler spends the night. Now, however, God in Jesus is permanently present to Israel by not lodging in an inn. The bands of cloth may allude to Wisdom 7:4-5, where King Solomon is said to be swaddled. Jesus indeed possesses royal dignity.

While relying upon the titles of the Davidic king in Isaiah 9:6, Luke substitutes his own, which comes from the Christian proclamation of Jesus. Jesus is a "Savior." In the Hebrew Scriptures this title refers to those who deliver God's people, e.g., the judges (see Jgs 3:9,15) and God himself (see Is 45:15,21). Caesar Augustus was known as savior of the whole world, especially in view of the peace he brought to the empire. By linking "Savior" and peace, Luke is suggesting that real peace comes only from Jesus.

Jesus is also "Messiah." From its Jewish roots this title designates Jesus as God's anointed agent who is the bearer of a new form of salvation. Luke, however, is careful to connect Jesus' messiahship with his suffering and death. "Was it not necessary that the Messiah should suffer these things and then enter into his glory?" (Lk 24:26). For Luke, titled people are committed people.

Today's Good News

These authors present us with a formidable challenge. Essentially, they urge us to discover the meaning of titles within the context of community. They impel us to look beyond the status implied by titles and bring to light those people who are to benefit from the title-bearers.

For example, the title "Mr. and Mrs." bespeaks mutual support and concern; the title of the married couple is a call to unflagging service. The title "father and mother" implies dedication to the members of the family; to acknowledge this title is to devote all their energies and talents to the common good. The title "teacher" expresses the giving of oneself to the total formation of those taught; it is the awareness that the success of one's pupils is the goal of the classroom enterprise. The title "employer" articulates the association of oneself with the needs as well as with the talents of others; the title suggests more than the overseer of the means of production—ideally it is a bond uniting owners and workers in a truly human experience of growth. For all such persons, titled people are committed people.

Points for Reflection and Discussion

1. What "titles" do you hold? To what and/or whom do your titles hold you accountable?

_____

_____

_____

_____

2. Imagine a newborn baby, wrest from his mother's womb into the midst of a cold and prickly stable/cave and hearing the sounds of animals competing with the sounds of angels. Listen to this baby's titles resound in your heart while your mind's eye sets the scene. Pray over the wonder of this moment.

_____

_____

_____

_____

Themes

Christmas, Savior
    C4, The Eucharist
    C10, Who is Jesus Christ?
    C16, The Dignity of Life
Commitment
    C3, The Sacrament of Confirmation
    C7, The Sacrament of Marriage
    C8, The Sacrament of Holy Orders
    C9, The People of God
    C13, Christian Moral Living
    C14, Social Justice

Reading 1 (ABC), Numbers 6:22-27

The Lord spoke to Moses, saying: Speak to Aaron and his sons, saying, Thus you shall bless the Israelites: You shall say to them, The Lord bless you and keep you; the Lord make his face to shine upon you, and be gracious to you; the Lord lift up his countenance upon you, and give you peace. So they shall put my name on the Israelites, and I will bless them.

Psalm 67:1-2,4-5,6-7 (R verse 1)

Reading 2, Galatians 4:4-7

When the fullness of time had come, God sent his Son, born of a woman, born under the law, in order to redeem those who were under the law, so that we might receive adoption as children. And because you are children, God has sent the Spirit of his Son into our hearts, crying, "Abba! Father!" So you are no longer a slave but a child, and if a child then also an heir, through God.

Gospel, Luke 2:16-21

[The shepherds] went with haste and found Mary and Joseph, and the child lying in the manger. When they saw this, they made known what had been told them about this child; and all who heard it were amazed at what the shepherds told them. But Mary treasured all these words and pondered them in her heart. The shepherds returned, glorifying and praising God for all they had heard and seen, as it had been told them.

After eight days had passed, it was time to circumcise the child; and he was called Jesus, the name given by the angel before he was conceived in the womb.

Theotokos

ELSIE HAINZ MCGRATH

Mary's oldest and most consistent "title" has been that of *Theotokos* (Mother of God). This is dogma, first defined at the Council of Ephesus in 431 A.D. It helps us to define Jesus as "true God and true man." Mary is called Mother of God not in the sense of having existed *before* God, but as affirmation of the Incarnation. Saint Cyril of Alexandria put it this way: "If we are to confess that Emmanuel is truly God, we must also confess that the Holy Virgin is *Theotokos;* for she bore according to the flesh the Word of God made flesh."

The letter Saint Paul wrote to Galatia (c 48-55) gives an earlier definition of Mary's maternity. That Jesus was "born of a woman" emphasizes the human condition of the baby; it was necessary that Jesus be fully human in order to accomplish the divine mission. That the Son was sent by God so we would be "no longer slaves" emphasizes the divinity of the baby; we could not be freed of the law through merely human intervention.

Proclaimed by Shepherds

Today's gospel celebrates Mary's maternity in still another way. An angel has visited the shepherds who are watching their flocks from the Tower of David that overlooked Bethlehem, and has announced the birth of the Messiah. We pick up the story at the point where the shepherds make their way down the hillside and see the Christ-child for themselves, whereupon they recount the angel's message to Mary and Joseph, praise God, and set about proclaiming his birth to all who would hear them.

Thus it is that the first ones to know about Jesus' birth are the very persons who are most despised of all by "good" Jews. Ordinary shepherds were *anathema* (excommunicated) for their lowly profession. Paradoxically, the shepherds in Bethlehem were of the highly esteemed caste of temple slaves. In fact, Jewish tradition held that the first announcement of the Messiah's coming would be made to shepherds in the Tower of David. These were *special* shepherds. They were in charge of the sheep that *would be sacrificed* in the Temple.

"But Mary treasured all these words and pondered them in her heart." We may or may not presume that she knew of the tradition about the Tower of David, as we wish, but shepherds appearing in her birthing chamber and announcing angels and heavenly hosts had to be unnerving! In her pondering, did she connect the fact that these men were in charge of the sheep that would be sacrificed? Did she wonder why the birth of her God-son was made known to temple slaves instead of temple priests? Did she realize, as she tried to comfort herself and her newborn babe in the cold, dark, smelly confines of a stable-cave, that this miraculous Nativity was destined for life and death among the *anawim* (the lowly ones of God)?

Today's Good News

It is fitting that the solemnity of the Mother of God is celebrated on the same day as the "World Day of Peace" because it has always been Mary who has inspired people to work for peace in the world. Witness the well-established devotions to Mary, and the numerous Marian apparitions calling for prayers for peace. Pope Paul VI first instituted the "World Day of Peace" on this day because the "Solemnity of Mary...is meant to commemorate the part played by Mary in this mystery of salvation...to exalt the singular dignity which this mystery brings to the holy Mother...for imploring to God, through the Queen of Peace, the supreme gift of peace." (*Devotion to the Blessed Virgin Mary*, Pope Paul VI.)

The Second Vatican Council further explicated the place of Mary in our world by stressing the "title" of Mother of the Church. Here the emphasis is on Mary's spiritual motherhood, scripturally established at Calvary when Jesus symbolically "gave" Mary over to all of us by telling the beloved disciple, "Here is your mother" (Jn 19:26-27). Because Mary is believed to be pure and holy, the perfect disciple who was assumed into heaven to be with God and watch over us, she is the fulfillment of the Church (the Body of Christ...the people of God...you and me). She is the person we need to emulate. Hers are the virtues we need to acquire. When we have accomplished her perfection, we too will have reached our fulfillment.

Points for Reflection and Discussion

1. Today's first reading gives us an ancient priestly blessing. Read it now, and reflect on it reverently. What is it saying to you?

_____

_____

_____

_____

2. Mary is believed to have been twelve or fourteen years old when Jesus was born. Imagine yourself in her situation (or in Joseph's)—giving birth to a baby in the middle of an alien land without even the comfort of a warm room and a bed, much less a physician or midwife. Talk about the experience.

_____

_____

_____

_____

Themes

Mary
   C9, The People of God
   C10, Who is Jesus Christ?
Parenthood
   C7, The Sacrament of Marriage
   C16, The Dignity of Life
Shepherd
   C8, The Sacrament of Holy Orders
   C14, Social Justice

Reading 1 (ABC), Malachi 3:1-4

The Lord God said: See, I am sending my messenger to prepare the way before me, and the Lord whom you seek will suddenly come to his temple. The messenger of the covenant in whom you delight—indeed, he is coming, says the Lord of hosts. But who can endure the day of his coming, and who can stand when he appears? For he is like a refiner's fire and like fullers' soap; he will sit as a refiner and purifier of silver, and he will purify the descendants of Levi and refine them like gold and silver, until they present offerings to the Lord in righteousness. Then the offering of Judah and Jerusalem will be pleasing to the Lord as in the days of old and as in former years.

Psalm 24:7,8,9,10 (*R verse 10*)

Reading 2 (ABC), Hebrews 2:14-18

Since…the children [of God] share flesh and blood, [Jesus] likewise shared the same things, so that through death he might destroy the one who has the power of death, that is, the devil, and free those who all their lives were held in slavery by the fear of death. For it is clear that he did not come to help angels, but the descendants of Abraham. Therefore he had to become like his brothers and sisters in every respect, so that he might be a merciful and faithful high priest in the service of God, to make a sacrifice of atonement for the sins of the people. Because he himself was tested by what he suffered, he is able to help those who are being tested.

Gospel (ABC), Luke 2:22-40

When the time came for their purification according to the law of Moses, [Mary and Joseph] brought [Jesus] up to Jerusalem to present him to the Lord (as it is written in the law of the Lord, "Every firstborn male shall be designated as holy to the Lord"), and they offered a sacrifice according to what is stated in the law of the Lord, "a pair of turtledoves or two young pigeons."

Now there was a man in Jerusalem whose name was Simeon; this man was righteous and devout, looking forward to the consolation of Israel, and the Holy Spirit rested on him. It had been revealed to him by the Holy Spirit that he would not see death before he had seen the Lord's Messiah. Guided by the Spirit, Simeon came into the temple; and when the parents brought in the child Jesus, to do for him what was customary under the law, Simeon took him in his arms and praised God, saying, "Master, now you are dismissing your servant in peace, according to your word; for my eyes have seen your salvation, which you have prepared in the presence of all peoples, a light for revelation to the Gentiles and for glory to your people Israel."

And the child's father and mother were amazed at what was being said about him. Then Simeon blessed them and said to his mother Mary, "This child is destined for the falling and the rising of many in Israel, and to be a sign that will be opposed so that the inner thoughts of many will be revealed—and a sword will pierce your own soul too."

There was also a prophet, Anna the daughter of Phanuel, of the tribe of Asher. She was of a great age, having lived with her husband seven years after her marriage, then as a widow to the age of eighty-four. She never left the temple but worshiped there with fasting and prayer night and day. At that moment she came, and began to praise God and to speak about the child to all who were looking for the redemption of Jerusalem.

When they had finished everything required by the law of the Lord, they returned to Galilee, to their own town of Nazareth. The child grew and became strong, filled with wisdom; and the favor of God was upon him.

Being Purified, Being Presented

ELSIE HAINZ MCGRATH

Today's gospel combines two rituals into one story. The first is the purification. "When the time came for *their* purification" is not a fully accurate statement. The law of Moses held that the *woman* who had delivered a child be "purified" in a Temple rite after the birth. This rite required a sacrifice. If the family was rich, the sacrifice was a lamb; if poor, two turtledoves were accepted (see Lv 12:1-8).

The presentation is another ritual, *bekor* in Hebrew. Only the firstborn son of a mother whose husband was not a priest (of the tribe of Levi) was presented. This presentation of the firstborn son was originally a human sacrifice (see Ex 13:1-2). Human sacrifice was not wholly discontinued until after the time of King David.

In today's account, Anna is the female counterpart to Simeon. Luke consistently gives us stories that illustrate men and women are equal and treated equally by Jesus. A "prophet," Anna was an equivalent of today's Sisters. She took vows of poverty and chastity, participated in daily prayer, and was committed to apostolic action.

A Sword to the Soul

Pope John Paul II says this about Simeon's words to Mary: They "seem like a second Annunciation, for they tell her of the actual historical situation in which the Son is to accomplish his mission, namely, in misunderstanding and sorrow. While this announcement on the one hand confirms her faith in the accomplishment of the divine promises of salvation, on the other hand it also reveals to her that she will have to live her obedience of faith in suffering, at the side of the suffering Savior, and that her motherhood will be mysterious and sorrowful" *(Mother of the Redeemer).*

The conclusion of Luke's account of these happenings is mysterious indeed. "When they had finished everything required by the law of the Lord, they returned to Galilee, to their own town of Nazareth. The child grew and became strong, filled with wisdom; and the favor of God was upon him." In short, there isn't much more to tell until Jesus begins his public ministry. There is the incident in the Temple when he is twelve, but for the most part his formative years are "hidden." These years of Mary's life are "hidden" too. Surely we may safely conjecture that as Jesus "grew and became strong," so did his mother.

The Messenger of the Covenant

"The Lord whom you seek will suddenly come into his temple," says Malachi in today's first reading. It is as if he is speaking directly to Simeon, who is "looking forward to the consolation of Israel." This "consolation" would be the comforter, the Messiah. Simeon was a minor judge who wanted to be freed from the disgrace and drudgery of his state in life. Considered a failure by his father, Simeon could not even use his full identifying name. Disconnected from his family heritage, he was in a very real sense under the yoke of the slavery of death and sin ("dismiss your servant in peace"). And suddenly the Lord was there, in the Temple, just as Malachi had promised.

Malachi means *messenger,* and his message today does appear to announce the coming of the Messiah in much the same way as John the Baptist announces him as an adult (see Jn 1:6-9). Very little is known about Malachi, not even when the book was written. It is a prophetic book and as such it gives its readers hope, but the hope offered seems to be more elusive and distant—maybe as distant as the birth of the Messiah.

Today's Good News

The Letter to the Hebrews reminds those of us who tend to get mired down in day-to-day problems and the catastrophic events of contemporary society that there is Light at the end of the tunnel. We need no longer be slaves to fear because our High Priest is both faithful and merciful. Our temptations to turn away from God are not abhorrent to our Lord because he was tempted in every way we are (see Lk 4:1-13; Mt 4:1-11; Mk 1:12-13); he was *one of us.* Death, whether death of body or soul or spirit, has been defeated by the One who humbled himself to be born into the degradation of human nature.

Mary's example for us, displayed once again in today's readings, is one of faithfulness and steadfastness. She kept all the laws of her Jewish faith, fulfilling the rituals demanded of herself and her son. She wondered at the prophecies she heard from Simeon and Anna, and went home to reverently ponder the meaning of it all. And she quietly and faithfully assumed the roles of wife and mother that she had committed herself to.

Points for Reflection and Discussion

1. Mary's example is one of fidelity to her commitments, no matter how difficult keeping them might be. Think about a commitment you have been faithful to despite temptations to break it. Has keeping that commitment strengthened you in any way(s)? If you're comfortable doing so, talk about that commitment and its effect on your life.

_____

_____

_____

_____

_____

2. How much do you think Mary understood about who Jesus was when she and Joseph presented him at the Temple?

_____

_____

_____

_____

Themes

Incarnation
    C1, The Sacraments: An Introduction
    C2, The Sacrament of Baptism
    C4, The Eucharist
    C10, Who is Jesus Christ?
Mary
    C7, The Sacrament of Marriage
Prophecy
    C3, The Sacrament of Confirmation

Reading 1 (ABC), 2 Samuel 7:4-5,12-14,16

The word of the Lord came to Nathan: Go and tell my servant David: "When your days are fulfilled and you lie down with your ancestors, I will raise up your offspring after you, who shall come forth from your body, and I will establish his kingdom. He shall build a house for my name, and I will establish the throne of his kingdom forever. I will be a father to him, and he shall be a son to me. Your house and your kingdom shall be made sure forever before me; your throne shall be established forever."

Psalm 89:1-2,3-4,26,28 (R verse 36)

Reading 2 (ABC), Romans 4:13,16-18,22

The promise that he would inherit the world did not come to Abraham or to his descendants through the law but through the righteousness of faith. For this reason it depends on faith, in order that the promise may rest on grace and be guaranteed to all his descendants, not only to the adherents of the law but also to those who share the faith of Abraham (for he is the father of all of us, as it is written, "I have made you the father of many nations")— in the presence of the God in whom he believed, who gives life to the dead and calls into existence the things that do not exist. Hoping against hope, he believed that he would become "the father of many nations," according to what was said, "So numerous shall your descendants be." Therefore his faith "was reckoned to him as righteousness."

Gospel (ABC), Matthew 1:16,18-21,24*

Jacob [was] the father of Joseph the husband of Mary, of whom Jesus was born, who is called the Messiah. Now the birth of Jesus the Messiah took place in this way. When his mother Mary had been engaged to Joseph, but before they lived together, she was found to be with child from the Holy Spirit. Her husband Joseph, being a righteous man and unwilling to expose her to public disgrace, planned to dismiss her quietly. But just when he had resolved to do this, an angel of the Lord appeared to him in a dream and said, "Joseph, son of David, do not be afraid to take Mary as your wife, for the child conceived in her is from the Holy Spirit. She will bear a son, and you are to name him Jesus, for he will save his people from their sins." When Joseph awoke from sleep, he did as the angel of the Lord commanded him; he took [Mary] as his wife.

*(or) Luke 2:41-51

Every year [Jesus'] parents went to Jerusalem for the festival of the Passover. And when he was twelve years old, they went up as usual for the festival. When the festival was ended and they started to return, the boy Jesus stayed behind in Jerusalem, but his parents did not know it. Assuming that he was in the group of travelers, they went a day's journey. Then they started to look for him among their relatives and friends.

When they did not find him, they returned to Jerusalem to search for him. After three days they found him in the temple, sitting among the teachers, listening to them and asking them questions. And all who heard him were amazed at his understanding and his answers.

When his parents saw him they were astonished; and his mother said to him, "Child, why have you treated us like this? Look, your father and I have been searching for you in great anxiety." He said to them, "Why were you searching for me? Did you not know that I must be in my Father's house?" But they did not understand what he said to them.

Then he went down with them and came to Nazareth, and was obedient to them.

Investing in the Future

JOHN F. CRAGHAN

Faith means the family's future. In the act of believing, we root ourselves in God but often hesitate to root ourselves in the lives of others. In the act of believing, we open ourselves up to God's person but are often reluctant to open ourselves up to other persons and their concerns. In the act of believing, we strengthen ourselves by leaning upon God but are often loath to strengthen ourselves by having others lean upon us. Faith directs us beyond the person of our God. By involving us in our God, faith also involves us in our God's world of problems.

Today's readings touch upon the faith of the Davidic king, of Abraham, and of Joseph. Their faith, however, is not limited to the world of purely personal concerns; rather, it is necessarily bound up with the good of their community. Faith means the family's future.

Faith and Family

Psalm 89 is probably a lament of the community (verses 38-51) that includes praise of Israel's God (verses 1-18) and the oracle to the Davidic dynasty assuring its kings of God's perpetual care and protection (verses 19-37). The psalm opens with the accent on God's favors in the past. In verses 3-4 there is the clear statement of God's unconditional promise to David and his line. As a father to the Davidic king (see Ps 2:7), this God is indeed "the Rock of my salvation!" (verse 26).

Beginning in verse 38, the psalm seems to question God's promise, e.g., "Lord, where is your steadfast love of old...?" (verse 49). Faced with some political crisis, the king and the community challenge their God to act on their behalf and resolve the problem. It is the faith of both the king and the community that makes such a demand possible. In this impasse, faith in the God of Israel means the family's future.

Father of Nations

In the passage from Romans, Paul illustrates the meaning of righteousness by discussing the faith of Abraham. Paul points out that the promise of inheritance depends on the righteousness of faith, not the Mosaic law. For Paul, to live by faith is to live by grace. Abraham's faith is not a purely private enterprise, however—it has impact on all, both Jews and Gentiles.

For Paul, Abraham's life means total dedication to God that, in turn, has impact on the community. Hence others will be the beneficiaries: "I have made you the father of many nations." Although his wife was barren and advanced in years, Abraham continued to believe on behalf of others: "'Look toward heaven and count the stars, if you are able to count them.' Then he said to him, 'So shall your descendants be'" (Gn 15:5). Clearly, Abraham's faith means the family's future.

Husband of Mary

Matthew concludes his genealogy (1:16) by registering Joseph as the son of Jacob. In this very same verse, however, he also observes that Jesus, the Messiah, is born of Mary, not Joseph. What follows in verses 18-25 is an expanded footnote that is intended to explain the irregularity of the genealogy. If Jesus does not have a human father, then how is it possible to call him "son of David" (1:1)? Matthew responds to the difficulty by noting that Joseph, although perplexed, was willing to accept legal paternity of Jesus because of the angel's revelation. Fittingly, Joseph is addressed in verse 20 as "son of David."

For Matthew, Joseph is a great example of faith ("righteous man"). He believes the angel's message that explains Mary's conception, namely, through the Holy Spirit. He also accepts the mission to act on behalf of Mary and the child. Matthew summarizes Joseph's faith by remarking: "He did as the angel of the Lord commanded him..." For Matthew, Joseph's faith means the family's future.

Today's Good News

These readings ought to challenge us to rethink our notion of faith. They urge us to move away from a purely one-on-one relationship with our God to a community-oriented relationship. In saying "we believe in God," we implicitly include the world of our community. Faith in this God is necessarily linked to this God's community—everyone.

For example, parents who devote themselves to the total education of their family demonstrate their faith. Educators who seek to form the whole person in view of society's needs prove their faith. The sick and the dying who see their condition as the opportunity to encourage others show their faith. Leaders in both civil and church society who view their position as the chance to improve the condition of others indicate their faith. All such people link their faith in God to the needs of others. For them faith clearly means the family's future.

Points for Reflection and Discussion

1. Today's readings emphasize the part faith has consistently played in the preservation of the Family of God. What part has faith played in the preservation of your biological family?

_____

_____

_____

_____

2. Society claims that faith is a private matter, something strictly between an individual and God. Scripture disputes that claim. Imagine what the world would be like if everyone followed the dictates of society. Imagine what the world would be like if everyone followed the dictates of Scripture. Discuss the differences.

_____

_____

_____

_____

Themes

Faith
  L2, Saying Yes to Jesus
  L4, The Nicene Creed
Family
  L7, The Meaning of Holy Week
  L8, Catechumenate Retreat Day
Future
  L3, Take a Look
  L5, The Way of the Cross

Reading 1 (ABC), Isaiah 7:10-14

The Lord spoke to Ahaz, saying, "Ask a sign of the Lord your God; let it be deep as Sheol or high as heaven." But Ahaz said, "I will not ask, and I will not put the Lord to the test."

Then Isaiah said: "Hear then, O house of David! Is it too little for you to weary mortals, that you weary my God also? Therefore the Lord himself will give you a sign. Look, the young woman is with child and shall bear a son, and shall name him Immanuel."

Psalm 40:6,7-8,9,10 (*R* verses 7-8)

Reading 2 (ABC), Hebrews 10:4-10

It is impossible for the blood of bulls and goats to take away sins. Consequently, when Christ came into the world, he said, "Sacrifices and offerings you have not desired, but a body you have prepared for me; in burnt offerings and sin offerings you have taken no pleasure. Then I said, 'See, God, I have come to do your will, O God' (in the scroll of the book it is written of me)."

When he said above, "You have neither desired nor taken pleasure in sacrifices and offerings and burnt offerings and sin offerings" (these are offered according to the law), then he added, "See, I have come to do your will." He abolishes the first in order to establish the second.

And it is by God's will that we have been sanctified through the offering of the body of Jesus Christ once for all.

Gospel (ABC), Luke 1:26-38

In the sixth month the angel Gabriel was sent by God to a town in Galilee called Nazareth, to a virgin engaged to a man whose name was Joseph, of the house of David. The virgin's name was Mary. And he came to her and said, "Greetings, favored one! The Lord is with you." But she was much perplexed by his words and pondered what sort of greeting this might be. The angel said to her, "Do not be afraid, Mary, for you have found favor with God. And now, you will conceive in your womb and bear a son, and you will name him Jesus. He will be great, and will be called the Son of the Most High, and the Lord God will give to him the throne of his ancestor David. He will reign over the house of Jacob forever, and of his kingdom there will be no end."

Mary said to the angel, "How can this be, since I am a virgin?" The angel said to her, "The Holy Spirit will come upon you, and the power of the Most High will overshadow you; therefore the child to be born will be holy; he will be called Son of God. And now, your relative Elizabeth in her old age has also conceived a son; and this is the sixth month for her who was said to be barren. For nothing will be impossible with God."

Then Mary said, "Here am I, the servant of the Lord; let it be with me according to your word." Then the angel departed from her.

God's Signposts

ELSIE HAINZ MCGRATH

Today's first reading has the prophet Isaiah wanting King Ahaz to ask God for a "sign" that the kingdom will be saved, but Ahaz refuses. He has already decided to allow Judah to become a vassal to Assyria, a means of saving himself from being deposed by the nations of Syria and Israel; his refusal to "test" the Lord is more probably a refusal to change his own mind.

The sign is given despite Ahaz's stubbornness: A woman is to bear a son named Immanuel, "for God is with us." The "young woman," often incorrectly translated as "virgin," is probably the wife of Ahaz. The child will consequently preserve the house of David from being overthrown.

Centuries later, the angel Gabriel greets Mary with the words, "The Lord is with you." Mary, a virgin, is to bear a son, "the Son of the Most High…(who)…will reign over the house of Jacob forever." Gabriel *volunteers* a sign, so that Mary may believe "nothing will be impossible with God"; her sign is to find her cousin to be also with child, even though beyond childbearing years.

Preserving the House of David

God is with the house of David, and the kingdom is preserved through new life. The annunciation to Mary differed from the annunciations to Ahaz (father of Hezekiah) and to Zechariah (father of John the Baptist) in significant ways, however. First, it was Mary herself—the mother, *not* the father—who received both the prophecy and the sign. And it was Mary's openness to God's promise of intimacy that made her pregnancy possible. The Annunciation, in fact, has little to do with motherhood and much to do with discipleship: Mary is the one who listens attentively, hears God's Word, and acts on it—precisely the means by which one comes to be called a disciple according to Jesus himself (see, for example, Lk 8:15,21;11:27-28; Acts 1:14).

The pivotal moment of Christian history was Mary's *fiat* to the angelic announcement. Her YES is our paradigm for all ages, which is why "all ages shall call me blessed." It was not *just* important to God that Mary say YES; it was *absolutely necessary* because redemption establishes a relationship between God and humanity that must be sealed at both ends by a free and personal decision. So it is that the celebration of the Annunciation is a "joint" celebration; we honor not only Mary's YES but God's initiative.

Today's Good News

Signs are given to us too, so we can recognize God's initiative in *our* lives, especially signs of new life. Remember when you or someone close to you was first discovered to be with a wanted child? Recall the joy, the wonder of the moment, of knowing that new life was beginning. With the joy and the wonder, though, there is usually a touch of fear, especially with the first child; even a questioning of how this can be happening. (Imagine how Mary must have felt!) And then the interminable waiting begins, always with at least a little discomfort and anxiety. The body grows heavy and awkward and tires too quickly. The joy of the announcement is forgotten and the experience of carrying this new life takes on an aura of death. But finally the baby emerges and fulfills the promise of that long-ago announcement. (Again, imagine how Mary must have felt!)

Signs of new life do not only come with announcements of pregnancy and births of babies, of course. How often do we reflect on the human cycle of death and life, for example. A grandparent dies, a baby is born. Is the *visible* new life (the baby) the *only* new life? Isn't the grandparent also experiencing new life—with God? Don't we often *feel* the presence of that grandparent, talk to him or her, experience consolation? Are not these experiences "signs" of life?

New life is most apparent through the change of the seasons. We *know* that the dead of winter is going to give way to the resurrection of spring—from gray and white to shades of pastel. We *know* that the resurrection of spring is going to give way to the fullness of lush green summer life. We *know* that the fullness of life is going to give way to the autumn of life—displayed in the glorious and multi-colored hues that richly epitomize the dignity and diversity of the wholly-mature. And we *know* that the autumn of life is going to give way to the dead of winter. The cycle repeats itself, year after year, generation after generation. Death continually gives way to life because death has no hold on us who believe in the Resurrection.

Points for Reflection and Discussion

1. Saint Paul tells us today that redemption can only come through a person. The burnt offerings of the past do not please God. A living person, one who listens to the Word and does the will of God, pleases God. That is why Mary is often referred to as co-redeemer. Without her humble cooperation there could not have been an Incarnation; without the Incarnation there could not have been the perfect sacrifice on Calvary; without Calvary there would be no Resurrection and no redemption. Reflect on this magnificent Mystery during the coming week.

_____

_____

_____

_____

_____

2. Write a letter to Mary and share it with the community.

_____

_____

_____

_____

_____

Themes

Annunciation, Discipleship, Mary
    L2, Saying Yes to Jesus
Redemption
    L1, What is Lent?
    L3, Take a Look
    L5, The Way of the Cross
    L7, The Meaning of Holy Week

Reading 1, Exodus 17:3-7

The people thirsted [in the wilderness] for water; and the people complained against Moses and said, "Why did you bring us out of Egypt, to kill us and our children and livestock with thirst?" So Moses cried out to the Lord, "What shall I do with this people? They are almost ready to stone me."

The Lord said to Moses, "Go on ahead of the people, and take some of the elders of Israel with you; take in your hand the staff with which you struck the Nile, and go. I will be standing there in front of you on the rock at Horeb. Strike the rock, and water will come out of it, so that the people may drink." Moses did so, in the sight of the elders of Israel.

He called the place Massah and Meribah, because the Israelites quarreled and tested the Lord, saying, "Is the Lord among us or not?"

Psalm 95:1-2,6-7,7-9 (R verses 7c, 8a)

Reading 2, Romans 5:1-2,5-8

Since we are justified by faith, we have peace with God through our Lord Jesus Christ, through whom we have obtained access to this grace in which we stand; and we boast in our hope of sharing the glory of God.

And hope does not disappoint us, because God's love has been poured into our hearts through the Holy Spirit that has been given to us. For while we were still weak, at the right time Christ died for the ungodly. Indeed, rarely will anyone die for a righteous person—though perhaps for a good person someone might actually dare to die. But God proves his love for us in that while we still were sinners Christ died for us.

Gospel, John 4:5-42

[Jesus] came to a Samaritan city called Sychar, near the plot of ground that Jacob had given to his son Joseph. Jacob's well was there, and Jesus, tired out by his journey, was sitting by the well. It was about noon.

A Samaritan woman came to draw water, and Jesus said to her, "Give me a drink." (His disciples had gone to the city to buy food.) The Samaritan woman said to him, "How is it that you, a Jew, ask a drink of me, a woman of Samaria?" (Jews do not share things in common with Samaritans.) Jesus answered her, "If you knew the gift of God, and who it is that is saying to you, 'Give me a drink,' you would have asked him, and he would have given you living water." The woman said to him, "Sir, you have no bucket, and the well is deep. Where do you get that living water? Are you greater than our ancestor Jacob, who gave us the well, and with his sons and his flocks drank from it?" Jesus said to her, "Everyone who drinks of this water will be thirsty again, but those who drink of the water that I will give them will never be thirsty. The water that I will give will become in them a spring of water gushing up to eternal life." The woman said to him, "Sir, give me this water, so that I may never be thirsty or have to keep coming here to draw water."

Jesus said to her, "Go, call your husband, and come back." The woman answered him, "I have no husband." Jesus said to her, "You are right in saying, 'I have no husband'; for you have had five husbands, and the one you have now is not your husband. What you have said is true!"

The woman said to him, "Sir, I see that you are a prophet. Our ancestors worshiped on this mountain, but you say that the place where people must worship is in Jerusalem." Jesus said to her, "Woman, believe me, the hour is coming when you will worship the Father neither on this mountain nor in Jerusalem. You worship what you do not know; we worship what we know, for salvation is from the Jews. But the hour is coming, and is now here, when the true worshipers will worship the Father in spirit and truth, for the Father seeks such as these to worship him. God is spirit, and those who worship him must worship in spirit and truth."

The woman said to him, "I know that Messiah is coming" (who is called Christ). "When he comes, he will proclaim all things to us." Jesus said to her, "I am he, the one who is speaking to you."

Just then his disciples came. They were astonished that he was speaking with a woman, but no one said, "What do you want?" or, "Why are you speaking with her?" Then the woman left her water jar and went back to the city. She said to the people, "Come and see a man who told me everything I have ever done! He cannot be the Messiah, can he?" They left the city and were on their way to him.

Meanwhile the disciples were urging him, "Rabbi, eat something." But he said to them, "I have food to eat that you do not know about." So the disciples said to one another, "Surely no one has brought him something to eat?" Jesus said to them, "My food is to do the will of him who sent me and to complete his work. Do you not say, 'Four months more, then comes the harvest'? But I tell you, look around you, and see how the fields are ripe for harvesting. The reaper is already receiving wages and is gathering fruit for eternal life, so that sower and reaper may rejoice together. For here the saying holds true, 'One sows and another reaps.' I sent you to reap that for which you did not labor. Others have labored, and you have entered into their labor."

Many Samaritans from that city believed in him because of the woman's testimony, "He told me everything I have ever done." So when the Samaritans came to him, they asked him to stay with them; and he stayed there two days. And many more believed because of his word. They said to the woman, "It is no longer because of what you said that we believe, for we have heard for ourselves, and we know that this is truly the Savior of the world."

Wellsprings

JOHN F. CRAGHAN

Love is its own reward. We live in a world of progress reports, work evaluations, and periodic reassessments. We hope to get a higher wage and/or a better position because of our improved output or more efficient management. We thereby assume that better performance means a better reward. In our *quid pro quo* atmosphere it is hard to believe love can be its own reward.

Today's readings treat the graciousness of our God, a graciousness not prompted by our work ethic or motivated by our compelling desire to succeed. It is a graciousness that is only explicable on the basis of our God's capacity to love for the sake of loving.

A second level in the narrative of Massah and Meribah is Israel's dispute with Yahweh over the question of the Exodus from Egypt. On this level the people's thirst serves as the occasion for attacking the very purpose of the Exodus: "Why did you bring us out of Egypt?" On this level, Israel rejects God's whole plan of salvation.

The primary tradition concentrates on Yahweh's graciousness for the people. In the primary tradition, the people merely quarrel with Moses and constrain him to meet their demands. Moses' cry to the Lord results in a positive and prompt reply. There is no threat of punishment for the people. God meets their needs because it is the nature of God to do so.

Love is Its Own Reward

In his Letter to the Romans, Paul observes that the state of being right with God brings about unshakable peace. Through Christ Jesus, the Christian has access to God's presence. Despite the ups and downs of life, the Christian has a hope rooted in God's Spirit. The gift of the Spirit is the assurance of God's love.

Paul insists that Christ freely chose to die for godless humans. The self-giving of Christ seems so incomprehensible, his death is the great proof of God's love.

John demonstrates in today's gospel the truth that the sending of the Son is grounded in God's love for the world (see Jn 3:16). It is only this love that can adequately explain the happenings in this episode.

Jesus brings living water, that is, God's revelation, to the Samaritans—renegade or at least second-class Jews. It is significant that Jesus chooses to talk not only with a Samaritan but with a Samaritan woman—this is indeed a reversal of acceptable practice in first-century Judaism in Palestine. The outcome is that the woman brings the message of Jesus to her people, who end up by accepting Jesus as the Savior of the world. John sees this as the fulfillment of Jesus' mission: "God did not send the Son into the world to condemn the world, but in order that the world might be saved through him" (Jn 3:17).

Today's Good News

We are directed to reach out to our family, to assist our friends, to love and work with all peoples not simply because we will be amply compensated but because it is the nature of our God to love with no strings attached. Hence to accept God is to accept God's worldview. Our family, our friends, and our business associates are worthy of gratuitous love because the essence of our God is to look to the welfare of others. In our pragmatic world, the upsetting message is that love is its own reward.

Points for Reflection and Discussion

1. Try to imagine loving some one as unconditionally as God loves every one. How would your life change?

_____

_____

_____

_____

2. The water of life is imaged throughout today's readings. Who has been a source of life-giving water for you?

_____

_____

_____

_____

Themes
Hope
   L1, What is Lent?
Love
   L2, Saying Yes to Jesus
Water
   L3, Take a Look

Reading 1, 1 Samuel 16:1,6-7,10-13

The Lord said to Samuel, "Fill your horn with oil and set out; I will send you to Jesse the Bethlehemite, for I have provided for myself a king among his sons."

When [the sons of Jesse] came, [Samuel] looked on Eliab and thought, "Surely the Lord's anointed is now before the Lord." But the Lord said to Samuel, "Do not look on his appearance or on the height of his stature, because I have rejected him; for the Lord does not see as mortals see; they look on the outward appearance, but the Lord looks on the heart."

Jesse made seven of his sons pass before Samuel, and Samuel said to Jesse, "The Lord has not chosen any of these." Samuel said to Jesse, "Are all your sons here?" And he said, "There remains yet the youngest, but he is keeping the sheep." And Samuel said to Jesse, "Send and bring him; for we will not sit down until he comes here." He sent and brought him in. Now he was ruddy, and had beautiful eyes, and was handsome. The Lord said, "Rise and anoint him; for this is the one."

Then Samuel took the horn of oil, and anointed him in the presence of his brothers; and the spirit of the Lord came mightily upon David from that day forward.

Psalm 23:1-3,3-4,5,6 (R verse 1)

Reading 2, Ephesians 5:8-14

Once you were darkness, but now in the Lord you are light. Live as children of light—for the fruit of the light is found in all that is good and right and true.

Try to find out what is pleasing to the Lord. Take no part in the unfruitful works of darkness, but instead expose them. For it is shameful even to mention what such people do secretly; but everything exposed by the light becomes visible, for everything that becomes visible is light. Therefore it says, "Sleeper, awake! Rise from the dead, and Christ will shine on you."

Gospel, John 9:1-41

As [Jesus] walked along, he saw a man blind from birth. His disciples asked him, "Rabbi, who sinned, this man or his parents, that he was born blind?" Jesus answered, "Neither this man nor his parents sinned; he was born blind so that God's works might be revealed in him. We must work the works of him who sent me while it is day; night is coming when no one can work. As long as I am in the world, I am the light of the world." When he had said this, he spat on the ground and made mud with the saliva and spread the mud on the man's eyes, saying to him, "Go, wash in the pool of Siloam" (which means Sent). Then he went and washed and came back able to see.

The neighbors and those who had seen him before as a beggar began to ask, "Is this not the man who used to sit and beg?" Some were saying, "It is he." Others were saying, "No, but it is someone like him." He kept saying, "I am the man." But they kept asking him, "Then how were your eyes opened?" He answered, "The man called Jesus made mud, spread it on my eyes, and said to me, 'Go to Siloam and wash.' Then I went and washed and received my sight." They said to him, "Where is he?" He said, "I do not know."

They brought to the Pharisees the man who had formerly been blind. Now it was a sabbath day when Jesus made the mud and opened his eyes. Then the Pharisees also began to ask him how he had received his sight. He said to them, "He put mud on my eyes. Then I washed, and now I see." Some of the Pharisees said, "This man is not from God, for he does not observe the sabbath." But others said, "How can a man who is a sinner perform such signs?" And they were divided. So they said again to the blind man, "What do you say about him? It was your eyes he opened." He said, "He is a prophet."

The Jews did not believe that he had been blind and had received his sight until they called the parents of the man who had received his sight and asked them, "Is this your son, who you say was born blind? How then does he now see?" His parents answered, "We know that this is our son, and that he was born blind; but we do not know how it is that now he sees, nor do we know who opened his eyes. Ask him; he is of age. He will speak for himself." His parents said this because they were afraid of the Jews; for the Jews had already agreed that anyone who confessed Jesus to be the Messiah would be put out of the synagogue. Therefore his parents said, "He is of age; ask him."

So for the second time they called the man who had been blind, and they said to him, "Give glory to God! We know that this man is a sinner." He answered, "I do not know whether he is a sinner. One thing I do know, that though I was blind, now I see." They said to him, "What did he do to you? How did he open your eyes?" He answered them, "I have told you already, and you would not listen. Why do you want to hear it again? Do you also want to become his disciples?" Then they reviled him, saying, "You are his disciple, but we are disciples of Moses. We know that God has spoken to Moses, but as for this man, we do not know where he comes from."

The man answered, "Here is an astonishing thing! You do not know where he comes from, and yet he opened my eyes. We know that God does not listen to sinners, but he does listen to one who worships him and obeys his will. Never since the world began has it been heard that anyone opened the eyes of a person born blind. If this man were not from God, he could do nothing." They answered him,

"You were born entirely in sins, and are you trying to teach us?" And they drove him out.

Jesus heard that they had driven him out, and when he found him, he said, "Do you believe in the Son of Man?" He answered, "And who is he, sir? Tell me, so that I may believe in him." Jesus said to him, "You have seen him, and the one speaking with you is he." He said, "Lord, I believe." And he worshiped him. Jesus said, "I came into this world for judgment so that those who do not see may see, and those who do see may become blind."

Some of the Pharisees near him heard this and said to him, "Surely we are not blind, are we?" Jesus said to them, "If you were blind, you would not have sin. But now that you say, 'We see,' your sin remains."

Points of View

JOHN F. CRAGHAN

Day after day we are offered a great number of facts, situations, events—especially in the media. We learn of murders, revolutions, natural disasters, and are required to assess all this material. Our conclusions to this process form our point of view about the world.

Today's readings dwell on light and darkness, sight and blindness, seeing and not seeing. They are timely reminders to reexamine our priorities and retest our standards for making judgments. They urge us to look within and ask whether or not our decisions are really Christian.

The author of 1 Samuel 16:1—2 Samuel 5:5 begins his narrative by painting an enthusiastic portrait of David's rise from a nobody to a royal somebody. He captures the upward movement of Israel's youthful hero. At the same time, he endorses key values of the decision-making process.

The story warns against judging by mere appearances since the well-to-do tend to be the elite. Hence there is the process whereby Samuel reviews the available sons of Jesse. The story highlights the motif of the selection of the most unlikely candidate. The shepherd boy, a marginal person, enters into the process and is ultimately chosen. God's Spirit can also rush on the lowly. Although the author notes David's handsome appearance, this is not the decisive factor because "the Lord looks on the heart."

Let There Be Light

The author of Ephesians contrasts the previously pagan lives of his audience with their new Christian lives by using the images of light and darkness, and the account from the Gospel of John contrasts the perceptions of the blind man and the Pharisees/Jews. The blind man progresses from darkness to light. Initially he regards Jesus as a man, but finally confesses that he is the Son of Man. The blind man sees (faith) that Jesus is "the light of the world."

The Pharisees/Jews first appear to accept the healing, but then begin to doubt that the man was blind from birth. They next deny Jesus' heavenly origins, and go on to mock the blind man. They adamantly refuse to see and thus end up blind.

Today's Good News

Taking this message to heart, modern Christians are called to look beyond appearances. We must decide whether the helpless, the indigent, the derelict are worthy of respect; or whether they are merely objects of disdain. These people are also the sisters and brothers of Jesus. It all depends on our point of view.

Modern Christians must judge wayward members of the family. Are they merely a disgrace to the family name? Or do they possibly exhibit genuine human qualities that we choose to ignore in order to concentrate on their clear excesses? It all depends on our point of view.

Modern Christians must evaluate the policies and programs of both Church and state. Are they right merely because authority has endorsed them? Do they really benefit the community? Or do too many people get hurt in the process of protecting the administration's policy? It all depends on our point of view.

Points for Reflection and Discussion

1. Do you generally derive your criteria for judgment from the gospel, or from the standard business procedures of our environment?

_____

_____

_____

2. Imagine yourself blind. Whom do you trust to lead you?

_____

_____

_____

Themes

Blindness
  L2, Saying Yes to Jesus
Conversion
  L3, Take a Look
Light
  L1, What is Lent?

Reading 1, Ezekiel 37:12-14

Thus says the Lord God: "I am going to open your graves, and bring you up from your graves, O my people; and I will bring you back to the land of Israel. And you shall know that I am the Lord, when I open your graves, and bring you up from your graves, O my people. I will put my spirit within you, and you shall live, and I will place you on your own soil; then you shall know that I, the Lord, have spoken and will act," says the Lord.

Psalm 130:1-2,3-4,5-6,7-8 (*R verse 7b*)

Reading 2, Romans 8:8-11

Those who are in the flesh cannot please God. But you are not in the flesh; you are in the Spirit, since the Spirit of God dwells in you. Anyone who does not have the Spirit of Christ does not belong to him. But if Christ is in you, though the body is dead because of sin, the Spirit is life because of righteousness. If the Spirit of him who raised Jesus from the dead dwells in you, he who raised Christ from the dead will give life to your mortal bodies also through his Spirit that dwells in you.

Gospel, John 11:1-45

Now a certain man was ill, Lazarus of Bethany, the village of Mary and her sister Martha. Mary was the one who anointed the Lord with perfume and wiped his feet with her hair; her brother Lazarus was ill.

So the sisters sent a message to Jesus, "Lord, he whom you love is ill." But when Jesus heard it, he said, "This illness does not lead to death; rather it is for God's glory, so that the Son of God may be glorified through it." Accordingly, though Jesus loved Martha and her sister and Lazarus, after having heard that Lazarus was ill, he stayed two days longer in the place where he was.

Then after this he said to the disciples, "Let us go to Judea again." The disciples said to him, "Rabbi, the Jews were just now trying to stone you, and are you going there again?" Jesus answered, "Are there not twelve hours of daylight? Those who walk during the day do not stumble, because they see the light of this world. But those who walk at night stumble, because the light is not in them."

After saying this, he told them, "Our friend Lazarus has fallen asleep, but I am going there to awaken him." The disciples said to him, "Lord, if he has fallen asleep, he will be all right." Jesus, however, had been speaking about his death, but they thought that he was referring merely to sleep. Then Jesus told them plainly, "Lazarus is dead. For your sake I am glad I was not there, so that you may believe. But let us go to him." Thomas, who was called the Twin, said to his fellow disciples, "Let us also go, that we may die with him."

When Jesus arrived, he found that Lazarus had already been in the tomb four days. Now Bethany was near Jerusalem, some two miles away, and many of the Jews had come to Martha and Mary to console them about their brother. When Martha heard that Jesus was coming, she went and met him, while Mary stayed at home. Martha said to Jesus, "Lord, if you had been here, my brother would not have died. But even now I know that God will give you whatever you ask of him." Jesus said to her, "Your brother will rise again." Martha said to him, "I know that he will rise again in the resurrection on the last day." Jesus said to her, "I am the resurrection and the life. Those who believe in me, even though they die, will live, and everyone who lives and believes in me will never die. Do you believe this?" She said to him, "Yes, Lord, I believe that you are the Messiah, the Son of God, the one coming into the world." When she had said this, she went back and called her sister Mary, and told her privately, "The Teacher is here and is calling for you." And when she heard it, she got up quickly and went to him. Now Jesus had not yet come to the village, but was still at the place where Martha had met him. The Jews who were with her in the house, consoling her, saw Mary get up quickly and go out. They followed her because they thought that she was going to the tomb to weep there.

When Mary came where Jesus was and saw him, she knelt at his feet and said to him, "Lord, if you had been here, my brother would not have died." When Jesus saw her weeping, and the Jews who came with her also weeping, he was greatly disturbed in spirit and deeply moved. He said, "Where have you laid him?" They said to him, "Lord, come and see." Jesus began to weep. So the Jews said, "See how he loved him!" But some of them said, "Could not he who opened the eyes of the blind man have kept this man from dying?"

Then Jesus, again greatly disturbed, came to the tomb. It was a cave, and a stone was lying against it. Jesus said, "Take away the stone." Martha, the sister of the dead man, said to him, "Lord, already there is a stench because he has been dead four days." Jesus said to her, "Did I not tell you that if you believed, you would see the glory of God?" So they took away the stone. And Jesus looked upward and said, "Father, I thank you for having heard me. I knew that you always hear me, but I have said this for the sake of the crowd standing here, so that they may believe that you sent me."

When he had said this, he cried with a loud voice, "Lazarus, come out!" The dead man came out, his hands and feet bound with strips of cloth, and his face wrapped in a cloth. Jesus said to them, "Unbind him, and let him go." Many of the Jews therefore, who had come with Mary and had seen what Jesus did, believed in him.

Dry Bones

JOHN F. CRAGHAN

We sometimes reach a point where despair takes over and depression reigns supreme. We feel overwhelmed by life's shocks and incapacitated by our own failure. Self-pity often becomes the expression of our profound misery. We feel we are old bones incapable of new life.

Today's readings deal with the very real problems of anxiety and hopelessness. Yet they clearly announce a God who becomes involved in human tragedy. This is the God of the living who chooses to become concerned because concern is a manifestation of life. This God unequivocally enables old bones to have new life.

Preaching to a depressed exilic audience in the aftermath of the destruction of Jerusalem, Ezekiel personally experiences their sense of frustration. He even quotes their expression of despair: "Our bones are dried up, and our hope is lost; we are cut off completely" (37:11). The prophet is transported by God's Spirit to a place littered with dry human bones. At the prophet's word, the bones are reconstituted into human bodies and the breath/spirit/wind brings the bodies to life. In Ezekiel's interpretation, the vision is applied to God's despondent people. The bones are the graves of that people who now come back to life and are promised resettlement in their own land. The message is that old bones can have new life.

In Romans 7:14-25, Paul paints a vivid picture of human agony. "I do not do the good I want, but the evil I do not want is what I do" (7:19). In chapter eight of Romans, however, Paul develops the theme of new hope because of the life-giving Spirit. Christians experience God's power whereby a genuine moral life is possible and the threat of condemnation is lifted.

In today's reading, Paul teaches that Christians who allow the Spirit to determine their moral values actually live out their profound association with Christ. Even though the Spirit does not remove physical death, the Spirit does bring to human life that transforming experience of being right with God (justice—a gratuitous gift) that leads to resurrection. For Paul, the message of God in Christ is that old bones can have new life.

The Glory of God

John recounts the raising of Lazarus as a sign that transforms tragedy into hope. Lazarus' illness and subsequent death are an occasion for the manifestation of God's glory. God's presence is made visible through deeds of power. The primary focus of this incident is the glory of the Father, not the assistance of a friend.

Faith goes hand in hand with glory. The miracle also glorifies Jesus, and the disciples' faith in Jesus will lead to the further display of God's glory (see also Jn 2:11). To accept Jesus is to make oneself open to that whole process of transformation. The disciple glorifies the Father just as the Son did by sharing in the passion/death/resurrection.

Today's Good News

Human despair takes many forms. Whatever form it takes, the process of overcoming despair is fundamentally the same. It is to be in the presence of God and to breathe the Spirit upon our world. Hope then becomes possible and life becomes livable.

To provide jobs for the unemployed is clearly in the tradition of Ezekiel: Graves open and the Spirit breathes new life. To care for the elderly and the shut-ins is certainly in the tradition of Paul: The Spirit influences our moral choices and outreach to others implies we belong to Christ. To alleviate the hunger of the world's stricken is obviously in the tradition of John. So too are the many acts of charity we all are called upon to perform. We thus manifest the glory of God and strengthen the faith of our sisters and brothers. We participate in God's great work of giving old bones new life.

Points for Reflection and Discussion

1. God is a God of the living. What area in your existence needs to be untied, as Lazarus was, in order to come back to life?

_____

_____

_____

_____

2. Do you fear death? Talk about your experiences of death.

_____

_____

_____

_____

Themes
Death
    L1, What is Lent?
Spirit
    L7, The Meaning of Holy Week

Reading 1 (ABC), Exodus 12:1-8,11-14

The Lord said to Moses and Aaron in the land of Egypt: This month shall mark for you the beginning of months; it shall be the first month of the year for you. Tell the whole congregation of Israel that on the tenth of this month they are to take a lamb for each family, a lamb for each household. If a household is too small for a whole lamb, it shall join its closest neighbor in obtaining one; the lamb shall be divided in proportion to the number of people who eat of it. Your lamb shall be without blemish, a year-old male; you may take it from the sheep or from the goats. You shall keep it until the fourteenth day of this month; then the whole assembled congregation of Israel shall slaughter it at twilight. They shall take some of the blood and put it on the two doorposts and the lintel of the houses in which they eat it. They shall eat the lamb that same night; they shall eat it roasted over the fire with unleavened bread and bitter herbs.

This is how you shall eat it: your loins girded, your sandals on your feet, and your staff in your hand; and you shall eat it hurriedly. It is the passover of the Lord. For I will pass through the land of Egypt that night, and I will strike down every firstborn in the land of Egypt, both human beings and animals; on all the gods of Egypt I will execute judgments: I am the Lord. The blood shall be a sign for you on the houses where you live: when I see the blood, I will pass over you, and no plague shall destroy you when I strike the land of Egypt. This day shall be a day of remembrance for you. You shall celebrate it as a festival to the Lord; throughout your generations you shall observe it as a perpetual ordinance.

Psalm 116:12-13,15-16,17-18 (R 1 Cor 10:16)

Reading 2 (ABC), 1 Corinthians 11:23-26

I received from the Lord what I also handed on to you, that the Lord Jesus on the night when he was betrayed took a loaf of bread, and when he had given thanks, he broke it and said, "This is my body that is for you. Do this in remembrance of me." In the same way he took the cup also, after supper, saying, "This cup is the new covenant in my blood. Do this, as often as you drink it, in remembrance of me." For as often as you eat this bread and drink the cup, you proclaim the Lord's death until he comes.

Gospel (ABC), John 13:1-15

Before the festival of the Passover, Jesus knew that his hour had come to depart from this world and go to the Father. Having loved his own who were in the world, he loved them to the end. The devil had already put it into the heart of Judas son of Simon Iscariot to betray him. And during supper Jesus, knowing that the Father had given all things into his hands, and that he had come from God and was going to God, got up from the table, took off his outer robe, and tied a towel around himself. Then he poured water into a basin and began to wash the disciples' feet and to wipe them with the towel that was tied around him. He came to Simon Peter, who said to him, "Lord, are you going to wash my feet?" Jesus answered, "You do not know now what I am doing, but later you will understand." Peter said to him, "You will never wash my feet." Jesus answered, "Unless I wash you, you have no share with me." Simon Peter said to him, "Lord, not my feet only but also my hands and my head!" Jesus said to him, "One who has bathed does not need to wash, except for the feet, but is entirely clean. And you are clean, though not all of you." For he knew who was to betray him; for this reason he said, "Not all of you are clean."

After he had washed their feet, had put on his robe, and had returned to the table, he said to them, "Do you know what I have done to you? You call me Teacher and Lord— and you are right, for that is what I am. So if I, your Lord and Teacher, have washed your feet, you also ought to wash one another's feet. For I have set you an example, that you also should do as I have done to you."

Service

JOHN F. CRAGHAN

Self-service is no service. Somehow we seem programmed to look only to our own concerns; we find it hard to include the concerns of others. We believe that we are to be served and waited upon; we find it difficult to serve and wait upon others. We are driven to pursue our personal advantage; we find it distasteful to pursue the advantage of others. Nonetheless the whole thrust of Holy Thursday is that to be Christian means to serve others. Hence self-service is no service.

An Unblemished Lamb

Originally the Passover was the feast of shepherds for the welfare of their flocks when they set out for new pasture grounds. It was a critical time in the spring when the young of the sheep and goats would be born. In this feast, the blood is smeared on the tent poles to ward off any danger to humans and animals.

In its Israelite context the Passover is the celebration of the new pasture grounds that follows the Exodus, i.e., the Promised Land. It is the celebration of the Lord's liberating action. The blood rite is now the link between the tenth plague and the Passover. The Lord will strike down the Egyptian firstborn but will pass over or spare the inhabitants of the blood-smeared houses.

In Christian use, and especially on Holy Thursday, Jesus is the Passover lamb who delivers the world from sin. There is a link, therefore, with the Passover lamb of Exodus whose blood delivered the Israelites from the "destroyer" (see Ex 12:23). In its Christian context, Jesus' self-giving in death is the supreme act whereby sin may be overcome. Hence it is that self-giving that looks to the needs of others. To that degree self-service is no service.

Remembering the Lord

The celebration of the Lord's Supper in Corinth involved two elements: a common meal in which one would share one's food and drink with other members of the community, and the Eucharist itself. It is clear from 1 Cor 11:17-22, however, that the Corinthian community was not really a community but an amalgam of various factions. The wealthier members arrived first and consumed the food and drink to the extent that some became intoxicated. The poorer members arrived later only to find that the meal was virtually ended, to such a degree that some of them went hungry.

At this point Paul upbraids his community, pointing out that the Corinthians are really unable to eat the Lord's Supper. Clearly their lack of charity does not dispose them to take part in the self-giving of Jesus. Paul quotes the tradition he received about the words of institution for the Eucharist. He insists that proclaiming the death of the Lord and remembrance imply a sharing now in the Lord's body and blood. But such sharing presupposes a bonded community, not a multiplication of factions. For Paul, Eucharist without community is no Eucharist. For Paul, self-service is no service.

Setting Examples

The opening verse of the gospel understands Jesus' death under two aspects: an act of love for his followers, and victory because of Jesus' return to the Father. In verse 2, the author links the foot washing with Jesus' death by noting the betrayal of Jesus and, in verse 3, by emphasizing Jesus' return to God. In verses 4-5, the foot washing is an act of humility by Jesus, in that he plays the role of a servant, a role that symbolizes his humiliation in death. Verses 6-10a give the first interpretation of Jesus' action, i.e., the foot washing makes the disciple capable of sharing eternal life with Jesus. This is further developed in verses 9-10a, which speak of bathing, i.e., baptism.

Verses 12-15 give the second interpretation of Jesus' action. The foot washing demonstrates Jesus' service for others—something that the followers of Jesus must imitate. Hence the foot washing is a reality that must be reproduced in the lives of the community. The authentic follower of Jesus will not shun washing the feet of other community members. To claim Jesus as Lord and Master means to make oneself servant and slave of all. Self-service is no service.

Today's Good News

The Passover ceremony of Exodus, the upbraiding of Paul at Corinth, and the symbolic action of Jesus in the gospel story are powerful reminders on Holy Thursday that we must look beyond ourselves and discover the world of pain and frustration of our sisters and brothers. They urge us to liberate our ego by service on behalf of others.

Husbands and wives who consistently consider each other's needs show the Christian way. Family members who regularly seek to alleviate problems reveal Christian values. Leaders who habitually spend time and energy in promoting the good of their people demonstrate genuine Christianity. Such people set examples for us; examples which show that self-service is no service.

Eucharist reflects a Lord and Master who is servant and slave. Eucharist takes Jesus' death-style and offers it as the community's lifestyle. To eat and drink with Jesus is to arise and offer oneself as food and drink for others. Eucharist clearly states that self-service is no service.

Points for Reflection and Discussion

1. Whom do you believe was most humbled by Jesus' washing of Peter's feet: Jesus or Peter? Why?

_____

_____

_____

2. Do you believe it is possible to truly celebrate Eucharist apart from a community? Why or why not?

_____

_____

_____

Themes
Community
    L4, The Nicene Creed
    L8, Catechumenate Retreat Day
Eucharist
    L2, Saying Yes to Jesus
    L7, The Meaning of Holy Week
Service
    L3, Take a Look

Reading 1 (ABC), Isaiah 52:13—53:12

See, my servant shall prosper; he shall be exalted and lifted up, and shall be very high. Just as there were many who were astonished at him—so marred was his appearance, beyond human semblance, and his form beyond that of mortals—so he shall startle many nations; kings shall shut their mouths because of him; for that which had not been told them they shall see, and that which they had not heard they shall contemplate.

Who has believed what we have heard? And to whom has the arm of the Lord been revealed? For he grew up before him like a young plant, and like a root out of dry ground; he had no form or majesty that we should look at him, nothing in his appearance that we should desire him. He was despised and rejected by others; a man of suffering and acquainted with infirmity; and as one from whom others hide their faces he was despised, and we held him of no account. Surely he has borne our infirmities and carried our diseases; yet we accounted him stricken, struck down by God, and afflicted. But he was wounded for our transgressions, crushed for our iniquities; upon him was the punishment that made us whole, and by his bruises we are healed. All we like sheep have gone astray; we have all turned to our own way, and the Lord has laid on him the iniquity of us all. He was oppressed, and he was afflicted, yet he did not open his mouth; like a lamb that is led to the slaughter, and like a sheep that before its shearers is silent, so he did not open his mouth. By a perversion of justice he was taken away. Who could have imagined his future? For he was cut off from the land of the living, stricken for the transgression of my people. They made his grave with the wicked and his tomb with the rich, although he had done no violence, and there was no deceit in his mouth. Yet it was the will of the Lord to crush him with pain.

When you make his life an offering for sin, he shall see his offspring, and shall prolong his days; through him the will of the Lord shall prosper. Out of his anguish he shall see light; he shall find satisfaction through his knowledge. The righteous one, my servant, shall make many righteous, and he shall bear their iniquities. Therefore I will allot him a portion with the great, and he shall divide the spoil with the strong; because he poured out himself to death, and was numbered with the transgressors; yet he bore the sin of many, and made intercession for the transgressors.

Psalm 31:1,5,11-12,14-15,16,24 (R Lk 23:46)

Reading 2 (ABC), Hebrews 4:14-16;5:7-9

Since we have a great high priest who has passed through the heavens, Jesus, the Son of God, let us hold fast to our confession. For we do not have a high priest who is unable to sympathize with our weaknesses, but we have one who in every respect has been tested as we are, yet without sin. Let us therefore approach the throne of grace with boldness, so that we may receive mercy and find grace to help in time of need.

In the days of his flesh, Jesus offered up prayers and supplications, with loud cries and tears, to the one who was able to save him from death, and he was heard because of his reverent submission. Although he was a Son, he learned obedience through what he suffered; and having been made perfect, he became the source of eternal salvation for all who obey him.

Gospel (ABC), John 18:1—19:42

Jesus went out with his disciples across the Kidron valley to a place where there was a garden, which he and his disciples entered. Now Judas, who betrayed him, also knew the place, because Jesus often met there with his disciples. So Judas brought a detachment of soldiers together with police from the chief priests and the Pharisees, and they came there with lanterns and torches and weapons. Then Jesus, knowing all that was to happen to him, came forward and asked them, "Whom are you looking for?" They answered, "Jesus of Nazareth." Jesus replied, "I am he." Judas, who betrayed him, was standing with them. When Jesus said to them, "I am he," they stepped back and fell to the ground. Again he asked them, "Whom are you looking for?" And they said, "Jesus of Nazareth." Jesus answered, "I told you that I am he. So if you are looking for me, let these men go." This was to fulfill the word that he had spoken, "I did not lose a single one of those whom you gave me."

Then Simon Peter, who had a sword, drew it, struck the high priest's slave, and cut off his right ear. The slave's name was Malchus. Jesus said to Peter, "Put your sword back into its sheath. Am I not to drink the cup that the Father has given me?" So the soldiers, their officer, and the Jewish police arrested Jesus and bound him. First they took him to Annas, who was the father-in-law of Caiaphas, the high priest that year. Caiaphas was the one who had advised the Jews that it was better to have one person die for the people.

Simon Peter and another disciple followed Jesus. Since that disciple was known to the high priest, he went with Jesus into the courtyard of the high priest, but Peter was standing outside at the gate. So the other disciple, who was known to the high priest, went out, spoke to the woman who guarded the gate, and brought Peter in. The woman said to Peter, "You are not also one of this man's disciples, are you?" He said, "I am not." Now the slaves and the police had made a charcoal fire because it was cold, and they were standing around it and warming themselves. Peter also was standing with them and warming himself.

Then the high priest questioned Jesus about his disciples and about his teaching. Jesus answered, "I have spoken openly to the world; I have always taught in synagogues and in the temple, where all the Jews come together. I have said nothing in secret. Why do you ask me? Ask those who heard what I said to them; they know what I said." When he had said this, one of the police standing nearby struck Jesus on the face, saying, "Is that how you answer the high priest?" Jesus answered, "If I have spoken wrongly, testify to the wrong. But if have spoken rightly, why do you strike me?" Then Annas sent him bound to Caiaphas the high priest.

Now Simon Peter was standing and warming himself. They asked him, "You are not also one of his disciples, are you?" He denied it and said, "I am not." One of the slaves of the high priest, a relative of the man whose ear Peter had cut off, asked, "Did I not see you in the garden with him?" Again Peter denied it, and at that moment the cock crowed.

Then they took Jesus from Caiaphas to Pilate's headquarters. It was early in the morning. They themselves did not enter the headquarters, so as to avoid ritual defilement and to be able to eat the Passover. So Pilate went out to them and said, "What accusation do you bring against this man?" They answered, "If this man were not a criminal, we would not have handed him over to you." Pilate said to them, "Take him yourselves and judge him according to your law." The Jews replied, "We are not permitted to put anyone to death." (This was to fulfill what Jesus had said when he indicated the kind of death he was to die.) Then Pilate entered the headquarters again, summoned Jesus, and asked him, "Are you the King of the Jews?" Jesus answered, "Do you ask this on your own, or did others tell you about me?" Pilate replied, "I am not a Jew, am I? Your own nation and the chief priests have handed you over to me. What have you done?" Jesus answered, "My kingdom is not from this world. If my kingdom were from this world, my followers would be fighting to keep me from being handed over to the Jews. But as it is, my kingdom is not from here." Pilate asked him, "So you are a king?" Jesus answered, "You say that I am a king. For this I was born, and for this I came into the world, to testify to the truth. Everyone who belongs to the truth listens to my voice." Pilate asked him, "What is truth?"

After he had said this, he went out to the Jews again and told them, "I find no case against him. But you have a custom that I release someone for you at the Passover. Do you want me to release for you the King of the Jews?" They shouted in reply, "Not this man, but Barabbas!" Now Barabbas was a bandit. Then Pilate took Jesus and had him flogged. And the soldiers wove a crown of thorns and put it on his head, and they dressed him in a purple robe. They kept coming up to him, saying, "Hail, King of the Jews!" and striking him on the face. Pilate went out again and said to them, "Look, I am bringing him out to you to let you know that I find no case against him." So Jesus came out, wearing the crown of thorns and the purple robe. Pilate said to them, "Here is the man!" When the chief priests and the police saw him, they shouted, "Crucify him! Crucify him!" Pilate said to them, "Take him yourselves and crucify him; I find no case against him." The Jews answered him, "We have a law, and according to that law he ought to die because he has claimed to be the Son of God." Now when Pilate heard this, he was more afraid than ever. He entered his headquarters again and asked Jesus, "Where are you from?" But Jesus gave him no answer. Pilate therefore said to him, "Do you refuse to speak to me? Do you not know that I have power to release you, and power to crucify you?" Jesus answered him, "You would have no power over me unless it had been given you from above; therefore the one who handed me over to you is guilty of a greater sin." From then on Pilate tried to release him, but the Jews cried out, "If you release this man, you are no friend of the emperor. Everyone who claims to be a king sets himself against the emperor."

When Pilate heard these words, he brought Jesus outside and sat on the judge's bench at a place called The Stone Pavement, or in Hebrew Gabbatha. Now it was the day of Preparation for the Passover; and it was about noon. He said to the Jews, "Here is your King!" They cried out, "Away with him! Away with him! Crucify him!" Pilate asked them, "Shall I crucify your King?" The chief priests answered, "We have no king but the emperor." Then he handed him over to them to be crucified.

So they took Jesus; and carrying the cross by himself, he went out to what is called The Place of the Skull, which in Hebrew is called Golgotha. There they crucified him, and with him two others, one on either side, with Jesus between them. Pilate also had an inscription written and put on the cross. It read, "Jesus of Nazareth, the King of the Jews." Many of the Jews read this inscription, because the place where Jesus was crucified was near the city; and it was written in Hebrew, in Latin, and in Greek. Then the chief priests of the Jews said to Pilate, "Do not write, 'The King of the Jews,' but, 'This man said, I am King of the Jews.'" Pilate answered, "What I have written I have written."

When the soldiers had crucified Jesus, they took his clothes and divided them into four parts, one for each soldier. They also took his tunic; now the tunic was seamless, woven in one piece from the top. So they said to one another, "Let us not tear it, but cast lots for it to see who will get it." This was to fulfill what the scripture says, "They divided my clothes among themselves, and for my clothing they cast lots." And that is what the soldiers did.

Meanwhile, standing near the cross of Jesus were his mother, and his mother's sister, Mary the wife of Clopas, and Mary Magdalene. When Jesus saw his mother and the disciple whom he loved standing beside her, he said to his mother, "Woman, here is your son." Then he said to the disciple, "Here is your mother." And from that hour the disciple took her into his own home. After this, when Jesus knew that all was now finished, he said (in order to fulfill the scripture), "I am thirsty." A jar full of sour wine was standing there. So they put a sponge full of the wine on a branch of hyssop and held it to his mouth. When Jesus had received the wine, he said, "It is finished." Then he bowed his head and gave up his spirit.

Since it was the day of Preparation, the Jews did not want the bodies left on the cross during the sabbath, especially because that sabbath was a day of great solemnity. So they asked Pilate to have the legs of the crucified men broken and the bodies removed. Then the soldiers came and broke the legs of the first and of the other who had been crucified with him. But when they came to Jesus and saw that he was already dead, they did not break his legs. Instead, one of the soldiers pierced his side with a spear, and at once blood and water came out. (He who saw this has testified so that you also may believe. His testimony is true, and he knows that he tells the truth.) These things occurred so that the scripture might be fulfilled, "None of his bones shall be broken." And again another passage of scripture says, "They will look on the one whom they have pierced."

After these things, Joseph of Arimathea, who was a disciple of Jesus, though a secret one because of his fear of the Jews, asked Pilate to let him take away the body of Jesus. Pilate gave him permission; so he came and removed his body. Nicodemus, who had at first come to Jesus by night, also came, bringing a mixture of myrrh and aloes, weighing about a hundred pounds. They took the body of Jesus and wrapped it with the spices in linen cloths, according to the burial custom of the Jews. Now there was a garden in the place where he was crucified, and in the garden there was a new tomb in which no one had ever been laid. And so, because it was the Jewish day of Preparation, and the tomb was nearby, they laid Jesus there.

Death Unto Life

John F. Craghan

Death brings life to the community. All too often we subscribe to the view that we are born for ourselves and we die for ourselves. Perhaps we also accept a dog-eat-dog philosophy and may even endorse belief in the survival of the fittest. We may tend to be isolationists, even when we interact with others. We may find it impossible to accept the paradoxical doctrine that death brings life to the community.

Today's readings are the very opposite of the isolationist philosophy. They point us in the direction of two individuals whose death culminated in life. Their death, however, was not a purely personal achievement. Rather, it was one that brought life to their community.

The first reading is the fourth Servant Song from the work of the anonymous exilic author, Second Isaiah (chapters 40—55). The Suffering Servant is quite likely the prophet himself and all those followers who heed God's word to leave exile in Babylon for a new life in Israel.

The song begins on a note of triumph, the exaltation of the Servant and the accomplishment of his mission. The song then describes the would-be triumph of the Servant's enemies, i.e., the disfigurement, death, and burial of the Servant as a criminal. Such a catastrophe obviously indicated the presence of sin. It was not the prophet's sin, however, but Israel's ("wounded for *our* transgressions, crushed for *our* iniquities"). The Servant, therefore, bore Israel's guilt and gave his life as a sin-offering (verse 10). The outcome of the Servant's action is redemption for Israel. In this passage death brings life to the community.

The second reading consists of two passages from Hebrews that emphasize Jesus' high-priestly office and its implications for believers. While the author acknowledges Jesus' special relationship with God, however, he also underlines the utter humanity of this high priest. Hence Jesus can fully understand the weakness of his people since he himself was often tempted.

In 5:7-9, while the author returns to the theme of Jesus' humanity ("loud cries and tears"), he also connects it with the theme of Jesus' exaltation. Jesus' obedience to the Father results in his priestly consecration. In turn, that consecration enables him to save those who obey him. Jesus' ultimate weakness, death on the cross, climaxes in his power as high priest whereby believers experience the source of salvation. Death brings life to the community.

A Lifegiving Passion

John's passion account has three main elements: Jesus' arrest and questioning (18:1-27), his trial before Pilate (18:28—19:16a), and his crucifixion (19:16b-42). Actually the word "passion" is something of a misnomer since Jesus' painful experience is only an aspect of his royal character. The reason for the crowning and mocking of Jesus, for example (19:2-3), is that Pilate has already proclaimed him a king (18:37). The cry, "Here is the man," is also part of the ritual of coronation—the people acknowledge Jesus as king. Finally, the crucifixion itself is Jesus' actual enthronement because the trilingual inscription (19:19-20) announces his kingship to the international community.

John presents an absolutely free and self-possessed Jesus who is the master of his own fate. Only in this gospel does Jesus respond to the indignities before the Jewish officials (18:21). In "lecturing" Pilate (19:9-11), Jesus implies that no one really takes his life away—rather, he lays it down freely. Unlike Matthew, Mark, and Luke, John has no Simon to help Jesus carry his cross. Jesus accepts his destiny alone in absolute freedom (19:17).

Among other special moments in this gospel is the flow of blood and water (19:34). The flow of water is linked to Jesus' own prophecy that from within him there would flow rivers of living water (7:37-38). John relates this to Jesus' giving up of his spirit (19:30). Jesus' death, therefore, is that moment of glorification when the Spirit is released upon the new community (7:39;20:22). Clearly, for the author of John, death brings life to the community.

Today's Good News

The Suffering Servant and the Jesus of both the Letter to the Hebrews and the Gospel of John must influence our way of thinking about life and death. These two realities are not isolated but intertwined. The experience of pain in self-giving must say something about genuine living.

There are the parents who provide for the total well-being of their families by daily sacrificing themselves. There are the politicians and other leaders who drain themselves for the people entrusted to their care. There are the friends of the sick, the lonely, the disabled; those who mend broken bones and broken hearts and broken spirits. These people, and all those like them, recognize that death truly does bring life to the community.

Points for Reflection and Discussion

1. Our Church does not celebrate the Liturgy of the Eucharist on Good Friday—the only day of the year that there is no eucharistic feast—because on this day we commemorate the death of the Lord Jesus. Allow his suffering and death to pierce your heart. Grieve for him—and for all God's people who suffer and die at the hands of ignorance and injustice.

———————————————————————

———————————————————————

———————————————————————

———————————————————————

———————————————————————

2. Do you find the passion according to John to be more of a "celebration" than the passions according to Mark and Matthew and Luke? Is it possible to really "celebrate" Christ's passion? Why or why not?

———————————————————————

———————————————————————

———————————————————————

———————————————————————

———————————————————————

Themes
Death
    L4, The Nicene Creed
    L7, The Meaning of Holy Week
Pain, Suffering
    L5, The Way of the Cross
Sin
    L1, What is Lent?
    L3, Take a Look
    L8, Catechumenate Retreat Day

Reading 1 (ABC), Genesis 1:1—2:2

In the beginning when God created the heavens and the earth, the earth was a formless void and darkness covered the face of the deep, while a wind from God swept over the face of the waters. Then God said, "Let there be light"; and there was light. And God saw that the light was good; and God separated the light from the darkness. God called the light Day, and the darkness he called Night. And there was evening and there was morning, the first day.

And God said, "Let there be a dome in the midst of the waters, and let it separate the waters from the waters." So God made the dome and separated the waters that were under the dome from the waters that were above the dome. And it was so. God called the dome Sky. And there was evening and there was morning, the second day.

And God said, "Let the waters under the sky be gathered together into one place, and let the dry land appear." And it was so. God called the dry land Earth, and the waters that were gathered together he called Seas. And God saw that it was good. Then God said, "Let the earth put forth vegetation: plants yielding seed, and fruit trees of every kind on earth that bear fruit with the seed in it." And it was so. The earth brought forth vegetation: plants yielding seed of every kind, and trees of every kind bearing fruit with the seed in it. And God saw that it was good. And there was evening and there was morning, the third day.

And God said, "Let there be lights in the dome of the sky to separate the day from the night; and let them be for signs and for seasons and for days and years, and let them be lights in the dome of the sky to give light upon the earth." And it was so. God made the two great lights—the greater light to rule the day and the lesser light to rule the night—and the stars. God set them in the dome of the sky to give light upon the earth, to rule over the day and over the night, and to separate the light from the darkness. And God saw that it was good. And there was evening and there was morning, the fourth day.

And God said, "Let the waters bring forth swarms of living creatures, and let birds fly above the earth across the dome of the sky." So God created the great sea monsters and every living creature that moves, of every kind, with which the waters swarm, and every winged bird of every kind. And God saw that it was good. God blessed them, saying, "Be fruitful and multiply and fill the waters in the seas, and let birds multiply on the earth." And there was evening and there was morning, the fifth day.

And God said, "Let the earth bring forth living creatures of every kind: cattle and creeping things and wild animals of the earth of every kind." And it was so. God made the wild animals of the earth of every kind, and the cattle of every kind, and everything that creeps upon the ground of every kind. And God saw that it was good. Then God said,

"Let us make humankind in our image, according to our likeness; and let them have dominion over the fish of the sea, and over the birds of the air, and over the cattle, and over all the wild animals of the earth, and over every creeping thing that creeps upon the earth." So God created humankind in his image, in the image of God he created them; male and female he created them. God blessed them, and God said to them, "Be fruitful and multiply, and fill the earth and subdue it; and have dominion over the fish of the sea and over the birds of the air and over every living thing that moves upon the earth." God said, "See, I have given you every plant yielding seed that is upon the face of all the earth, and every tree with seed in its fruit; you shall have them for food. And to every beast of the earth, and to every bird of the air, and to everything that creeps on the earth, everything that has the breath of life, I have given every green plant for food." And it was so. God saw everything that he had made, and indeed, it was very good. And there was evening and there was morning, the sixth day.

Thus the heavens and the earth were finished, and all their multitude. And on the seventh day God finished the work that he had done, and he rested on the seventh day from all the work that he had done.

Psalm 104:1-2,5-6,10,12,13-14,24,35 (R verse 30)

(or) Psalm 33:4-5,6-7,12-13,20,22 (R verse 5)

Reading 3 (ABC), Exodus 14:15—15:1

The Lord said to Moses, "Why do you cry out to me? Tell the Israelites to go forward. But you lift up your staff, and stretch out your hand over the sea and divide it, that the Israelites may go into the sea on dry ground. Then I will harden the hearts of the Egyptians so that they will go in after them; and so I will gain glory for myself over Pharaoh and all his army, his chariots, and his chariot drivers. And the Egyptians shall know that I am the Lord, when I have gained glory for myself over Pharaoh, his chariots, and his chariot drivers."

The angel of God who was going before the Israelite army moved and went behind them; and the pillar of cloud moved from in front of them and took its place behind them. It came between the army of Egypt and the army of Israel. And so the cloud was there with the darkness, and it lit up the night; one did not come near the other all night. Then Moses stretched out his hand over the sea. The Lord drove the sea back by a strong east wind all night, and turned the sea into dry land; and the waters were divided. The Israelites went into the sea on dry ground, the waters forming a wall for them on their right and on their left. The Egyptians pursued, and went into the sea after them, all of Pharaoh's horses, chariots, and chariot drivers.

At the morning watch the Lord in the pillar of fire and cloud looked down upon the Egyptian army, and threw the Egyptian army into panic. He clogged their chariot wheels so that they turned with difficulty. The Egyptians said, "Let us flee from the Israelites, for the Lord is fighting for them against Egypt." Then the Lord said to Moses, "Stretch out your hand over the sea, so that the water may come back upon the Egyptians, upon their chariots and chariot drivers." So Moses stretched out his hand over the sea, and at dawn the sea returned to its normal depth. As the Egyptians fled before it, the Lord tossed the Egyptians into the sea. The waters returned and covered the chariots and the chariot drivers, the entire army of Pharaoh that had followed them into the sea; not one of them remained. But the Israelites walked on dry ground through the sea, the waters forming a wall for them on their right and on their left.

Thus the Lord saved Israel that day from the Egyptians; and Israel saw the Egyptians dead on the seashore. Israel saw the great work that the Lord did against the Egyptians. So the people feared the Lord and believed in the Lord and in his servant Moses.

Then Moses and the Israelites sang this song to the Lord: "I will sing to the Lord, for he has triumphed gloriously; horse and rider he has thrown into the sea."

Exodus 15:1-2,3-5,6-7,17-18 (R verse 1)

Epistle (ABC), Romans 6:3-11

Do you not know that all of us who have been baptized into Christ Jesus were baptized into his death? Therefore we have been buried with him by baptism into death, so that, just as Christ was raised from the dead by the glory of the Father, so we too might walk in newness of life. For if we have been united with him in a death like his, we will certainly be united with him in a resurrection like his. We know that our old self was crucified with him so that the body of sin might be destroyed, and we might no longer be enslaved to sin. For whoever has died is freed from sin. But if we have died with Christ, we believe that we will also live with him. We know that Christ, being raised from the dead, will never die again; death no longer has dominion over him. The death he died, he died to sin, once for all; but the life he lives, he lives to God. So you also must consider yourselves dead to sin and alive to God in Christ Jesus.

Psalm 118:1-2,16-17,22-23 (R Alleluia! Alleluia!)

Gospel (A), Matthew 28:1-10

After the sabbath, as the first day of the week was dawning, Mary Magdalene and the other Mary went to see the tomb. And suddenly there was a great earthquake; for an angel of the Lord, descending from heaven, came and rolled back the stone and sat on it. His appearance was like lightning, and his clothing white as snow. For fear of him the guards shook and became like dead men. But the angel said to the women, "Do not be afraid; I know that you are looking for Jesus who was crucified. He is not here; for he has been raised, as he said. Come, see the place where he lay. Then go quickly and tell his disciples, 'He has been raised from the dead, and indeed he is going ahead of you to Galilee; there you will see him.' This is my message for you." So they left the tomb quickly with fear and great joy, and ran to tell his disciples. Suddenly Jesus met them and said, "Greetings!" And they came to him, took hold of his feet, and worshiped him. Then Jesus said to them, "Do not be afraid; go and tell my brothers to go to Galilee; there they will see me."

Gospel (B), Mark 16:1-8

When the sabbath was over, Mary Magdalene, and Mary the mother of James, and Salome bought spices, so that they might go and anoint [Jesus]. And very early on the first day of the week, when the sun had risen, they went to the tomb. They had been saying to one another, "Who will roll away the stone for us from the entrance to the tomb?" When they looked up, they saw that the stone, which was very large, had already been rolled back. As they entered the tomb, they saw a young man, dressed in a white robe, sitting on the right side; and they were alarmed. But he said to them, "Do not be alarmed; you are looking for Jesus of Nazareth, who was crucified. He has been raised; he is not here. Look, there is the place they laid him. But go, tell his disciples and Peter that he is going ahead of you to Galilee; there you will see him, just as he told you."

So they went out and fled from the tomb, for terror and amazement had seized them; and they said nothing to anyone, for they were afraid.

Gospel (C), Luke 24:1-12

On the first day of the week, at early dawn, [the women] came to the tomb, taking the spices that they had prepared. They found the stone rolled away from the tomb, but when they went in, they did not find the body. While they were perplexed about this, suddenly two men in dazzling clothes stood beside them. The women were terrified and bowed their faces to the ground, but the men said to them, "Why do you look for the living among the dead? He is not here, but has risen. Remember how he told you, while he was still in Galilee, that the Son of Man must be handed over to sinners, and be crucified, and on the third day rise again." Then they remembered his words, and returning from the tomb, they told all this to the eleven and to all the rest. Now it was Mary Magdalene, Joanna, Mary the mother of James, and the other women with them who told this to the apostles. But these words seemed to them an idle tale, and they did not believe them. But Peter got up and ran to the tomb; stooping and looking in, he saw the linen cloths by themselves; then he went home, amazed at what had happened.

Victory

JOHN F. CRAGHAN

To celebrate Easter is to celebrate God's victory over death. Easter smacks of eggs, new clothes, and the promise of spring. In these examples the least common denominator is life of some type. From a biblical point of view, however, life and death take on special nuances. Thus life is the reality of community with God while death is the absence of community with God (see Ez 33:1-16). To celebrate Easter, therefore, is to celebrate the restoration of community with God through Jesus.

The Easter Vigil offers a wealth of biblical passages dealing with the theme of God's victory over death. Here we will limit our consideration to God's victory at the Red Sea (Ex 14:15—15:1), Paul's proclamation of victory over sin and death in baptism (Rom 6:3-11), and the discovery of the empty tomb (Mt 28:1-10; Mk 16:1-8; Lk 24:1-12).

The biblical traditions do not offer a blow-by-blow account of Israel's crossing of the Red Sea simply because the necessary sources are wanting. The Bible does provide a variety of traditions depicting the Lord as the Divine Warrior who uses military prowess to deliver his people. In this Easter Vigil passage there are three such traditions.

In the earliest account (15:1-18,21) the Lord defeats the Egyptians by creating a storm at sea that sinks their chariots and contributes to their death by drowning (15:8-10). While there is only an allusion to the safe passage of the Israelites, there is the clear statement of the utter destruction of the enemy.

In the second account (14:19-20,21b,24-25,27b,30-31) the Lord drives back the sea with a strong easterly wind and just before dawn startles the Egyptians with a glance that provokes military chaos. When the sea resumes its normal depth, the Lord throws the retreating Egyptians into its midst.

In the third account (14:21a,22-23,26-27a,28-29) dry land appears for the safe passage of the Israelites with the water forming something like walls to their right and left. The Egyptians pursue the Israelites on this dry land but the returning waters then engulf the entire Egyptian army.

In the celebration of the Easter Vigil this biblical text takes on special meaning. The waters of the Red Sea now refer to Jesus' experience of death and new life. God intervenes to turn the waters into a destructive force for the Egyptians. The Lord's victory over death is the Resurrection of Jesus. Hence to celebrate Easter is to celebrate this victory over death.

Past, Present, Future

In the passage from Romans, Paul deals with three time zones. The past is the time of baptism and hence immersion into Jesus' passion, death, and Resurrection. The future is the time of completion when the Second Coming of Jesus will occur. The present is the moment of ethical action. The Christian who has a past in Christ and so awaits the Second Coming must demonstrate life in Christ here and now.

Through baptism the Christian shares the transforming experiences of Jesus' death and Resurrection. Passing over our being raised together with Christ, Paul focuses on the implications of baptism. We thus begin a new mode of being that looks forward to the Second Coming. Though death has been vanquished, we can still sin. It is only an ongoing Christian life that demonstrates Jesus' death and Resurrection experience. Hence to celebrate Easter is to celebrate this victory over death.

The Empty Tomb

In Mark, the young man announces the Christian belief in the death and Resurrection of Jesus. While Jesus of Nazareth is the Crucified One, he is now the Raised One. In the Christian paradox death gives way to life. Omitting any post-resurrection appearances, Mark seems to suggest that the Resurrection is not the final moment—indeed life must go on. But it must be a life influenced by Jesus' triumph over death. To celebrate Easter is to celebrate this victory over death.

In Matthew, at the approach of the women there is an earthquake that calls to mind the earthquake at the time of Jesus' death (27:51-54). It announces the shaking of the world's foundations at Jesus' conquest of death. The posture of the angel, i.e., sitting on the stone, also underlines Jesus' victory. The message of the angel proclaims the startling reality in Mark that the Crucified One is now the Raised One. To celebrate Easter is to celebrate this victory over death.

In Luke, the story of the empty tomb is a study in contrasts. Although the women are authoritative witnesses, they do not arrive at faith. The two men scold the women for not understanding the message of Jesus that spoke of his Resurrection. The women then report their findings to the Eleven but encounter only ridicule. Finally *the* authority of the group, Peter, is overwhelmed by his own visit to the tomb but still cannot grasp the meaning of the event. It is only the presence of the Lord that will make Peter (24:34) and the others (24:13-32, 35-49) believers. Only then will the disciples be able to accept the truth that to celebrate Easter is to celebrate victory over death.

Today's Good News

This victory over death announced so powerfully in Romans and the gospels and reinterpreted in the crossing of the Red Sea must have profound repercussions on us. We are bidden to break out into *Alleluias* of Easter joy. However, the *Alleluias* must be more than the expression of happiness at the Easter Vigil. They must pervade our entire lives.

Perhaps we need to reflect on this question: Where is death (i.e., the absence of community with God) present in our daily lives? This may force us to examine our relationships. We may be led to examine our marriages, our ways of dealing with family members, our interaction with others at work, or any number of other relationships. If we seriously hamper community with our sisters and brothers, we seriously hurt our community with God. Against the background of *Alleluias*, we must bring about genuine life in these and other situations. Only then will we be able to state that to celebrate Easter is to celebrate this victory over death.

Points for Reflection and Discussion

1. Reflect on the question posed above: Where is death (i.e., absence of community with God) present in your daily life? What will you do to change death into life?

_____

_____

_____

_____

2. Take some time to read and reflect on all the readings that can be used in the Easter Vigil celebration: #2, Gn 22:1-18: #4, Is 54:5-14; #5, Is 55:1-11; #6, Bar 3:9-15,32–4:4; #7 Ez 36:16-28.

_____

_____

_____

_____

Themes

Life, Resurrection
  M1, Conversion: A Lifelong Process
  M3, Your Special Gifts
  M6, Discernment
  M7, Holiness
Relationships
  M2, The Laity: Called to Build God's Kingdom
  M4, Family Life
  M5, Your Prayer Life
  M8, Evangelization

Reading 1 (ABC), Acts 1:1-11

In the first book, Theophilus, I wrote about all that Jesus did and taught from the beginning until the day when he was taken up to heaven, after giving instructions through the Holy Spirit to the apostles whom he had chosen. After his suffering he presented himself alive to them by many convincing proofs, appearing to them during forty days and speaking about the kingdom of God. While staying with them, he ordered them not to leave Jerusalem, but to wait there for the promise of the Father. "This," he said, "is what you have heard from me; for John baptized with water, but you will be baptized with the Holy Spirit not many days from now." So when they had come together, they asked him, "Lord, is this the time when you will restore the kingdom to Israel?" He replied, "It is not for you to know the times or periods that the Father has set by his own authority. But you will receive power when the Holy Spirit has come upon you; and you will be my witnesses in Jerusalem, in all Judea and Samaria, and to the ends of the earth."

When he had said this, as they were watching, he was lifted up, and a cloud took him out of their sight. While he was going and they were gazing up toward heaven, suddenly two men in white robes stood by them. They said, "Men of Galilee, why do you stand looking up toward heaven? This Jesus, who has been taken up from you into heaven, will come in the same way as you saw him go into heaven."

Psalm 47:1-2,5-6,7-8 (R verse 5)

Reading 2 (ABC), Ephesians 1:17-23*

I pray that the God of our Lord Jesus Christ, the Father of glory, may give you a spirit of wisdom and revelation as you come to know him, so that, with the eyes of your heart enlightened, you may know what is the hope to which he has called you, what are the riches of his glorious inheritance among the saints, and what is the immeasurable greatness of his power for us who believe, according to the working of his great power. God put this power to work in Christ when he raised him from the dead and seated him at his right hand in the heavenly places, far above all rule and authority and power and dominion, and above every name that is named, not only in this age but also in the age to come. And he has put all things under his feet and has made him the head over all things for the church, which is his body, the fullness of him who fills all in all.

*In Canada the Second Reading for *Cycle B* is Ephesians 4:1-13; the Second Reading for *Cycle C* is Hebrews 9:24-28;10:19-23

Gospel (A), Matthew 28:16-20

The eleven disciples went to Galilee, to the mountain to which Jesus had directed them. When they saw him, they worshiped him; but some doubted. And Jesus came and said to them, "All authority in heaven and on earth has been given to me. Go therefore and make disciples of all nations, baptizing them in the name of the Father and of the Son and of the Holy Spirit, and teaching them to obey everything that I have commanded you. And remember, I am with you always, to the end of the age."

Gospel (B), Mark 16:15-20

[Jesus] said to [the apostles], "Go into all the world and proclaim the good news to the whole creation. The one who believes and is baptized will be saved; but the one who does not believe will be condemned. And these signs will accompany those who believe: by using my name they will cast out demons; they will speak in new tongues; they will pick up snakes in their hands, and if they drink any deadly thing, it will not hurt them; they will lay their hands on the sick, and they will recover." So then the Lord Jesus, after he had spoken to them, was taken up into heaven and sat down at the right hand of God. And they went out and proclaimed the good news everywhere, while the Lord worked with them and confirmed the message by the signs that accompanied it.

Gospel (C), Luke 24:46-53

[Jesus] said to [the apostles], "Thus it is written, that the Messiah is to suffer and to rise from the dead on the third day, and that repentance and forgiveness of sins is to be proclaimed in his name to all nations, beginning from Jerusalem. You are witnesses of these things. And see, I am sending upon you what my Father promised; so stay here in the city until you have been clothed with power from on high." Then he led them out as far as Bethany, and, lifting up his hands, he blessed them. While he was blessing them, he withdrew from them and was carried up into heaven. And they worshiped him, and returned to Jerusalem with great joy; and they were continually in the temple blessing God.

The Promise

ELSIE HAINZ MCGRATH

It was necessary that the Risen Jesus spend some time with his friends. They needed the reassurance that seeing and touching gives to people—the proof that he truly had been raised to new, transfigured life-after-death. Thomas was not the only one who had to see in order to believe!

But if Jesus had just hung around earth for the rest of his risen life, what would we—who hadn't seen him die to begin with—accept as proof of new, transfigured life-after-death? What would we have learned about our own lives? And what would Jesus have done with his promise?

The Power

The disciples were anxious for answers. They asked, "Lord, is this the time when you will restore the kingdom to Israel?" They thought "the promise of the Father" would bring about an age of political sovereignty such as the nation had enjoyed under the reign of King David. Jesus' answer made clear that this was not what the promise was all about. Neither would the promise give them a glimpse of the *eschaton,* for "it is not for you to know the times or periods that the Father has set" for the end of time. The promise was not going to make their lives easier by restoring national dominance or by granting divine insight; it was, in fact, destined to "muddy the waters" of their baptisms. When they received the Spirit they too, would be baptized in fire. They would be empowered to take on the role of Christ: to teach and to nourish and to serve; to be ignored and to hunger and to die.

The larger purpose of Jesus' Resurrection is revealed to us in the story of his Ascension: the Church and its mission. That mission is the *kerygma,* the proclamation of the Good News throughout the entire world, and it is to be done by people who are afraid and filled with doubts. Only Jesus' passion and death, Resurrection and Ascension can overcome the skepticism and unbelief of his most ardent followers.

Today's Good News

The promise of the Spirit was a promise that was to be fulfilled on Pentecost, but which continues to be fulfilled *every* day in *every* lifetime. The Holy Spirit gives us the very mind and heart and power of our Lord, enabling us to carry on his work of redemption in our sinful world. That mission is the most striking manifestation of the triumphant power of God.

Ascension brings our Lord closer to us than he was to the apostles in his Risen body. Ascension is less about what God has done for the Son than it is about what God has done—and continues to do—for us through the Son. As the Letter to the Ephesians tells us: "[the Father] has put all things under [Jesus'] feet and has made him the head over all things for the church, which is his body, the fullness of him who fills all in all."

Points for Reflection and Discussion

1. Have you ever thought that the apostles were "lucky" to have known Jesus?; that belief would be easier "if only" you could see him face-to-face? Have you ever wondered why it took them so long to "get it"?

_____

_____

_____

_____

2. Think about the awesomeness of God being "just one of the guys." Imagine that your best friend is God Incarnate. What would you do differently if you knew he or she was God? Would belief be easier?

_____

_____

_____

_____

Themes

Ascension, Christ, Holy Spirit
    M3, Your Special Gifts
    M6, Discernment
Church
    M2, The Laity: Called to Build God's Kingdom
    M4, Family Life
    M7, Holiness
    M8, Evangelization

Reading 1 (ABC), Isaiah 49:1-6

Listen to me, O coastlands, pay attention, you peoples from far away! The Lord called me before I was born, while I was in my mother's womb he named me. He made my mouth like a sharp sword, in the shadow of his hand he hid me; he made me a polished arrow, in his quiver he hid me away. And he said to me, "You are my servant, Israel, in whom I will be glorified." But I said, "I have labored in vain, I have spent my strength for nothing and vanity; yet surely my cause is with the Lord, and my reward with my God."

And now the Lord says, who formed me in the womb to be his servant, to bring Jacob back to him, and that Israel might be gathered to him, for I am honored in the sight of the Lord, and my God has become my strength—he says, "It is too light a thing that you should be my servant to raise up the tribes of Jacob and to restore the survivors of Israel; I will give you as a light to the nations, that my salvation may reach to the end of the earth."

Psalm 139:1-3,13-14,14-15 (*R* verse 14)

Reading 2 (ABC), Acts 13:22-26

Paul spoke in the synagogue: "[God] made David…king [of our ancestors]. In his testimony about him [God] said, 'I have found David, son of Jesse, to be a man after my heart, who will carry out all my wishes.' Of this man's posterity God has brought to Israel a Savior, Jesus, as he promised; before his coming John had already proclaimed a baptism of repentance to all the people of Israel. And as John was finishing his work, he said, 'What do you suppose that I am? I am not he. No, but one is coming after me; I am not worthy to untie the thong of the sandals on his feet.'

"You descendants of Abraham's family, and others who fear God, to us the message of this salvation has been sent."

Gospel (ABC), Luke 1:57-66,80

The time came for Elizabeth to give birth, and she bore a son. Her neighbors and relatives heard that the Lord had shown his great mercy to her, and they rejoiced with her. On the eighth day they came to circumcise the child, and they were going to name him Zechariah after his father. But his mother said, "No; he is to be called John." They said to her, "None of your relatives has this name."

Then they began motioning to his father to find out what name he wanted to give him. He asked for a writing tablet and wrote, "His name is John." And all of them were amazed. Immediately his mouth was opened and his tongue freed, and he began to speak, praising God.

Fear came over all their neighbors, and all these things were talked about throughout the entire hill country of Judea. All who heard them pondered them and said, "What then will this child become?" For, indeed, the hand of the Lord was with him.

The child grew and became strong in spirit, and he was in the wilderness until the day he appeared publicly to Israel.

Being a Prophet

JOHN F. CRAGHAN

Prophetic title means prophetic service. Prophet is both the title and the challenge that we receive at baptism. We are pleased with the title but often displeased with the service involved. We are elated to be known as God's spokespersons but less elated to act as spokespersons, i.e., by reaching out to others. We are gratified to be called God's criticizers (we tell it the way it really is) and God's energizers (we tell it the way it can be). But we are less gratified when we must actually involve ourselves in the plight of others. We bask in the beauty of the name "prophet" but we cower in the reality of that title.

Today's readings deal with the reality of being prophets. They situate the prophetic role within the context of the community. The one who is called by God is called to serve the community. Hence the movement is ever outward—from the prophet to the people. Prophetic title means prophetic service.

A Light to the Nations

The first reading is the second Servant Song from the work of the anonymous exilic author, Second Isaiah (chapters 40—55). The Suffering Servant is quite likely the prophet himself and all those followers who heed God's word to leave exile in Babylon for a new life in Israel. As the passage points out, however, the prophetic vocation of the Servant necessarily involves service.

In Second Isaiah both name and reality of prophet come together in terms of service. After the prophet mentions his prophetic calling from his mother's womb (see Jer 1:5), he describes the implications of that calling. He is the one through whom the Lord will show his glory (verse 3), through whom Jacob will be brought back (verse 5), through whom the survivors of Israel will be restored (verse 6). His vocation also includes the Gentiles, however—he will serve as their light (verse 6). Despite God's protection and care ("sharp sword" and "polished arrow"), he is afflicted and discouraged. He feels as though he has labored and spent himself in vain.

But he is confident that the Lord will sustain him in his trial with his enemy. Here prophetic title means prophetic service.

In Acts, Paul's sermon in the synagogue at Pisidian Antioch is Luke's model sermon for the proclamation of the Good News to Israel. Here Paul addresses Jews living outside the Holy Land and pagans who accepted Israel's ethical monotheism but did not keep the entire Mosaic Law ("others who fear God"). In verses 16-25, Luke develops God's plan as it leads from Israel to the Christian Church.

A Voice in the Wilderness

In verses 22-23, Luke moves quickly from David to Jesus by way of John the Baptist. John's prophetic career is one of service, i.e., he is to prepare God's people by preaching a baptism of repentance (see Lk 1:76-77). He is a herald who announces the coming of "one who is more powerful" (Lk 3:16). John acknowledges that his whole career is in view of the one the thong of whose sandals he is not worthy to untie (verse 25). Prophetic title means prophetic service.

The gospel is the account of the birth and naming of the Baptist. Elizabeth's delivery is reminiscent of the Hebrew Scriptures where the barren wives of the patriarchs bear a child (or children) and thus provoke an atmosphere of great joy. On the occasion of John's circumcision and name-giving the neighbors learn of the divinely-arranged conception/birth. These neighbors also begin to grasp the future greatness of this child when Elizabeth and Zechariah agree on his unexpected name of John. Zechariah's regained speech increases the neighbors' amazement. This is also Luke's device for anticipating John's greatness.

In verse 80, Luke adopts another motif from the Hebrew Scriptures, i.e., the growth and maturity of the child (see Gn 21:8; Jgs 13:24-25; 1 Sm 2:21). The phrase "in spirit" suggests John's spirit-influenced prophetic mission. It may also, however, imply the Holy Spirit (see Lk 1:15,41,67). What is certainly clear is John's sojourn in the desert, the place of revelation. As a prophet, he will remain there until his heraldic proclamation of "the one who is coming" (see Lk 3:15-17).

Today's Good News

These readings draw us away from an ego-centered notion of prophetic ministry to one of communal service. The figures of the Suffering Servant and John the Baptist evoke the image of one called by God to attend to the needs and concerns of the community.

Family members who devote their time and energy to minister to each other vindicate their prophetic title, for example, as do workers who see their jobs as the opportunity to contribute to the common good. All those in leadership positions who employ their influence and power to promote justice for all justify their prophetic title, as do peacemakers who use their talents to overcome hate and foster reconciliation between families and friends. All such people insist on the proper and sacramental marriage of prophecy and service. For them prophetic title means prophetic service.

Points for Reflection and Discussion

1. Have you ever thought of yourself as "prophet"? As "servant"?

_____

_____

_____

_____

2. Prophets point the way to persons greater than themselves. Talk about some modern-day prophets and the world's general response to them.

_____

_____

_____

_____

Themes

Baptism
  Q2, What Do Catholics Believe?
  M1, Conversion: A Lifelong Process

Prophet
  Q12, Catholics and Church
  M3, Your Special Gifts
  M6, Discernment

Service
  Q6, The Saints
  Q7, Mary
  Q9, Who's Who in the Church
  M2, The Laity: Called to Build God's Kingdom
  M8, Evangelization

Reading 1 (ABC), Acts 12:1-11

King Herod laid violent hands upon some who belonged to the church. He had James, the brother of John, killed with the sword. After he saw that it pleased the Jews, he proceeded to arrest Peter also. (This was during the festival of Unleavened Bread.) When he had seized him, he put him in prison and handed him over to four squads of soldiers to guard him, intending to bring him out to the people after the Passover. While Peter was kept in prison, the church prayed fervently to God for him. The very night before Herod was going to bring him out, Peter, bound with two chains, was sleeping between two soldiers, while guards in front of the door were keeping watch over the prison. Suddenly an angel of the Lord appeared and a light shone in the cell. He tapped Peter on the side and woke him, saying, "Get up quickly." And the chains fell off his wrists. The angel said to him, "Fasten your belt and put on your sandals." He did so. Then he said to him, "Wrap your cloak around you and follow me."

Peter went out and followed him; he did not realize that what was happening with the angel's help was real; he thought he was seeing a vision. After they had passed the first and the second guard, they came before the iron gate leading into the city. It opened for them of its own accord, and they went outside and walked along a lane, when suddenly the angel left him.

Then Peter came to himself and said, "Now I am sure that the Lord has sent his angel and rescued me from the hands of Herod and from all that the Jewish people were expecting."

Psalm 34:1-2,3-4,5-6,7-8 (R verse 4)

Reading 2 (ABC), 2 Timothy 4:6-8,17-18

Paul wrote: As for me, I am already being poured out as a libation, and the time of my departure has come. I have fought the good fight, I have finished the race, I have kept the faith. From now on there is reserved for me the crown of righteousness, which the Lord, the righteous judge, will give me on that day, and not only to me but also to all who have longed for his appearing.

The Lord stood by me and gave me strength, so that through me the message might be fully proclaimed and all the Gentiles might hear it. So I was rescued from the lion's mouth. The Lord will rescue me from every evil attack and save me for his heavenly kingdom. To him be the glory forever and ever. Amen.

Gospel (ABC), Matthew 16:13-19

When Jesus came into the district of Caesarea Philippi, he asked his disciples, "Who do people say that the Son of Man is?" And they said, "Some say John the Baptist, but others Elijah, and still others Jeremiah or one of the prophets." He said to them, "But who do you say that I am?" Simon Peter answered, "You are the Messiah, the Son of the living God."

And Jesus answered him, "Blessed are you, Simon son of Jonah! For flesh and blood has not revealed this to you, but my Father in heaven. And I tell you, you are Peter, and on this rock I will build my church, and the gates of Hades will not prevail against it. I will give you the keys of the kingdom of heaven, and whatever you bind on earth will be bound in heaven, and whatever you loose on earth will be loosed in heaven."

Giving Gifts

JOHN F. CRAGHAN

If we are not careful, we can hoard our talents, our gifts, our possessions and property. We somehow think that our efforts to acquire them preclude sharing them with others. Today's readings demand that we reassess our attitudes towards gifts, talents, and personal possessions. The example of Peter and Paul drives us from the limited domain of private possessions into the greater area of communal concern. These examples state unequivocally that private gifts and talents are really public property.

In the Acts of the Apostles, Luke selects Peter as his first hero (to be followed by Paul in chapters 16—21). Peter shares the gift of the Good News he received from Jesus with the Gentiles (chapters 10—11). Peter's personal experience of the Christian message becomes his gift to Jews and Gentiles alike.

Since persecution is often the catalyst for growth (Acts 12:24), Luke tells the story of Peter's imprisonment and miraculous escape. Despite the tight security, God masterminds the escape, while Peter remains completely passive.

Luke asserts that God will provide for the people in times of persecution. He also implies that the escape is calculated to allow Peter to continue his mission. Luke observes that after explaining his miraculous deliverance to the local Christian community, Peter left them to go off to another place. The deliverance, a genuine gift from God, becomes part of Peter's message to be shared with others.

The Legacy of Leadership

In exhorting his audience to preach solid doctrine, to accept suffering, and to continue their ministry faithfully, the author of Second Timothy offers the example of the apostle Paul. He presents this plea as if it were Paul's last will and testament. Noting Paul's sacrificial death ("libation"), he encourages the readers to use their gifts and talents for others as Paul did.

The author recounts the apostle's deliverance, noting that the rescue from the lion's jaws was not merely a personal favor. Paul's talents and gifts benefited the common good, "so that through me the preaching task might be completed and all the nations might hear the gospel" (4:17). Paul's example of self-giving is to become the contagious legacy of the community. We are not to retain the Lord's gifts for ourselves but to share them with others.

The gospel passage is recorded by all three synoptic authors (Mark, Matthew, Luke). In Mark, Peter identified Jesus as the Messiah (8:29). In Luke, Peter calls Jesus the Messiah of God (9:20). In Matthew, Peter adds, "[you are] the Son of the living God!" (16:16). Peter's perception of Jesus as the transcendent Son of God is due, not to mere human nature (literally "flesh and blood") but to a revelation from the Father (16:17; see Gal 1:15-16). This realization of Peter's giftedness prompts Matthew to have Jesus confer a leadership role on Peter. "Rock" suggests the unshakableness he will provide for Jesus' community (Mt 7:24-27). Not even the insatiable appetite of the nether world ("the jaws of death," Song 8:6) will prevail against it.

The reference to the keys of the kingdom recalls the authority of a prime minister (Is 22:22) and indicates that Peter has the power to teach people the way to reach the kingdom (Mt 23:13).

For Matthew, Peter does not stand in splendid isolation from the rest of the community. His position as rock and his power of binding and loosing are not purely personal privileges. They presume the welfare of the entire community. In the Gospel of Matthew, therefore, Peter gives an example of how personal gifts are to be shared with the entire Christian community.

Today's Good News

Our personal gifts are manifold. We may find that we have talents for consoling, healing, teaching, leading, and so forth. These may be talents that have been acquired only at great price and after much sacrifice. While we tend to clutch them as a miser's booty, Peter and Paul suggest that these talents are not ours alone. Since we are all members of the community, the talents and gifts that we possess become the common possession of the entire Christian community.

When talents are hoarded for personal use, they atrophy. Sharing one's talents, gifts, and possessions enriches them. Such an awareness calls for a new set of priorities. The question must now be, how can I share my gift with you?; not, how can I use my gift for personal gain? The gift is perfected in the act of giving, not in the act of hoarding. Ultimately, to receive a gift from God is to receive a call to give that gift to the human community. Personal gifts, by Christian definition, are to be shared with others.

Points for Reflection and Discussion

1. What special gifts and talents have you been given by God? How do you best share them with others?

_____

_____

_____

_____

2. Today's readings remind us that authority and power ("crown of righteous"; "rock") can only work if used in service to others ("bound in chains"; "poured out like a libation"). What authority and power do you have? How do you exercise it?

_____

_____

_____

_____

Themes

Authority
  Q9, Who's Who in the Church
Gifts
  M3, Your Special Gifts
Ministry
  Q12, Catholics and Church
  M2, The Laity: Called to Build God's Kingdom
  M8, Evangelization

Reading 1 (ABC), Daniel 7:9-10,13-14

As I watched, thrones were set in place, and an Ancient One took his throne, his clothing was white as snow, and the hair of his head like pure wool; his throne was fiery flames, and its wheels were burning fire. A stream of fire issued and flowed out from his presence. A thousand thousands served him, and ten thousand times ten thousand stood attending him. The court sat in judgment, and the books were opened.

As I watched in the night visions, I saw one like a human being coming with the clouds of heaven. And he came to the Ancient One and was presented before him. To him was given dominion and glory and kingship, that all peoples, nations, and languages should serve him. His dominion is an everlasting dominion that shall not pass away, and his kingship is one that shall never be destroyed.

Psalm 97:1-2,5-6,9,12 (*R* verses 1 and 9)

Reading 2 (ABC), 2 Peter 1:16-19

We did not follow cleverly devised myths when we made known to you the power and coming of our Lord Jesus Christ, but we had been eyewitnesses of his majesty. For he received honor and glory from God the Father when that voice was conveyed to him by the Majestic Glory, saying, "This is my Son, my Beloved, with whom I am well pleased." We ourselves heard this voice come from heaven, while we were with him on the holy mountain. So we have the prophetic message more fully confirmed. You will do well to be attentive to this as to a lamp shining in a dark place, until the day dawns and the morning star rises in your hearts.

Gospel (A), Matthew 17:1-9

Jesus took with him Peter and James and his brother John and led them up a high mountain, by themselves. And he was transfigured before them, and his face shone like the sun, and his clothes became dazzling white. Suddenly there appeared to them Moses and Elijah, talking with him. Then Peter said to Jesus, "Lord, it is good for us to be here; if you wish, I will make three dwellings here, one for you, one for Moses, and one for Elijah."

While he was still speaking, suddenly a bright cloud overshadowed them, and from the cloud a voice said, "This is my Son, the Beloved; with him I am well pleased; listen to him!" When the disciples heard this, they fell to the ground and were overcome by fear. But Jesus came and touched them, saying, "Get up and do not be afraid." And when they looked up, they saw no one except Jesus himself alone.

As they were coming down the mountain, Jesus ordered them, "Tell no one about the vision until after the Son of Man has been raised from the dead."

Gospel (B), Mark 9:2-10

Jesus took with him Peter and James and John, and led them up a high mountain apart, by themselves. And he was transfigured before them, and his clothes became dazzling white, such as no one on earth could bleach them. And there appeared to them Elijah with Moses, who were talking with Jesus. Then Peter said to Jesus, "Rabbi, it is good for us to be here; let us make three dwellings, one for you, one for Moses, and one for Elijah." He did not know what to say, for they were terrified.

Then a cloud overshadowed them, and from the cloud there came a voice, "This is my Son, the Beloved; listen to him!" Suddenly when they looked around, they saw no one with them any more, but only Jesus.

As they were coming down the mountain, he ordered them to tell no one about what they had seen, until after the Son of Man had risen from the dead. So they kept the matter to themselves, questioning what this rising from the dead could mean.

Gospel (C), Luke 9:28-36

Jesus took with him Peter and John and James, and went up on the mountain to pray. And while he was praying, the appearance of his face changed, and his clothes became dazzling white. Suddenly they saw two men, Moses and Elijah, talking to him. They appeared in glory and were speaking of his departure, which he was about to accomplish at Jerusalem.

Now Peter and his companions were weighed down with sleep; but since they had stayed awake, they saw his glory and the two men who stood with him. Just as they were leaving him, Peter said to Jesus, "Master, it is good for us to be here; let us make three dwellings, one for you, one for Moses, and one for Elijah"—not knowing what he said. While he was saying this, a cloud came and overshadowed them; and they were terrified as they entered the cloud.

Then from the cloud came a voice that said, "This is my Son, my Chosen; listen to him!" When the voice had spoken, Jesus was found alone. And they kept silent and in those days told no one any of the things they had seen.

To Be Transfigured

ELSIE HAINZ MCGRATH

What did the transfiguration mean for Peter and James and John? What does it mean for us? We catch a clue in today's second reading. The Letter of Peter was clearly written in hindsight—after the Resurrection. It reiterates the events of the mountaintop as fact—an eye-witness account being put forward as proof of the *Parousia*, the Second Coming of Christ. Peter and James and John, in looking back on the events of that glorious day, interpret the transfiguration in light of the Resurrection. They were given a glimpse of the King of Glory while he was still among them as a mere man. Clearly, Jesus reigns in transfigured splendor with his *Abba* Father. God attested to this when stating that Jesus was "my Son." Clearly, Jesus will make a second transfigured appearance.

An Everlasting Dominion

The first reading today gives us a sample of *apocalyptic*, that style of writing which was to exert tremendous influence during the next few centuries in the Church. Its means is to use events from past and present history in such a way that they are perceived as future prophecies; its purpose is to provide hope to people who are facing seemingly insurmountable crises.

As the story establishes before today's reading picks it up, four beasts have to be destroyed before "one like a human being" is given everlasting dominion by the "Ancient One." These four beasts have been identified by scholars as the four successive pagan empires of the Babylonians, the Medes, the Persians, and the Greeks. The readers knew that *only* the Greek empire, under the obsessively cruel rule of Antiochus IV Epiphanes, still oppressed them. The message of hope was clear to them, therefore: the others eventually fell, so will this one.

The Christian interpretation of today's reading has remained unchanged throughout the centuries: *all* injustice will eventually cease, *all* evil rulers will eventually fall, and Christ will come again to reign in glory forever.

Today's Good News

Peter wanted to stay on the mountaintop, to pitch tents and maybe start a campfire. And why not? The apostles heard the voice of God, and they believed, and they obeyed—but they didn't understand. (Such a thing could not have been understood on the other side of the Resurrection.) Still they went back down the mountain, back to the "real" world of work and worry, of temptation and rejection. But they had only to close their eyes and bring back the vision of the mountaintop to feel the closeness they had shared.

And so do we. The message of the Transfiguration story—for us today and for Peter and James and John two thousand years ago—is that the Son of God brings change and turns death into life. And sometimes we are graced with glimpses of the reign of God. They get us through the hard times down in the valleys; they take us to the heady and transfiguring peaks of the mountaintops.

Points for Reflection and Discussion

1. Talk about a transfiguring experience in your life. Did you want to leave the experience? Did leaving it bring new and unexpected spiritual growth?

_____

_____

_____

_____

2. Some Scripture scholars think the transfiguration story is actually a post-resurrection story; that it didn't happen before Easter. What do you think? Why?

_____

_____

_____

_____

_____

Themes

Revelation
   Q12, Catholics and Church
   M1, Conversion: A Lifelong Process

Second Coming
   Q2, What Do Catholics Believe?
   M8, Evangelization

Transfiguration
   Q5, How Do Catholics Interpret the Bible?
   M7, Holiness

Reading 1 (ABC), Revelation 11:19;12:1-6,10

God's temple in heaven was opened, and the ark of his covenant was seen within his temple. A great portent appeared in heaven: a woman clothed with the sun, with the moon under her feet, and on her head a crown of twelve stars. She was pregnant and was crying out in birthpangs, in the agony of giving birth.

Then another portent appeared in heaven: a great red dragon, with seven heads and ten horns, and seven diadems on his heads. His tail swept down a third of the stars of heaven and threw them to the earth. Then the dragon stood before the woman who was about to bear a child, so that he might devour her child as soon as it was born.

And she gave birth to a son, a male child, who is to rule all the nations with a rod of iron. But her child was snatched away and taken to God and to his throne; and the woman fled into the wilderness, where she has a place prepared by God, so that there she can be nourished for one thousand two hundred sixty days.

Then I heard a loud voice in heaven, proclaiming, "Now have come the salvation and the power and the kingdom of our God and the authority of his Messiah."

Psalm 45:9-10,11,12,14,15,17 (*R verse 9*)

Reading 2 (ABC), 1 Corinthians 15:20-26

Christ has been raised from the dead, the first fruits of those who have died. For since death came through a human being, the resurrection of the dead has also come through a human being; for as all die in Adam, so all will be made alive in Christ. But each in his own order: Christ the first fruits, then at his coming those who belong to Christ. Then comes the end, when he hands over the kingdom to God the Father, after he has destroyed every ruler and every authority and power. For he must reign until he has put all his enemies under his feet. The last enemy to be destroyed is death.

Gospel (ABC), Luke 1:39-56

Mary set out and went with haste to a Judean town in the hill country, where she entered the house of Zechariah and greeted Elizabeth. When Elizabeth heard Mary's greeting, the child leaped in her womb. And Elizabeth was filled with the Holy Spirit and exclaimed with a loud cry, "Blessed are you among women, and blessed is the fruit of your womb. And why has this happened to me, that the mother of my Lord comes to me? For as soon as I heard the sound of your greeting, the child in my womb leaped for joy. And blessed is she who believed that there would be a fulfillment of what was spoken to her by the Lord."

And Mary said, "My soul magnifies the Lord, and my spirit rejoices in God my Savior, for he has looked with favor on the lowliness of his servant. Surely, from now on all generations will call me blessed; for the Mighty One has done great things for me, and holy is his name. His mercy is for those who fear him from generation to generation. He has shown strength with his arm; he has scattered the proud in the thoughts of their hearts. He has brought down the powerful from their thrones, and lifted up the lowly; he has filled the hungry with good things, and sent the rich away empty. He has helped his servant Israel, in remembrance of his mercy, according to the promise he made to our ancestors, to Abraham and to his descendants forever." And Mary remained with her about three months and then returned to her home.

The Assumption

ELSIE HAINZ MCGRATH

As early as the fifth century, Christians celebrated a "Memorial of Mary" on the fifteenth of August. This evolved into what was called the feast of the Dormition (or "falling asleep") of the Virgin. In other words, Mary died but her body did not corrupt; rather, it was assumed into heaven. The Assumption, then, is a truth that emerged from the faith of the people because Christians simply could not imagine that Mary's body was separated from her soul and suffered decay when she died. It has been a part of the Church's lived Tradition and, as such, was proclaimed dogma in 1950. The Church believes that "Mary is one with the risen Christ in the fullness of her personality" (*Behold Your Mother* [1973], National Council of Catholic Bishops).

Queen of Heaven

The Book of Revelation dates back to the Church's beginnings. It is believed to have been written during the Roman reign of Domitian (A.D. 81-96), a particularly violent persecutor of Christians. The literary genre of *apocalyptic* was well-known in times of crises; it gave the people cause for hope in the midst of despair. With symbolic numbers and colors, clothing and metals, writers conveyed the promise that God would be the ultimate victor in whatever war was being waged against them.

As today's reading indicates, Revelation, which is the only wholly apocalyptic writing in the New Testament, is also filled with images of a woman who is the queen of heaven. The characteristic sun, moon, and stars are typical of high goddesses in the ancient world. While the woman's identity is not fully revealed, Church Tradition has universally held her to be Mary.

Today's reading has the queen of heaven (thus the spouse of the king—God) suffering the pains of child-birth for the sake of delivering the Messiah—the Savior of the world. She faces the mythological dragon, used in ancient literature to represent the oppressor, whether Nero or Satan, and when the baby is born he is immediately rescued from the grips of the oppressor by God. This is a sign that the child will truly usher in world peace and justice, a sign here reinforced by the heavenly proclamation. The woman, having successfully birthed her godly son, is transported to the desert where she may in safety and privileged privacy complete her time of ritual purification.

The Canticle of Mary

Luke's Gospel tells the story of Mary's visitation. She enters the home of Elizabeth and Zechariah, and the babe in Elizabeth's womb immediately recognizes the babe in Mary's womb. If that isn't amazing enough, Elizabeth herself recognizes the babe in Mary's womb—and no one even knew she was pregnant yet! But the focus is not on the special children—neither Jesus the Christ nor John the Baptizer. The focus is on *Mary*—the *mother* of the Lord. Mary herself recognizes this, and sings a canticle of praise. "Surely, from now on all generations will call *me* blessed; for the Mighty One has done great things *for me.*"

This canticle has been the Church's prayer, in the Liturgy of the Hours, for "all generations." Recited daily, it stands as a reminder of perfect faithfulness to those who would be faithful—Mary's own humble testimony to the greatness of God and the wonderful things God will wrought in the lives of those who trust.

Today's Good News

Saint Paul tells us that "Christ has been raised from the dead, the first fruits of those who have died." In other words, what was done for Christ will be done for all of us. When he comes again we will be raised to heaven with him, body and soul, but this cannot happen until all the forces that stint our full humanity ("rule, authority, and power") are destroyed. In other words, we must become perfect, as our Lord is perfect, in order to attain our heavenly home.

Mary's assumption into heaven, then, theologically points to what we believe God will do for us. She was "the handmaid of the Lord" who agreed that "it be done to me according to your will." Perfect humanity mirrors divinity, and so she has taken her rightful place beside God—as Mother of the Redeemer, as spouse of the Creator, as representative of the Church—as Queen of Heaven. Body and soul, we too will someday be raised to new life in the kingdom of God.

Points for Reflection and Discussion

1. How is Mary most relatable for you (as mother or sister...as human or super-human...as accessible or unreachable...)?

_____

_____

_____

_____

_____

2. Pray the canticle of Mary slowly and reverently. Try to imagine that you are Mary as you say the words. How do you feel?

_____

_____

_____

_____

_____

Themes
Assumption, Mary
    Q7, Mary
    M7, Holiness
Redemption
    Q2, What Do Catholics Believe?
    M1, Conversion: A Lifelong Process

Reading 1 (ABC), Numbers 21:4-9

From Mount Hor they set out by the way to the Red Sea, to go around the land of Edom; but the people became impatient on the way. The people spoke against God and against Moses, "Why have you brought us up out of Egypt to die in the wilderness? For there is no food and no water, and we detest this miserable food." Then the Lord sent poisonous serpents among the people, and they bit the people, so that many Israelites died. The people came to Moses and said, "We have sinned by speaking against the Lord and against you; pray to the Lord to take away the serpents from us." So Moses prayed for the people.

And the Lord said to Moses, "Make a poisonous serpent, and set it on a pole; and everyone who is bitten shall look at it and live." So Moses made a serpent of bronze, and put it upon a pole; and whenever a serpent bit someone, that person would look at the serpent of bronze and live.

Psalm 78:1-2,34-35,36-37,38 (*R verse 7*)

Reading 2 (ABC), Philippians 2:6-11

Though he was in the form of God, [Jesus] did not regard equality with God as something to be exploited, but emptied himself, taking the form of a slave, being born in human likeness. And being found in human form, he humbled himself and became obedient to the point of death—even death on a cross. Therefore God also highly exalted him and gave him the name that is above every name, so that at the name of Jesus every knee should bend, in heaven and on earth and under the earth, and every tongue should confess that Jesus Christ is Lord, to the glory of God the Father.

Gospel (ABC), John 3:13-17

Jesus said to Nicodemus: "No one has ascended into heaven except the one who descended from heaven, the Son of Man. And just as Moses lifted up the serpent in the wilderness, so must the Son of Man be lifted up, that whoever believes in him may have eternal life.

"For God so loved the world that he gave his only Son, so that everyone who believes in him may not perish but may have eternal life. Indeed, God did not send the Son into the world to condemn the world, but in order that the world might be saved through him."

Reaching the Top

JOHN F. CRAGHAN

In our conversations and perhaps even in our prayers we dream about making it big and getting to the top. We rehearse the steps necessary for our climb upward. If other people become obstacles in our path, we quietly yet effectively set them aside. We give gifts only to the extent that they will enhance our prestige. We have failed to learn that giving oneself is the way to reach the top.

Today's readings focus on the challenge of giving oneself for the sake of others. They offer us a different formula for success and prosperity. Only those who give themselves in service for others really win esteem. Paradoxically, it is the symbol of the cross that casts its shadow across our gift-giving and provides a model of action for reaching the top. It implies that self-giving can be truly self-fulfilling.

Psalm 78 is a historical epic that provides a lesson for modern living. The psalmist invites the audience to reflect on Israel's history and learn from it. In verses 12-32, the psalmist recites Israel's wilderness experience. Though God was exceedingly gracious during the years the people lived in the desert, Israel responded through rebellion, which in turn provoked God's anger. Anger, however, was not present in God's final reply. Despite Israel's rejection, Israel's God will not be outdone. In verses 33-39, the psalmist appeals to the audience to see God's marvelous plan at work. In this scenario, sin brings punishment, which then becomes the occasion for the people's repentance. In the end, the people's repentance moves God to grant forgiveness.

In this reflection, Israel's God grows in strength by understanding the weakness of Israel. Without condoning sin, the psalmist paints a picture of a God who achieves greatness by bending low to assist the weak people. God's concern for the people is rewarded by their reverence and esteem.

The Name Above All Names

In his letter, Paul seeks to motivate the charity of the Philippians by incorporating (with some additions) a Jewish-Christian hymn into his text. It stands to reason that since Jesus was totally sinless, he should not have been subject to death and corruption (see Wis 2:23). Nevertheless, he put aside his prerogatives and took on a life of suffering and frustration.

Rejecting his privileged status, Jesus went even further. He descended to the very depths of death through his death on the cross. But Jesus' death would not be God's last word. God accepted the self-giving of the Son and exalted him, conferring on him the title and authority previously reserved to God, namely, "Lord." Consequently, everyone that is in the heavens, on the earth, and under the earth (see Is 45:2) must "confess that JESUS CHRIST IS LORD to the glory of God the Father." Jesus demonstrates that by giving oneself for the good of others, one can truly make it to the top.

To Be Lifted Up

In his conversation with Nicodemus, Jesus affirms that he alone has direct vision of God (Jn 3:13; see Prv 30:3-4). Next, Jesus addresses Nicodemus' question about being born again (see Jn 3:4). He explains how this new sense of being born flows from the mystery of the crucifixion/resurrection/ascension. Referring to Israel's experience in the desert mentioned in today's first reading, Jesus appeals to the crucifixion. Ironically, "being lifted up" on the cross is only the start of the process that will culminate in "being lifted up" in glory (see Jn 8:28;12:32). Ultimately all believers will experience this new life as a result of this total process of being uplifted (see Jn 7:37-39).

John next joins Jesus' exaltation with the notion of gift-giving. Like Abraham sacrificing Isaac, God the Father loves the world so much that he is willing to give his only Son so that all may benefit (see Gn 22:2,12,18). By giving his Son, the Father ultimately gives himself, that is, he sends his Son "that the world might be saved through him" (Jn 3:17). By linking the sending of the beloved Son ever so intimately with the self-giving on Calvary, John affirms that giving oneself in service is truly making it to the top.

Today's Good News

We naturally seek "to be lifted up." We want to be recognized as truly successful people. On a worldly level, this may lead us to disregard our responsibilities toward others and see them as mere stepping-stones in our upward climb. In such a pursuit, we have opted for only one interpretation of "being lifted up," namely, that of exaltation at the expense of others.

Today's feast challenges us by presenting an entirely different approach. The Triumph of the Cross affirms that only those who give themselves in the service of others ultimately make it to the top. In the language of Paul, it is only self-emptying that is self-fulfilling. The symbol of the cross shows that there is strength in weakness. Jesus demonstrates that it is in the giving of self that one really gains prominence. The Lord of glory is first the Jesus of pain. The cross is Christianity's most powerful symbol that giving oneself in service to others is truly the way to make it to the top.

Points for Reflection and Discussion

1. Seriously reflect on the fact that the humility of the cross is the triumph of the Church. Do you bear your cross humbly or triumphantly?

_____

_____

_____

_____

2. Do you find it hard to let go of your crosses? Why or why not? Does turning them over to Jesus lighten your load? If so, how?

_____

_____

_____

_____

Themes

Cross, Lord, Salvation
Q2, What Do Catholics Believe?

Reading 1 (ABC), Revelation 7:2-4,9-14

I, [John], saw an angel ascending from the rising of the sun, having the seal of the living God, and he called with a loud voice to the four angels who had been given power to damage earth and sea, saying, "Do not damage the earth or the sea or the trees, until we have marked the servants of our God with a seal on their foreheads." And I heard the number of those who were sealed, one hundred forty-four thousand, sealed out of every tribe of the people of Israel.

After this I looked, and there was a great multitude that no one could count, from every nation, from all tribes and peoples and languages, standing before the throne and before the Lamb, robed in white, with palm branches in their hands. They cried out in a loud voice, saying, "Salvation belongs to our God who is seated on the throne, and to the Lamb!" And all the angels stood around the throne and around the elders and the four living creatures, and they fell on their faces before the throne and worshiped God, singing, "Amen! Blessing and glory and wisdom and thanksgiving and honor and power and might be to our God forever and ever! Amen."

Then one of the elders addressed me, saying, "Who are these, robed in white, and where have they come from?" I said to him, "Sir, you are the one that knows." Then he said to me, "These are they who have come out of the great ordeal; they have washed their robes and made them white in the blood of the Lamb."

Psalm 24:1-2,3-4,5-6 (*R* verses 7 and 10)

Reading 2 (ABC), 1 John 3:1-3

See what love the Father has given us, that we should be called children of God; and that is what we are. The reason the world does not know us is that it did not know him. Beloved, we are God's children now; what we will be has not yet been revealed. What we do know is this: when he is revealed, we will be like him, for we will see him as he is. And all who have this hope in him purify themselves, just as he is pure.

Gospel (ABC), Matthew 5:1-12

When Jesus saw the crowds, he went up the mountain; and after he sat down, his disciples came to him. Then he began to speak, and taught them, saying:

"Blessed are the poor in spirit, for theirs is the kingdom of heaven.

"Blessed are those who mourn, for they will be comforted.

"Blessed are the meek, for they will inherit the earth.

"Blessed are those who hunger and thirst for righteousness, for they will be filled.

"Blessed are the merciful, for they will receive mercy.

"Blessed are the pure in heart, for they will see God.

"Blessed are the peacemakers, for they will be called children of God.

"Blessed are those who are persecuted for righteousness' sake, for theirs is the kingdom of heaven.

"Blessed are you when people revile you and persecute you and utter all kinds of evil against you falsely on my account. Rejoice and be glad, for your reward is great in heaven."

Freedom Fighters

JOHN F. CRAGHAN

We sometimes imagine the saints to be rather esoteric types. We see them as the recipients of special revelations and the devotees of mystical experiences. We imagine them to be divorced from our "real" world. We cannot conceive of them as people with a crusade or a cause. Since saints populate never-never land, we automatically exclude the possibility that they are freedom fighters.

Today's readings see the saints in the context of freedom. They are the people who decide upon a course of action and pursue it relentlessly. Since they opt for God's vision, they refuse to be tied down by any force or power opposed to that vision. Each day they reject whatever detracts from the love of God and of others. In this setting saints are clearly freedom fighters.

Robes of White

The Book of Revelation responds to a persecution of Christians in Asia Minor toward the end of the first century A.D. The refusal to worship the Roman emperor could have dire consequences, including death. Writing from Patmos, some fifty miles southwest of Ephesus, the author provides an interlude between the breaking of the sixth (6:12-17) and the seventh (8:1) seals. In 7:1-8, he speaks of God's care for the Church on earth and, in 7:9-17, of God's reception of glory from the Church in heaven. The seal shows that the elect are divine property. The number 144,000 attempts to capture—with no attempt at mathematical precision—the multitude of the true Israel.

In verses 9-12, the jubilant Christians appear in full glory. Their palm branches bespeak their victory. Verse 14 identifies them further. They have survived the great period of trial, namely, the persecution. While the martyrs are certainly included, this verse also envisions all Christians who choose to be faithful during crises. By sharing in Christ's death, they have kept themselves pure ("white robes"). Saints are freedom fighters.

The author of First John, writing around A.D. 100, sometime after the composition of the fourth gospel, addresses the question of secession within his community. Some groups have left the community and established independent associations to preach and teach a doctrine different from the author's. Such groups have rejected basic beliefs about Jesus (see 4:1-3). Moreover, there are fundamental differences between the author's community and these dissident groups over matters of sin and judgment.

In the midst of troubles, the community is urged to reflect on their relationship with the Father through the Son and to act upon it. In effect, the invitation is a call to exercise freedom by mirroring the perfection ("pure") of God.

Inheriting the Kingdom

In this keynote address, namely, the Sermon on the Mount, Matthew presents Jesus' vision of the kingdom. He brings together those qualities that pronounce a person truly fortunate or blessed. The first four beatitudes (5:3-6) emphasize a passive attitude (the mournful, the meek...) while the fifth, sixth, and seventh (verses 7-10) stress an active involvement (merciful, peacemakers...). The final beatitude (verses 11-12) focuses on persecution.

The eighth beatitude probably refers to the situation of Matthew's Jewish-Christian community. They still bear scars connected to their separation from Judaism. Developing this theme, Matthew has Jesus address the disciples directly, warning them about the harassment (persecution) they will endure in living the Christian life. He also underlines the personal relationship between Jesus and the disciples ("on my account").

Today's Good News

Today's feast is a marvelous opportunity to recall the "saints" in our own lives. We naturally think of parents, relatives, and friends who daily undertook the task of living the Christian life. They were freedom fighters insofar as they rejected other interests and pursuits to devote their time and energy to good. In their dedication, they experienced pain and frustration because freedom is not exempt from these. In recalling them on this feast, we truly honor them by applying their pursuit of freedom to our lives. In this way the chain of service is continued. We, the saints of the present world, are called to be freedom fighters.

Points for Reflection and Discussion

1. Who are the "saints" in your everyday life? Why?

_____

_____

_____

_____

2. How would you define "freedom" in light of sainthood?

_____

_____

_____

_____

Themes

Freedom
  M3, Your Special Gifts
  M7, Holiness
Revelation
  Q5, How Do Catholics Interpret the Bible?
  Q12, Catholics and Church
  M5, Your Prayer Life
  M6, Discernment
Saints
  Q6, The Saints
  M2, The Laity: Called to Build God's Kingdom

Reading 1 (ABC), Daniel 12:1-3

At that time Michael, the great prince, the protector of your people, shall arise. There shall be a time of anguish, such as has never occurred since nations first came into existence. But at that time your people shall be delivered, everyone who is found written in the book. Many of those who sleep in the dust of the earth shall awake, some to everlasting life, and some to shame and everlasting contempt. Those who are wise shall shine like the brightness of the sky, and those who lead many to righteousness, like the stars forever and ever.

Psalm 23:1-3,3-4,5,6 (*R* verse 1)

Reading 2 (ABC), Rom 8:31-35,37-39

If God is for us, who is against us? He who did not withhold his own Son, but gave him up for all of us, will he not with him also give us everything else? Who will bring any charge against God's elect? It is God who justifies. Who is to condemn? It is Christ Jesus, who died, yes, who was raised, who is at the right hand of God, who indeed intercedes for us. Who will separate us from the love of Christ? Will hardship, or distress, or persecution, or famine, or nakedness, or peril, or sword? In all these things we are more than conquerors through him who loved us. For I am convinced that neither death, nor life, nor angels, nor rulers, nor things present, nor things to come, nor powers, nor height, nor depth, nor anything else in all creation, will be able to separate us from the love of God in Christ Jesus our Lord.

Gospel (ABC), John 17:24-26

Jesus prayed and said: "Father, I desire that those also, whom you have given me, may be with me where I am, to see my glory, which you have given me because you loved me before the foundation of the world.

"Righteous Father, the world does not know you, but I know you; and these know that you have sent me. I made your name known to them, and I will make it known, so that the love with which you have loved me may be in them, and I in them."

*These are only suggested readings for All Souls Day. Any readings from the liturgical Masses for the Dead may be used today.

Life Everlasting

JOHN F. CRAGHAN

We have a penchant for forgetting. We easily succumb to the debilitating disease of "out of sight, out of mind." Though loved ones have graced our lives with support and dedication, we tend to forget them once they are dead. Somehow it is so difficult to bridge the chasm between the great deeds of our beloved dead and the faulty performance of our memories.

Today's readings are designed to jar our sense of recollection. They all converge on a God who does not forget the people and their accomplishments. They emphasize that God cannot overlook the goodness of others. We might say God has instant recall. The feats of the faithful departed are very much alive. By definition, in fact, God proclaims, "I will never forget my people."

A Glimmer of Hope

Around 165 B.C., the author of Daniel sought to offer encouragement to the Jews during the persecution of the Seleucid king, Antiochus IV Epiphanes (see 1 Mc 1—6; 2 Mc 4—9). Today's first reading is the conclusion of his most elaborate *apocalypse*. An angel explains the vision to Daniel, who in turn communicates the message of hope to his beleaguered community. The triumph of Michael is symbolic of the triumph of the faithful people of God.

This is the first biblical passage that clearly speaks about the resurrection of the dead. The author does not envision a universal resurrection: only those who merit eternal reward or punishment will rise. In this passage, the author singles out Israel's wise teachers among those who will rise in glory. He praises the example of the Maccabean martyrs who have offered their lives for their religious convictions (see Is 53:12).

Significantly, the author speaks about those whose names are written in the book. In both Israel (see Ex 32:32-33; Ps 69:29) and the ancient Near East such a book recorded the names of those who belonged to the community. In this instance those listed in the book are specifically those Jews who have persevered and who will, therefore, be delivered. The book and its record of loyal followers proclaims, "I will never forget my faithful people."

Nothing Can Separate Us From the Love of God

Today's passage from the second reading is Paul's triumphant conclusion to chapters 5—8. This section implicitly raises the questions: Will God continue to remember us?; will God continue to provide for us? At the great judgment scene the Judge will decide in favor of the faithful. Christ who died for all people will continue, in his risen life, to support them and serve as the advocate at their trial.

In this heavenly scene there is no obstacle that can separate loyal Christians from God's abiding love. No matter what the force, God's overwhelming love, manifest in the person of Christ Jesus, will continue to protect the faithful. This love clearly proclaims, "I will never forget my creatures."

Today's gospel is the end of Jesus' high-priestly prayer (Jn 17:1-26). As Moses blessed the Israelites before he died (see Dt 33), Jesus blesses his community for the final time. He expresses the wish that believers should be with him in heaven to share a final revelation of his own glory. Since these believers have been his intimates on earth, it is only right that they should enjoy lasting union with Jesus in eternity. The dynamic love between Father and Son is the basis of Christian unity. Such unity perpetuates that love and is the assurance that God is incapable of ever forgetting "my own."

Today's Good News

There are, of course, many ways in which we can remember our dead. We can page through family photo albums and review our home movies. We can recall both the humorous and the tragic events in their lives. We can reflect on their wise sayings and timely advice. The danger remains, however, that the past is condemned to be simply the past.

Let the past be the catalyst for the present and the future. Let the love and devotion of parents be the inspiration in our family circle. Let the patience and understanding of relatives and friends be the springboard for our gentleness and tolerance at our jobs. Let the generosity and self-giving of our forbearers in community have an impact on our social life. Ultimately, to remember is to let the past influence the present and the future. In such a way we are loyal to the author of Daniel, to Paul, and to John, all of whom clearly proclaim, "God never forgets the people and their goodness." We must likewise recall and benefit from the good deeds of our ancestors.

Points for Reflection and Discussion

1. After you get over missing them, do you often think about those who have died? Do you ever wonder where they are or what they are doing?

_____

_____

_____

_____

2. Stories keep memories alive—even for those who may never have known the stories' characters. Do you tell stories about long-ago relatives and friends—maybe even some you never knew but remember from the stories that were told to you?

_____

_____

_____

_____

_____

Themes
Death
    Q2, What Do Catholics Believe?
Life
    Q6, The Saints
    M1, Conversion: A Lifelong Process
Remembrance
    Q3, What is the Meaning of the Mass?
    Q11, Catholic Practices

Reading 1 (ABC), 2 Chronicles 5:6-10,13—6:2

King Solomon and all the congregation of Israel, who had assembled before him, were before the ark, sacrificing so many sheep and oxen that they could not be numbered or counted. Then the priests brought the ark of the covenant of the Lord to its place, in the inner sanctuary of the house, in the most holy place, underneath the wings of the cherubim. For the cherubim spread out their wings over the place of the ark, so that the cherubim made a covering above the ark and its poles. The poles were so long that the ends of the poles were seen from the holy place in front of the inner sanctuary; but they could not be seen from outside; they are there to this day. There was nothing in the ark except the two tablets that Moses put there at Horeb, where the Lord made a covenant with the people of Israel after they came out of Egypt.

It was the duty of the trumpeters and singers to make themselves heard in unison in praise and thanksgiving to the Lord, and when the song was raised, with trumpets and cymbals and other musical instruments, in praise to the Lord, "For he is good, for his steadfast love endures forever," the house, the house of the Lord, was filled with a cloud, so that the priests could not stand to minister because of the cloud; for the glory of the Lord filled the house of God.

Then Solomon said, "The Lord has said that he would reside in thick darkness. I have built you an exalted house, a place for you to reside in forever."

Psalm 122:1-2,3-4,4-5,8-9 (R verse 1)

Reading 2 (ABC), 1 Corinthians 3:9-13,16-17

You are God's building. According to the grace of God given to me, like a skilled master builder I laid a foundation, and someone else is building on it. Each builder must choose with care how to build on it. For no one can lay any foundation other than the one that has been laid; that foundation is Jesus Christ. Now if anyone builds on the foundation with gold, silver, precious stones, wood, hay, straw—the work of each builder will become visible, for the Day will disclose it, because it will be revealed with fire, and the fire will test what sort of work each has done.

Do you not know that you are God's temple and that God's Spirit dwells in you? If anyone destroys God's temple, God will destroy that person. For God's temple is holy, and you are that temple.

Gospel (ABC), Luke 19:1-10

[Jesus] entered Jericho and was passing through it. A man was there named Zacchaeus; he was a chief tax collector and was rich. He was trying to see who Jesus was, but on account of the crowd he could not, because he was short in stature. So he ran ahead and climbed a sycamore tree to see him, because he was going to pass that way. When Jesus came to the place, he looked up and said to him, "Zacchaeus, hurry and come down; for I must stay at your house today."

So he hurried down and was happy to welcome him. All who saw it began to grumble and said, "He has gone to be the guest of one who is a sinner." Zacchaeus stood there and said to the Lord, "Look, half of my possessions, Lord, I will give to the poor; and if I have defrauded anyone of anything, I will pay back four times as much." Then Jesus said to him, "Today salvation has come to this house, because he too is a son of Abraham. For the Son of Man came to seek out and to save the lost."

* These readings have been selected from among the many Scripture readings designated as suitable for today from the Masses for the Dedication of a Church.

Building Churches

JOHN F. CRAGHAN

We seem to easily isolate ourselves from the woes of others, to deem aloofness a blessing. We preserve our personal relationship with our God but elect to bypass the community. Today's readings focus on the presence of God among the community of believers. They demonstrate a presence that goes beyond church walls to the heart of each believer. This presence is not a static presence, but one that provokes action. God's presence in and through believers is a contagious experience. It has the capacity to penetrate the world of others and offer new dimensions of hope. God's presence, therefore, means that we must reach out and touch someone.

Writing around 520 B.C., the author of today's passage from Second Chronicles attempts to involve God's community in the rebuilding of the Temple. (The neo-Babylonians had destroyed it in 586 B.C.) He paints a grandiose picture of the dedication of Solomon's temple. The priests place the Ark (the container for the two tablets and the footstool of Israel's invisible God) in the Holy of Holies, the innermost sanctuary. At this point the musicians celebrate the awesome spectacle by singing the refrain of Psalm 136. In turn, the Lord signals acceptance of this house by filling it with a cloud. The cloud manifests God's power and might. It shows God's "glory" (Ex 16:7; Nm 14:22). For the author, God's people enjoy this divine presence because they have busied themselves with the process of reconstruction. In so doing they have reached out and touched the presence of God.

The Holy Temple of God

For Paul, the Christian community is an organic unity (see 1 Cor 12:12-31). Everyone in this community both gives and receives. In today's passage Paul emphasizes the quality of the Corinthians' contributions. In addition to building on the right foundation, they are to employ adequate building materials. The materials necessary for building the community and making Christ present are love, joy, patience, peace, and the like (see Col 3:12-17).

The Second Coming of Christ ("the Day") will assess the quality of the workmanship. Worse than the use of substandard materials, however, is the attempt to destroy the Christian community. All such attempts are basically egocentric. They focus on self and not the community (see 1 Cor 8:11-12). Believers are to reveal God's presence within them by good works. This is the holiness that results from love in action (see Phil 2: 14-16). For Paul too, the presence of Christ is recognized as Christians reach out and touch others in a spirit of love.

Salvation

In the gospel episode, Luke insists that the mission of Jesus of Nazareth is to search out and save the lost (see Ez 34:16). Jesus singles out a wealthy tax collector—an occupation that made Zacchaeus especially odious to fellow Jews. The Jews label Zacchaeus a sinner and conclude that it is improper for Jesus to lodge with him. At this point Zacchaeus bristles. He announces that henceforth he will give half of his wealth to the poor. He also states that in the event of extortion he offers four times the amount in question. In Luke's view, Zacchaeus has as great a claim on Jesus as any other descendant of Abraham.

By using the adverb "today" twice in the story, Luke insists on the presence of salvation in the person of Jesus (see also Lk 2:11;23:43). Jesus' coming to Zacchaeus' house is actually part of the Father's plan. "I must stay" implies necessity. It behooves Jesus to stay with Zacchaeus. Here the presence of Christ connotes mercy and forgiveness.

In this story there is a twofold reaching out. Despite the objections of the crowd, Jesus reaches out to Zacchaeus. Because of Jesus' generosity, Zacchaeus reaches out to the poor. The presence of Jesus in Zacchaeus' house is only fitting. For Luke too, the message is clearly stated: Reach out and touch someone.

Today's Good News

Our God is a God of disguises. God chooses individual believers as appropriate dwelling places. This is a God who transcends the sacred space of churches to reside in the body (temple) of individual Christians. God is not just present in churches and chapels. God is present in the kindly deeds of all Christian people. By their loving actions, Christians become living churches, dwelling places for God in today's world. Christians must reach out and touch all people who seek to enjoy the presence of the all-holy One of Israel. They must bring Christ's love to those who yearn to come in contact with the mercy and concern of this God.

Points for Reflection and Discussion

1. Think about being a holy temple of God. Imagine those who would come to you, as temple. What is your response to them?

_____

_____

_____

_____

2. How would the world be different if everyone built churches of flesh—communities of people—instead of churches of stone?

_____

_____

_____

_____

Themes

Church
    Q8, Places in the Catholic Church
    Q12, Catholics and Church
    M2, The Laity: Called to Build God's Kingdom
Holiness
    Q6, The Saints
    M3, Your Special Gifts
    M7, Holiness
Salvation
    Q1, Journey of Faith
    M1, Conversion: A Lifelong Process

Gathering Prayers During Inquiry

Prayer

Loving and merciful God, we gather today because we have faith in you. We want our faith to grow, as our knowledge of you and of one another grows. We ask your blessings on us and our efforts as we begin this new journey of faith in our lives. We pray in the name of Jesus.
Amen

Prayer

Gracious God, we gather once again as your people embarked on a journey of faith. We pray for the courage to voice those things we find troubling or confusing about the Catholic Church, so that our understanding may increase and our quest for knowledge may bring us ever closer to you who are All Knowing.
Amen

Prayer

God of all, we thank you for being with us on our journey of faith. We marvel at the friendships that are being formed as we share our stories—the fascinating ways in which they are different and yet the same. We are no longer alone in our desire for knowledge and understanding—for you are with us, and we are with one another.
Amen

Prayer

How marvelous are your ways, O Lord, our God! Again we ask your blessings upon us as our journey continues. Soon we will be making a turn in the road, pledging our faith-lives to the Catholic Church in fidelity and prayer and continued study. Our hearts are filled with gratitude and awe. How marvelous are your ways, O Lord, our God!
Amen

Gathering Prayers During Catechumenate

Prayer

Dear God, we gather together today and reflect upon your Word. It is another beginning for us, as each new day is another beginning. Please hear our prayer and help us to see that you are present and active in our lives today just as you were present and active in the lives of our ancestors—those whose stories we hear each week in the Liturgy of the Word.
Amen

Prayer

Creator God, we bow before you and ask your blessing upon our hearts and upon our minds, so that we may be drawn ever closer to your infinite love in our sharing of your scriptural presence. Our hearts are restless until they rest in you, O God, for you are our heart's one true desire. Speak your Words to us, O God; write them on our hearts.
Amen

Prayer

Eternal Lord, our appetites will not be sated, for you have put a hunger within us that can only be filled by your Word of everlasting life. You, who are all things to all people, speak to us out of our need. Give us the ears to hear so that our words can speak to our sisters and brothers in their need.
Amen

Prayer

Yahweh God, we have journeyed so far together with you! We have been challenged, and we have been consoled. We have been hurt, and we have been healed. We asked to know your ways, O Lord, and fleetingly we have. We approach another turn in the road. Abba, instill in us the steadfast faith that will allow us to stay the course.
Amen

Gathering Prayers During Lent

Prayer

Father-Mother God, help us to accept the suffering in our lives as faithfully as your Son did, as we begin our journey down his Lenten path. Sustain us in our own desert experience, so that our hunger for your life-giving sustenance may never be compromised by grasping at worldly riches and power. We pray these things of you in the blessed Name of Jesus.
Amen

Prayer

We pray, dear God, that you do not leave us orphaned on our journey. Hear us, O God, as we profess our faith in you, Father, Son, and Spirit; and in your living Church of yesterday, today, and tomorrow; and in the everlasting life of all your saints. Illumine our hearts and our minds with your love.
Amen

Prayer

Jesus, our friend and brother, we feel your agony and your anguish. We offer love, and the work of our hands, to sustain you on your Way—the way that we all must follow as we aspire to our own glorious resurrection. We are your Body, the Church, and we place our hope in you.
Amen

Prayer

Sing Hosanna to our Lord! Gentle Jesus, we waffle between praises and curses, first celebrating with you and then hiding from you—while you steadfastly love us and serve us. We eventually bow down, paying homage to your bruised and lifeless body, for it is in you that we have our being. And, behold, you make all things new! Hosanna in the highest!
Amen

Gathering Prayers During Mystagogy

Prayer

Lord of life, what a glorious God you are! We now are truly a new creation, and still you have not finished with us! We begin to fathom the mysteries of our heart. We recognize you, eternal Lord, in the faces of one another, in the service of strangers, ...in the breaking of bread.
We say Alleluia! Amen!

Prayer

Giver of all good things, as we move along your Way we sense the path leads to everywhere and nowhere. We pray for the stillness that will allow our hearts to hear you in the midst of our noisiness. We pray for the grace to touch others' hearts with your tender mercy and steadfast love. We pray, Abba, and we do not know the words. Lord, hear our prayer.
Amen

Prayer

Prayer is a hunger that grows within us, Lord. We are trying to be your hands...your ears...your mouth—but sometimes it is so hard, Lord. We want nothing more than to be with you, but you demand more in order for that to happen. You demand that we BE you! Keep telling us we really can do it, Lord. Thy will be done!
Amen

Prayer

Eternal and loving God of all, though our journey is common its paths are divergent. You have given us means of sustaining one another along your Way, and what has been given us must now be distributed to those poor who have need of it. You promise the Spirit will guide us. We do believe, Lord; help our unbelief.
Amen

## *Dismissal Prayers During Inquiry*	## *Dismissal Prayers During Catechumenate*
Prayer Loving and merciful God, as we come to the end of our time together today we give you thanks for sparks of insight. We believe you have blessed us with faith, and that you bless our efforts to come to know you better. We thank you in the name of Jesus. Amen	*Prayer* Dear God, as we have reflected on your Word today we have gained a new awareness of how the stories of our lives intertwine. In sharing your stories of yesterday, we experience your dynamic presence in our own stories of today. May we never tire of sharing your stories—and ours. Amen
Prayer Gracious God, we marvel at our increasing courage to speak and to question, and at the increase of peace that comes with our increase of understanding and knowledge about the Catholic Church. All-Knowing God, keep our appetites for knowledge and understanding whetted. Amen	*Prayer* Creator God, it seems your words are truly written upon our hearts. It is only our minds that impede their journey and keep us from the holy wholeness for which you have formed us. We are grateful for the opening of our minds that allows our restless hearts to beat more nearly with your own Sacred Heart. Amen
Prayer God of all, our stories of faith bind us ever more closely into a Christian community. As we invest in one another's lives we seem to be bolstered by a sense of unity even though we are surely a diverse group! We feel your presence among us, Lord; we give you thanks. Amen	*Prayer* Eternal God of all, hunger for your words of life grows with our sharing of those words. We thank you for all that we have heard today, and we ask that we continue to hear your words every day of our lives. We ask not only for ourselves, God, but for all those to whom we can speak in your holy Name. Amen
Prayer How marvelous are your ways, O Lord, our God! We ask your blessings, and we receive them. We are confident, as we face this turn in our journey-of-faith road, that you walk beside us, and so our journey becomes easier even as it becomes more difficult! How marvelous are your ways, O Lord, our God! Amen	*Prayer* Yahweh God, as the road makes another major turn in our journey of faith we breath deeply and say AMEN: Amen for all that has been, and Amen for all that will yet be. We approach a stretch of desert with anxious hearts. Amen, Abba!